MW01156434

Marijuana Grower's Insider's Guide

"*The Insider's Guide* is **the** definitive guide to growing marijuana."

– *High Times*

"If ever a subject had a definitive work, this book is it."

–*The Tab*

"A new home-reference handbook on marijuana cultivation indoors, in the greenhouse, in garden plots, in soil, under hydroponic conditions, and just about any other way that the plant can be grown."

– *American Library Association Booklist*

"Whether you are interested in recent innovations in horticultural techniques, or in maximizing THC content; need pointers on how to keep rats from chewing on your plant or, if you're just curious as to how this multi-billion dollar a year cash crop is cultivated, all the answers are here in the *Marijuana Grower's Insider's Guide*."

– *The Occidental*

Marijuana Grower's Insider's Guide

by

Mel Frank

Red Eye Press
Los Angeles, California

All photographs and photomicrographs by Mel Frank unless otherwise noted. Photomicrographs taken with a Zeiss optical microscope with an Olympus camera body. Illumination is by incident sunlight or daylight and magnification is given to the original photographic negative. Photographs were taken with a Leica R3 and Leica R4, or an Olympus OM-1 or Olympus OM-2. Most exposures are with Kodachrome 64, Kodak Tri-Ex and Plus-X , 35mm film.

Cover photograph: Mel Frank
Cover Design: Larry White
Typesetting & Electronic pasteup: Nancy Anderson

Copyright © 1988 by Mel Frank
Los Angeles, California
All rights reserved

Published and Distributed by:

Red Eye Press
P.O. Box 65751
Los Angeles, CA 90065-0751

ISBN: 0-929349-00-8

Library of Congress Cataloguing-in-Publication Data

Frank, Mel.
  Marijuana grower's insider's guide.

  Includes index.
  1. Cannabis. 2. Marijuana. I. Title.
SB295.C35F74 1988   633.7'9   88-30668
ISBN 0-929349-00-8

Printed and bound in the United States of America
First Printing - December, 1988
Print #   11 12 13 14 15 16 17 18 19

"It is a plant — this thing that we are about to discuss: a green plant, a very abundant and ubiquitous plant, an unusually valuable economic plant, possibly a dangerous plant, certainly in many ways a mysterious plant."

Dr. Richard Evans Schultes
Random Thoughts and Queries
on the Botany of Cannabis

"Dope will get you through times of no money better than money will get you through times of no dope."

The Fabulous Furry Freak Brothers

"The plant is Cannabis — the plant we know as hemp or marijuana — a mysterious plant, a powerful plant, a plant of great importance in the history of humankind for thousands of years. In our modern times this ancient plant still plays a formidable role. The questions raised by its use concern our societies, our cultures, our politics, our religions, and actually our perceptions of reality — need I say more?"

Mel Frank

The material in this book is presented as information which should be available to the public. Neither the publisher nor author advocate breaking any law. However, we urge readers to support the efforts of NORML, CALM and other groups in their efforts to secure the passage of sensible and fair marijuana legislation.

Dedicated to Sandy Weinstein

(1941-1987)

Sandy was one of the finest human beings we ever knew. He lived his life quietly exemplifying the best of human qualities. The world is poorer in his absence, and all of us who knew him miss him dearly.

Sandy

IN CASE OF
EMERGENCY--
BREAK GLASS

Table of Contents

Day of the Triffids.

Preface

Many of you at some time have tried to grow marijuana. Very likely you buried some seeds in a flower pot, added some water, and put the pot on a windowsill. When the seeds sprouted, you watered them faithfully every day. The plants grew for perhaps a few months to 18 inches, at which time you cut them down, and harvested four disappointing joints. It need not have been this way.

The purpose of this book is to let you know how home gardeners successfully grow high quality marijuana, no matter where they live, or whether they've ever grown a plant before. Anyone can grow high-quality grass easily and inexpensively. Regular and even casual users of marijuana eventually realize they need not spend hundreds of dollars for decent marijuana when they could grow superior smoke for relatively little expense.

Estimates of the number of Americans who smoke marijuana range from 18 to 35 million people. Perhaps 40 million people smoke marijuana occasionally. About 500,000 people are arrested annually in the U.S.A. for marijuana offenses. The Drug Enforcement Administration (DEA) estimates that in 1984, Americans consumed about 9,400 tons of marijuana, of which 12 percent, or more than 1,100 tons, were grown domestically. The National Organization for the Reform of Marijuana Laws (NORML) claims that as much as 60 percent of the marijuana consumed in the U.S.A. is homegrown. Although estimates from the DEA and pro-marijuana groups differ greatly, both sides agree that the domestically grown crop is worth, at a minimum, at least 16 billion dollars. This means that marijuana is second only to corn as America's foremost, agricultural cash crop.

One Florida police study found that 50 percent of the people arrested for marijuana offenses admitted that they had grown marijuana or had tried to at some time. Clearly, there is a lot of grass being grown and the reasons might be mercenary or economical, or a concern by growers that they don't know what is in the grass they're smoking. Consumers rightfully worry that commercial grass is adulterated with other drugs, or is contaminated with herbicides (paraquat, which the U.S. government funds for spraying in Mexico), pesticides, or other foreign substances. Also, some consumers are reluctant to associate with any drug dealers who may be unsavory or distribute other drugs. I hope that soon the folly, discrimination, and economic insanity of the present marijuana laws will change to a more enlightened and fair system through legalization, regulation, and taxation on the production of this desirable weed. While the present laws remain, concerned consumers have no other recourse than to grow marijuana of known purity and quality for their own protection.

Most gardeners find that learning to nurture and respond to their plants is a valuable and most humanizing experience, even if they never harvest a joint. Actually, even the most inexperienced gardeners should have few problems in harvesting a potent crop if they have some basic knowledge of the plant beforehand and a little foresight and insight into what it takes. Even the most inexperienced gardeners will learn all they need from this book.

If you grow your own flowers or vegetables, you probably understand why the process of starting a seed, nurturing the plant, and then smoking your own pure, uncontaminated, and potent homegrown can be one of the most satisfying and rewarding of experiences. If you've never grown a plant before, skim through this book in one sitting; imagine how growers decide their options, and then envision what you would do in your imaginary garden to help bring your plants to a healthy and potent maturity.

Author's Acknowledgments and Thanks

This book was made possible only through the efforts of many people. I would like to thank each grower who opened his or her heart and garden to me. Your experiences enlightened and introduced me to situations and problems I'd never seen or imagined. Your openness, experiences, and love will help others through this book.

I would like to acknowledge certain growers for their unique contributions. My gratitude to my friends in Alameda, Calavaras, Calistoga, Humboldt, Los Angeles, Merced, Mendocino, Orange, San Francisco, San Diego, and Sonoma counties in California. Also thanks to those friends in Massachusetts, Vermont, Connecticut, New York City and upstate New York, New Jersey, Pennsylvania, Florida, Mississippi, Arkansas, Texas, Georgia, Colorado, Utah, Oregon, Hawaii, and Jamaica. Some of you now reside in carefree Amsterdam, and I thank you also.

Specifically, I want to acknowledge the contributions of Rob Greenberg, Aiden Kelly, and C.D.R. for editing; Linda P. Kallan, Ellen Laincz, and Oliver Williams for their drawings, charts and maps; Danny Kallan for the final proof reading; Marianne for her many body parts to show relative size in photographs; Nancy Anderson for electronic typesetting, the index, and her indispensable help and advice.

Special thanks to C.R., L.K., M.M., P.R., J.& L. K., my friends in New York for your help and confidence in me. My encouragement and support goes to the people at CALM and NORML for their ongoing and worthwhile efforts. Also thanks to J.C., K.W., R.T., T.E., P.W., B.B, S.S, and C.T. And in San Francisco thanks to M.M., C.M., T.C., S.A., and D.M. To all of you who wrote to me, your letters were invaluable, and much appreciated.

I was fortunate to have had the use of and help from the following libraries: Bronx Botanical Gardens, City College of New York, Harvard Botanical Museum, New York City Public Libraries, University of California at Berkeley and Irvine, U.C. Medical Library in San Francisco, University of Mississippi at Oxford, and the Fitz Hugh Ludlow Memorial Library in San Francisco.

Author's Note

This book introduces the novice to the many ways marijuana is grown, and guides both the apprentice and the experienced grower through the setup and maintenance of his or her garden. It does not need to be read cover to cover. You'll find this book most useful as a reference guide that answers your questions and offers solutions to your problems as they appear.

There is a comprehensive Table of Contents, 26 chapters with more than 60 subentries, and an Index to help you find the pages that should address your questions. I've learned it's better to repeat certain important points and facts in several appropriate places rather than for the reader to somehow miss a crucial point. Please bear these redundancies with me.

Almost any problem should be addressed somewhere in this book. I know from twenty years of experience that the answers are here, but you must ask the questions in an appropriate context. Skim this book at first to familiarize yourself with the areas covered and the layout; then use this book as a reference to answer any questions as they surface.

There are nearly as many ways to grow marijuana as there are marijuana growers. Cultivation is not a complicated process (after all, marijuana is a weed), and I hope I haven't made it appear complicated. Some chapters may seem excessively detailed, but this is because I've tried to anticipate the most common problems, or address difficulties you may never see. Your questions about the plants and cultivation will become more complex as you gain experience. This book should serve as a useful guide long after your first reading and initial harvest.

Use of Registered Trademarks

The following is a list of registered trademarks for companies and products referred to in this book:

Agro-lite	Gro-lux	Rootone
Angel City	Grow	Safe-T-Vapor
Applied Hydroponics	Hartz	Safer
Arab	Hi-Bloom	Seal-a-Meal
Astrolon	High Times	Sears
Attack	Holiday	Seek
Bandini	Hydrofarm	Sinsemilla Tips
Black Gold	Hydrolife	Siphotrol
Bloom	Ivory	Solar Shuttle
Captan	Jefferson	Sudbury
Chacon	Jiffy-7	Sun-Circle
Daconil 2787	Jiffy-mix	Super Metalarc
Dansco	Kodak	Super Soil
Deep Feed	Liquid Iron	Swiss Farms
Dexol	Miracid	Sylvania Safeline
Dipel	Miracle-Gro	Tanglefoot
Duro-lite	N. American Phillips	Thuricide
Duro-test	Nitron	Transplantone
Dyna-gro	Optimarc	True-Ban
Eco-grow	Ortho	Vigoro
Fluomeric	Ortho-Mix	Vita-lite
Funginex	Pentrex	W/S Gro-lux
Filon	Peters	Watt-Miser
GE Safe-T-Gard	PlantGro	Whirly-gig
Germain's	Ra-Pid-Gro	Windex
		Zip-lock

Any registered or trademarked product not on this list is an unintentional omission by the author. Any omissions will be corrected in subsequent printings after notification to the publisher. For the reader's convenience, many of the products referred to in the text are available from suppliers listed at the end of this book.

Part I
About the Marijuana Plant

Chapter 1

Introduction to *Cannabis*
A Brief History

Legally defined, marijuana consists of the dried leaves and flowers of the plant *Cannabis sativa*. *Cannabis* is one of the most ancient and historically important of cultivated plants. *Cannabis* has been cultivated for at least 6,000 years. Particularly in China, the transition of stone-age hunter/gathers into agricultural villagers took place partly because people could grow *Cannabis* and create many useful products from this multipurpose plant.

From the *Cannabis* stem comes hemp, a very long, strong fiber used to make rope, nets, cloth, and paper of renowned durability. Stone-age Chinese may have replaced their animal skins with clothing made from hemp fiber. Cloth developed from the making of hemp fishing nets with progressively finer weaves. The oldest paper known is made from hemp fibers. This paper was recovered from grave sites in the *Shensi* province in China; it's more than 2,100 years old. Hemp paper is prized for its longevity and resistance to tearing. Some fine Bibles, rare books and manuscripts, and some paper money are still made from hemp fiber.

The dried leaves and flowers are what constitute marijuana but they also were used, along with the root, in the preparation of numerous medicines. The oldest known book of pharmacology (the *Pên-ts'ao Ching*) written about 4,000 years ago in China, prescribes marijuana preparations for the treatment of malaria, beriberi, constipation, rheumatic pains, absentmindedness, and "female disorders" (probably menstrual cramps). For millenia, doctors and healers around the world prescribed marijuana preparations for various ailments until the late Nineteenth Century when marijuana started to be replaced by aspirin. The Marijuana Tax Act of 1937 effectively outlawed marijuana, and ended doctors' ability to prescribe marijuana for medicinal purposes in the U.S.A.

Cannabis seeds were a staple food for many thousands of years — one of the ancient "grains" of China — until they were displaced by the introduction of new, more palatable grains about 2,000 years ago. *Cannabis* seeds are still cultivated in the U.S.S.R., Chile, and several other countries for animal and bird feed, and primarily for the seed's oil. Once pressed from the seed, *Cannabis* oil is similar to linseed oil, and can be used for fuel and lubrication, and in the making of paints and varnishes.

Quite naturally, such a useful plant was carried from its native Asia throughout the civilized world. Cultivated *Cannabis* quickly spread westward, and by Roman times was raised in almost every European country. Europeans also grew *Cannabis* for medicine, but primarily cultivated for hemp fiber to make rope, cloth, and paper. In western Asia and Africa, marijuana was the preferred product to hemp, and marijuana was smoked ritually and for pleasure.

The Pilgrims who came from England in 1632 brought hemp seed to make rope and home-spun cloth. Hemp fiber was so important to the British navy for ships' rigging that colonists were paid bounties to plant hemp; in some states penalties were imposed on colonists who wouldn't plant hemp. The hemp industry grew to such an extent that by the Civil War, hemp was second only to cotton in the agricultural industries of the South.

Cannabis now grows throughout the world from near the Arctic Circle to the Equator, and from sea level to above 7,000 feet in the Himalayas. It is, in fact, the most widely distributed of all cultivated plants, a fact that attests to the plant's tenacity and adaptability as well as to its usefulness, versatility, and economic value.

Unlike many cultivated plants, *Cannabis* never lost its ability to survive without human help. Whenever ecological conditions permit, *Cannabis* "escapes" cultivation and becomes weedy by establishing "wild" populations. Weedy *Cannabis* still flourishes throughout the U.S., except in the arid and mountainous areas of the West and in the Southeast. The largest stands grow in the corn belt of the Midwest; these are the remnants of hemp farms planted during World War II to offset a wartime rope shortage.

Such an adaptable plant, when brought to a wide range of environments, and then bred and grown for products from the stem, from the seed, or from the leaves and flowers, understandably evolved into many distinctive ecotypes and cultivated varieties. These different varieties adapted to local growing conditions and are particularly suited for their intended use. Hence there is an incredible diversity within this single species of *Cannabis sativa*.

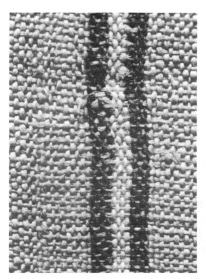

Figure 1. The making of nets eventually developed into cloth making. (Hemp and contemporary hemp textiles from Japan.)

Hemp varieties with long fibers come from tall, straight-stemmed plants. Seed varieties either produce large amounts of seeds on bushy plants, or have large seeds very rich in oil. Weedy plants are hardy, can live with little water or nutrients, and develop small seeds that sprout only under the right conditions. Most important to the readers of this book are the marijuana varieties, which vary in their overall sizes and yields, in the color of seeds and flowers, in when they flower, in their tastes and fragrances, and above all, in their potencies.

For the most part, potency (how strong or psychoactive the marijuana) is a genetic factor. The potency of a plant is inherited from its mother (the seed bearer) and its father (the pollen maker). Growers should plant seeds from marijuana that they have smoked and liked, because the marijuana from these seeds will be similar in potency to the potency inherited from their parents. The marijuana grower's goal is to choose seeds from potent grass and to nurture the plants to a healthy, fully developed maturity. Nature and the plant will take care of the rest.

Before Cultivation Begins

Marijuana is a notoriously hardy, fast growing weed that survives extreme heat, mild frosts, droughts, and deluges. Few diseases seriously effect marijuana, and insects and animals generally have little impact on overall growth and yield once the vulnerable seedling stage is past. Mere survival, though, is not the point. Your goal is to raise healthy, potent, and fully matured plants.

Every seed contains a certain potential for growth, overall size, and potency. Given the seed's potential, the environment then determines the actual size and potency of the plant. In an ideal environment, some marijuana varieties grow from a sprout to 18 feet tall in only six months, and yield up to five pounds of buds.

Indoors there is seldom enough space or light to support such robust growth. Consequently, indoor plants are much smaller, sometimes reaching only three or four feet tall, and they yield about half an ounce of buds, although much larger plants easily and more often are grown indoors.

Overview of Marijuana's Life Cycle

Marijuana is an annual; a single season completes a generation and all hope for the future is left to the seeds. In nature, seeds germinate when the warmth and rains of spring encourage the start of

Figure 2. Germination sequence. The future of the species and the hopes of marijuana growers are held within the seeds.

Figure 3. *Left*: A single male flower (x4). *Photo by R. Harris. Right*: Full view of male (staminate) marijuana flowers.

a new season and life cycle. The first pair of leaves that appear on a sprout are entire (they have smooth edges), and they were part of the embryo contained within the seed. The appearance of the second pair begins the seedling stage. The seedling's leaves differ from the embryonic leaves in having serrated margins (toothed edges), and being larger. The first leaves usually have a single, spearhead-shaped blade. With the next pair of leaves, each leaf is larger, and usually has three blades. A basic pattern has been set: each new pair of leaves is larger and has more blades per leaf, until the leaves reach a maximum size and number of blades per leaf usually nine or eleven (although 19 blades on an 18 inch long leaf have been seen).

The **seedling** stage is completed four to six weeks into growth. Next begins **vegetative growth** (middle stage of life). This is the time of maximum growth, during which branches appear and form the plant into its distinctive shape. After another few weeks, leaf pairs that had been opposite each other (opposite phyllotaxy) begin to form in a staggered position along the top of the stem (alternate phyllotaxy), a sign that the plant is preparing itself for the start of sexual maturation.

Marijuana is *dioecious*, which means that male and female flowers appear on separate plants, and that each plant is then

Figure 4. *Left:* Female (pistillate) flowers form in collections called "buds".
Right: Buds may collect in dense masses called "colas" by maturation.

considered either a male or a female plant. During the stage of
preflowering, (a two-week period prior to flowering), the plant goes
through a quiescent period; rapid growth slows while the plant
prepares itself for the growth of flowers.

A description of the **flowering** stage for both male and female
plants appears in Chapter 18. Briefly, males produce pollen-bearing
flowers, and females produce seed-bearing flowers. Females are the
preferred plant for marijuana because their flower clusters (buds)
are more potent and because they yield better marijuana than do
male plants. The familiar "buds" of commercial grass are in fact
collections of hundreds of individual female flowers that form in
masses called "buds" or "colas".*

Once the male drops pollen and seeds mature on the female,
both plants normally die. This ends a generation, but artificial
lighting allows you to alter many aspects of the plant's life, by knowl-
edgeable modification of the plant's life processes, and mani-
pulation of its normal life cycle. You'll learn these techniques in subsequent chapters. It's actually possible to grow a single plant for several years, or its clones for the rest of your life.

---

*The terminology generally agreed upon is that in marijuana, a bud is a
collection of female flowers that form an individual cluster. Colas are collections of buds.

Growth and the Concept of Limiting Factors

Marijuana grows best in fertile, well draining soil that gets plenty of water and is exposed to bright light, and a warm, airy atmosphere. To reduce the complexities of the environment into factors over which a gardener can maintain some control, think of the environment as consisting of four basic growth factors: **light, air, water,** and **soil**. Plants live and grow by using:

(1) **light energy** to make food and biological energy for growth from

(2) **carbon dioxide** (CO_2) and oxygen from the air,

(3) **water** from the air and soil and

(4) **minerals** (nutrients or fertilizers) absorbed from the soil.

air
sky
land
water
touch me
keep me child
simple
and in rythm
with the earth

Figure 5. From *Poems and Pictures II* by Charles Chase.

Each of these four growth factors is like a link in a chain, and the plant grows no faster than the weakest link will allow. For example, if there is not much light, weak light limits growth no matter how abundant the water is, or how fertile the soil may be. In the same sense, if soil nutrients are scarce, growth is limited by the amount of nutrients, no matter how much light, air, or water is given.

Of course, no grower can know exactly if all four growth factors are in perfect balance, but there is no need to know. Only after growers have watered and fertilized the plants to near excess do they need to recognize that low light is the reason their plants are not growing faster. I've seen growers drowning their plants or poisoning them with too much fertilizer when they've had them growing under a 60-watt light bulb and could not understand why they weren't ten feet tall.

A grower does need a sense of balance and a general sensitivity towards what makes plants grow. Hopefully, this book will help you gain this understanding and sensitivity. A brief reading should relieve you of undue worries and misconceptions, and help persuade you to avoid such things as too much watering or fertilizing. A few read-throughs, a little observation, and some common sense should be all a sensible grower needs to grow a healthy, potent crop.

One final thought on what constitutes common sense when it comes to plants. **Don't overdo it!** The demise of many a plant comes from trying to force the issue. If directions prescribe a teaspoon of fertilizer, won't three teaspoons be three times as good? No! Plants do quite well given sensible care, so help them do what comes naturally and never try to force them.

The first crop is always a learning experience and even when the harvest is wonderfully successful, every grower believes that the next will be even better, and generally this is true. Also, each crop gets easier, because questions get answered and doubts gradually disappear, until the process of caring for your crop becomes second nature and more fun than smoking the harvest. Any experienced grower will probably say, "There's no place I'd rather be and nothing I'd rather be doing than sitting among my plants giving them a little TLC (**Tender, Loving, Care**).

Indoors or Outdoors: Electric or Natural Light

The question of where to grow and whether to use natural or electric light depends on your situation: the space you have, the time and funds you have, and the quantity of grass you want to harvest. For example, a moderate weekend smoker easily could supply all of the grass he or she might want with a modest indoor setup: a garden under an eight-foot fluorescent fixture, or in a sunny window or back porch. A household that consumes more than an ounce weekly would need a couple of 1,000-watt HID's (high-intensity discharge lamps, which are halide and sodium-vapor lamps), a greenhouse, or a backyard plot.

Sunlight is free; use it whenever possible. The main problem with sunlit gardens is visibility. Window gardens or backyard plots must not be visible to passers-by or to the curious. Greenhouses may innocently attract attention even when using greenhouse plastics that transmit light yet obscure the greenhouses' contents. Furthermore, sunlit gardens usually must be started in the spring and harvested in the fall, following the natural seasonal growth cycle. This restriction can be modified with supplemental lighting and shades (which is covered in Chapters 6 and 7). Under exclusively electric lights, growers decide when to start the plants, when the plants will begin to flower, and when they'll be ready to harvest. Controlling the basic elements of the environment is then fairly simple and straightforward; indoors there is little concern with wind and rain, cold, poor soil, or whether it's springtime or the dead of winter.

Security

Security is the first consideration when setting up any garden. Gardeners should take special care that their gardens and lights aren't visible from outside or accessible to unexpected visitors. Even where marijuana growing is legal, theft is a major concern. Growers must carefully consider the consequences before they tell anyone about their garden, and must exercise caution whenever anyone comes to visit. An unfortunate fact of life is that envy, revenge, greed, and misplaced morality has made thieves or informers of acquaintances and former friends.

Unlike sunlight, electric lights cost money to buy and operate. First consider the minimal cost for a modest fluorescent garden, or the expense of a multi-lamp HID garden. Electric light gardens require more frequent care than sunlit gardens; on the other hand, they can be cared for at any time since they are inside, and the lights can be on at any time that fits the gardener's schedule. Electric-light gardens are perfect for the working apartment dweller.

You can hide electric-light gardens in closed rooms, basements, attics, closets or garages. Even when hidden, large HID gardens may arouse suspicions of the utility company. Large metal halide lamps (MH's), the main light source for many gardeners, draw almost 1,100 watts each. If three or more lamps are used, the utility company may wonder why your electric bill has suddenly gotten so high, and they may make inquiries about your electric usage or investigate a possible short or other problem along your lines. Growers who manage large electric light gardens sometimes run their lights at night when other tenants are asleep, so that the meter reader doesn't see the electric meter "spinning" when he reads the usage meter. In a home situation, commercial growers limit their electrical consumption so that their usage is less obvious to the electric company. If asked, the best excuse is that you've installed electric heating or central air conditioning.

Large HID gardens may be too noisy. Ballasts may hum loudly, and light balancers (if installed) may cause considerable vibrations. Ballasts manufactured by Jefferson are purportedly the quietest.

Commercial growers who are concerned about the scent of their marijuana may choose to run their lights and ventilation fans at night, when their neighbors are asleep. Consider all possible problems first, before you set up your system, especially if it's a large commercial operation. Small gardens need no special security precautions. But don't tell anyone about the garden, and keep the garden hidden from unexpected visitors.

Warning: if your property can be shown to have been purchased with funds from illicit drug sales, it can be confiscated; a vehicle used to transport illegal drugs or to transport materials used in an illegal garden is also subject to confiscation.

At this point, skim the chapters in Part II. Then decide between two basic options within a fundamental decision: to grow or not to grow; if the choice is to grow, grow with either electric light or natural light. The rest of the information provided here is common to both "yes" situations. However you imagine that you'll be growing, you'll find useful information in all chapters. Skim this book once or twice, and carefully consider what is said about growing in general before you make any decisions.

Marijuana growing is fun, and more rewarding than you might imagine. In all states except Alaska, growing is illegal, so take some time to consider all of the consequences. The purpose of this book is not to encourage you to grow illegally, but to report how growing is done legally, and how it may be done when growing is decriminalized. I hope a thorough reading of this book gives you foresight, a good idea of what to expect, and solutions to the problems you might confront.

Starting in 1968, I've experienced more wonderful harvests than I can count, and I've smoked myself into happy oblivion with home-grown more times than I can remember (the excellent quality of the dope definitely affected my memory). Good luck and many happy harvests.

Figure 6. Skylights can support huge plants.

Part II
How to Get Started

Chapter 2

Electric Lights for Plant Growth

The light system is the heart of any electric light garden. The amount of light and space your plants have determines how fast, large, and robust the plants will grow. In a well-maintained garden it's relatively simple to supply indoor plants with all the water, air, and nutrients they need, so that light becomes the only limiting factor which might restrict growth. The amount of light also determines the garden's dimensions, the overall size of the plants, and even what varieties of marijuana a grower chooses to cultivate. Skim these chapters on light in your first reading, but read them carefully and often when contemplating the start of a garden. Most other aspects of gardening can be considered when you come to them, but the kind of lights and the amount of light that illuminates a garden must be decided before any seed is sown.

Any whitish electric light fosters plant growth. However, several types of lamps are manufactured specifically for plant growth, and many other lamps that were originally intended for vision work at least as well and often better for growing plants. This chapter describes the most popular, effective and efficient types of lights used to grow marijuana or any other plant. Chapters 6 and 7 describe growing under natural light in window gardens, greenhouses, and outdoor plots.

Primary Light Sources: Types of Lamps

Fluorescents (Modest Indoor Gardens)

Fluorescents are common, inexpensive, cheap to run, and effective in illuminating **modest** indoor marijuana gardens. Fluorescent fixtures contain a ballast and two end sockets in which the tube (bulb or lamp) is held. If possible, purchase fixtures with built-in

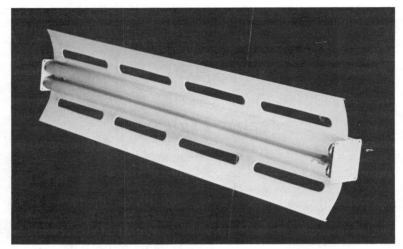

Figure 7. Fluorescent fixture with reflector and heat vents.

reflectors. There are innumerable types of fluorescent tubes, and many lengths and wattages available to the homegrower. Only those sizes and types that are the most effective as growing lamps are described here.

Fluorescents have gotten a bad rap from many growers who were disappointed with the results. Good results require almost daily care **while the plants are flowering.** Fluorescents generate weaker light than other recommended lamps. While flowering, plants must be carefully tended to keep the tops of all plants at the same height and as close to the fluorescents as possible, otherwise the final crop will amount to no more than some skimpy buds and a lot of leaf (see the section Promoting Even Growth in Chapter 15). Many fine crops are raised under fluorescents by conscientious growers who spend the necessary time and who are sensitive to the plants' needs. Fluorescents are an inexpensive alternative to other lamps for the **moderate** smoker who can't invest much money or devote much space to a larger light system. The type of light makes little difference to the potency.

Fluorescent fixtures may be found or scavenged, tubes are cheap, and the garden contributes little to the electric bills. On the other hand, if cost and space are no object, High Intensity Discharge lamps (see HID's later in this chapter) support larger and more robust plants, and require less careful attention and less frequent care.

Figure 8. Keep fluorescents close to the plants' tops.

Fluorescents are cheaper and better than HID's for rooting clones, raising males for pollen, and starting seedlings up to about eight weeks of growth before they are transferred to an HID system; on all of these, the high energy output and expense of HID's is wasted. Commercial growers use fluorescents to start plants when they rotate crops to successively larger light systems, particularly when using High Pressure Sodium (HPS, a type of HID) lamps.

Ironically, some of the largest commercial indoor gardens use the lowly fluorescent exclusively. These "growing factories" use growing shelves and clones for rotating fast turnover gardens. For the homegrower growing for personal use, a shelf garden under fluorescents might be your best option in terms of your initial cost, electrical consumption and subterfuge. (See Shelf Gardens in Chapter 5).

Standard Fluorescent Fixtures

Standard Fluorescents (the long tubes you see in industrial and some home lighting) come in lengths from six inches to 12 feet, and all of them use about ten watts per linear foot. This means that a standard four-foot fixture with its tube uses about 40 watts per tube and an eight-footer uses about 80 watts. These two sizes, four-foot and eight-foot lengths, are the most common sizes available and the most popular with marijuana growers. You can find tubes of five, six, and seven-foot lengths, and you should use them if they will fit your space.

Any tube less than four feet long emits too little light to grow a vigorous crop of marijuana. Tubes longer than eight feet are hard to find and somewhat unwieldy to raise and lower, but they work very well if you have the space.

Fluorescents are also manufactured in *efficient use* tubes. GE sells their Watt-Miser line and Sylvania has their SuperSaver line. Europeans look for TL tubes, and most manufacturers sell a line of watt-saving standard fluorescents which emit more light per watts consumed than standard tubes. Typically, "watt-saving" tubes consume about 20 percent less electricity and emit ten percent less light than standard tubes. Look for these watt-saving lines when setting up a large shelf garden where you're concerned about electrical consumption. Many fluorescents are manufactured as "power twists" or "power grooves." These tubes have indentations or are twisted, which gives the bulb more surface area, and they emit about ten to 15 percent more light per watt consumed. Most manufacturers offer tubes in "efficient use", "power groove", and "higher output versions".

Figure 9. Afghani/hybrids (foreground) have good colas even under fluorescents. Plants are three feet tall after 15 weeks, and are ready for harvest.

Higher-Output Fluorescents

Fluorescents also come in higher wattage sizes, the most common being **Very High Output (VHO)** at 215 watts per eight-foot tube, and **High Output (HO)** at 110 watts per eight-foot tube. VHO's emit about 2.25 times as much light, and consume almost three times as much power, as standard fluorescents of the same length. They also require a special VHO fixture (a VHO ballast and end sockets). HO tubes also require an HO ballast and different end sockets than standard bulbs use. HO's use about 45 to 50 percent more electricity and emit about 45 percent more light than standard fluorescents of the same length. VHO and HO tubes in four-foot lengths are rated at about half the wattage of the eight-foot tubes. HO tubes in five, six, and seven-foot lengths with correspondingly higher wattages are hard to find, but they can be ordered. VHO tubes also come in five-foot and six-foot lengths. For better results, always use the longest tube you can fit in your prospective garden.

Generally, VHO and HO "watt-saving" tubes consume less watts with a correspondingly lower output in overall light. In other words, they aren't necessarily more efficient, they just put out proportionally less light, while they consume correspondingly fewer watts. A "watt-saving" eight-foot VHO consumes about 185 watts, and a "watt-saving" eight-foot HO uses about 95 watts.

Although all higher-output fluorescents work well for growing marijuana, VHO's are not better than HID lamps (see next section); they cost about the same, and the light system is more unwieldy and less efficient in terms of light delivered per watt consumed. Setup and care is easier with HID's lamps; when the plants get larger, growth is more robust under the higher intensity of HID lamps. However, HO tubes draw less current, are cheaper, and work very well with moderate electric costs after the initial investment in the HO fixture.

One advantage of fluorescent tubes is that they may conform to an odd space with limited headroom such as a shelf, overhead closet, attic, crawl space, half-basement, nook, or space beneath a loft bed; they come in many lengths and take up less **vertical** space for gardening than HID's.

HID's: Metal Halides (MH's) and
Sodium Vapor Lamps (HPS's)

Metal Halides (MH) lamps and High Pressure Sodium Vapor (HPS) lamps are the most effective and efficient electric light sources available to the indoor gardener. These bulbs are a point source of light, rather than a linear source like fluorescents. Because the light radiates from a point, it's more intense and can penetrate leaves and illuminate a **deeper cubic** area than fluorescents. **A 1,000-watt HID will grow larger plants with a deeper layer of worthwhile buds than five VHO fluorescents using 1,075 watts.**

Both MH and HPS bulbs come in many sizes: the halides range from 175 to 1,500 watts; the sodium vapor bulbs from 35 to 1,500 watts. For most situations I recommend only two sizes, 400 and 1,000 watts, and only a few basic bulb types which are listed later. A 1,500-watt bulb lasts only 25 percent as long as the smaller sizes do, including the 1,000-watt bulb, so 1,500-watt bulbs are not recommended because of excessive bulb costs. Most bulbs of less than 400-watts are not as effective for plant growth, and it's considerably more expensive for growers to set up several smaller units than to use either of the two larger, recommended sizes. The GE Watt-Miser or similarly efficient bulbs of 325-watts, and the Duro-test Optimarc of 250-watts are the only smaller bulbs recommended for typical gardens. With special circumstances — for instance, if the only

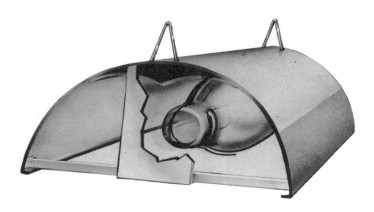

Figure 10. A metal halide mounted in a horizontal, double parabolic reflector. Courtesy of *Applied Hydroponics*.

place you can grow is in a small closet, consider buying a smaller, horizontally mounted MH or HPS. These **mini-horizontals** range from a 150-watt HPS or 175-watt MH to the 250-watt sizes. The horizontal fixture delivers from 20 to 45 percent more light to the plants than conventional, vertically hung bulbs. The smallest versions come in self-contained units with the ballast built into the fixture. In an area three to five feet square, mini-horizontals are a simple, moderate, yet very effective source of lighting for a personal mini-garden. **The most productive, modest setup you can buy is a 400 watt HPS with a horizontal reflector.** It doesn't add much to your electric bill, and the bulb lasts for about three years. For about the same costs, one 400-watt HPS may yield three times as much as a 320 watt fluorescent system.

MH lamps require a special ballast for the corresponding lamp size; a 400-watt ballast runs any 400-watt MH, and a 1,000-watt ballast runs any 1,000-watt MH. HPS bulbs require their own particular ballast which should be purchased along with the HPS bulb.

Light Balancers (Movers)

Light balancers (also called movers) are mechanical arms from which hang MH or HPS bulbs; their small motors move the lights slowly across a garden. Light balancers come in two basic configurations, linear or circular. Linear balancers move the lights back and

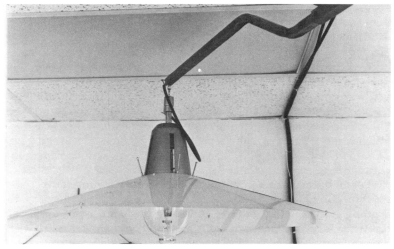

Figure 11. An MH lamp on a Sun-Circle light balancer.

forth along a linear track, and are best employed in a rectangular garden. Circular balancers either rotate the lights continuously in a circle, or move 180 degrees and back to repeat a cycle. After the initial cost, light balancers save considerable electrical costs, considering the extended area that they illuminate versus their running costs, which are negligible (only 14 to 24 watts). Light balancers increase the effective size of any garden significantly without additional bulbs or any appreciable increase in electrical costs.

Supplemental Lights: Types of Lamps

The supplemental lights described here are best used when the grower wishes to supplement or add more light to an existing light system or to a natural light garden. For extending the photoperiod any lamp will do (see Chapter 4).

Mercury Vapor

Mercury Vapor lamps can be screwed into a standard incandescent light socket, yet they produce a lot of light. Mercury lamps are relatively inefficient in terms of usable light versus electrical consumption. Use mercury vapor bulbs only to add light to a natural light garden. Mercury vapor bulbs do produce a very high intensity light compared to most bulbs that work in a standard light socket. The best bulb in terms of light-spectrum is the **Duro-test Fluomeric Safe-T-Vapor** lamp, because, as the name implies, the bulb is safe to use in home situations, and the light spectrum is excellent for growing plants whereas the light spectrum of other mercury vapor lamps is quite poor. Wattages range from 160 watts up to 1,250 watts, (although bulbs with wattages higher than 250 watts from Duro-test or Duro-lite may not be available by the time you read this book). Buy mercury vapor lamps with built-in reflective coatings, and mount them as you would a spotlight. The Fluomeric is an excellent bulb to supplement natural light, but any HID is more economical and a better light to use as a sole source of light. A 400-watt MH or HPS covers more area with considerably cheaper bulb replacement costs.

For supplementing natural light, mercury vapor lamps add much useful light, and when extending the photoperiod there is no shading from a bulky fixture. Installing the lamp is as simple as screwing it into a standard light socket. The disadvantages with mercury vapor lamps are that they burn hot like a spotlight, and the area they illuminate is a smaller area than that from a comparable

HID. For simply extending the photoperiod in a natural light garden, any type of lamp will do. The new, low-wattage MH and HPS lamps in self-contained horizontal fixtures are cheaper than mercury vapor lamps in the long run and actually, they're more effective in terms of plant growth. These self-contained mini-horizontals are highly recommended for both mini-gardens and as supplemental lights.

Circular and "U" Shaped Fluorescents

Circular fluorescents need no special fixture to operate. They are self-ballasted and designed to operate in an incandescent socket (typical table lamp socket). Hang them around the garden's perimeter or position them in stand-up lamps in standard light sockets. The wattages range from 20 to 44 watts and you should use the highest wattage available (circular fluorescents over 22 watts need a special fixture). Usually growers use these bulbs to increase light during flowering so the best, most common bulb to use is the Warm White which is strong in the red band, the preferred light for flowering. Circular fluorescents are excellent for supplementing light or for extending the photoperiod in natural-light gardens, since they require no special fixtures and they shade little of the garden from natural light. Circular fluorescents take up little room, and are inexpensive and easy to employ. A 44-watt GE Watt-Miser emits

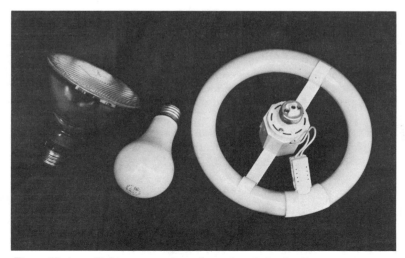

Figure 12. A spotlight, common incandescent, and circular fluorescent.

more light (lumens) than a 100-watt incandescent. Circular bulbs are about 16" in diameter for the largest (40 to 44-watt) size. "U" shaped fluorescents are much like circular fluorescents, but require a special fixture and ballast. Their only practical use is when the space available is restricted, although some growers use them to illuminate the lower branches in small gardens. Circular fluorescents are equally effective and are easier to set-up. "U"-shaped fluorescents come in sizes from 25 to 40 watts; a 40-watt tube is nine inches wide and about two feet long. Circular lamps work better, since they require no special fixture, and their overall cost is much less.

Low-Pressure Sodium Lamps

Low-Pressure Sodium Lamps (LPS) are offered by a few distributors that advertise in marijuana publications. The LPS is the most efficient of all lamps in converting electricity to light. However the bulb is monochromatic; that is, it produces light in a single, narrow band at about 589 nanometers, in the orange part of the visible spectrum. Although its yellow/orange light is slightly outside of the desirable red part of the spectrum, its high output versus electrical consumption makes it a good performer as supplemental light. LPS lamps must only be used to supplement natural light, fluorescents, or MH lamps. Plants elongate and grow abnormally when cultivated solely under LPS lamps.

The most popular sizes offered to marijuana growers are the 135 and 180 watt sizes manufactured by North American Phillips. These require an LPS fixture that looks somewhat like a slightly oversized four foot fluorescent fixture. In any halide or natural light garden, a supplemental LPS very effectively adds much useful light near the red end of the spectrum to promote flowering.

An LPS has the unique property of maintaining the same lumen output throughout its lifetime. The bulb gives no indication of age before it suddenly ceases working after about 18,000 hours of use. Because the bulb contains sodium, be particularly cautious when using water near either an operating or a discarded bulb. Sodium explodes when it contacts water.

Standard and Plant-Gro
Incandescents and Spotlights

Incandescents are the standard screw-in bulb that we're all familiar with. They are inefficient lamps, produce an unbalanced spectrum (mostly red, orange, and yellow), are very hot, and can burn the plants. Their advantages are that in a pinch, before you can set up other lights, they are cheap, easily found, and easy to set up on the perimeter of a garden.

Spotlights are actually focused incandescents. The spectrum is a slight improvement on incandescents. They also are very hot and can burn the plants.

"Plant-gro" versions of both incandescents and spotlights are available in garden shops. They are coated to improve the light spectrum for growing plants, but they still burn hot and are inefficient. Replace them with other supplemental lights, such as self-contained mini-HID's, LPS's, circular fluorescents, or mercury vapor lamps in any extended operation.

Where to Use Supplemental Lights

Use supplemental lights to extend the natural daylength or to increase the light in natural light gardens. Their advantages (except for "U" shaped fluorescents and LPS's) are that they require no special fixture other than an ordinary light socket; they don't have a bulky fixture that shades natural light; they are lightweight and easy to hang or position around the perimeter of any garden. All of these lights work well enough as supplements, but MH's or HPS's and fluorescents work much better as sole sources of electric light.

Types of Bulbs and the Light Spectrum

The white light of electric lamps consists of all the colors (wavelengths) of the visible spectrum (colors of the rainbow). Electric lights differ in the amount of light radiated in each color band: this gives them their characteristic color tone or degree of whiteness. For example, an incandescent bulb (common table lamp) generates mostly red, orange, and yellow light but very little blue light; hence it appears orange/yellowish. White fluorescents have a more balanced spectrum; so they appear white. You can trust your eyes to tell you whether a bulb predominates in blue or red because it will have a bluish-white color or a softer, pinkish tone. A glance at a metal halide (MH) tells you that its spectrum favors blue because of its blue-white color. High Pressure Sodium vapor lamps (HPS's) appear pinkish-orange; their spectrum is much richer in the yellow, orange and red regions of the light spectrum.

Plants use light energy primarily in the blue and red regions of the light spectrum to carry on photosynthesis and chlorosynthesis, the two life processes that plants use to transform light energy into

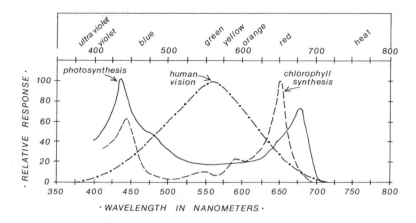

Figure 13. The action spectra of chlorosynthesis and photosynthesis compared to that of human vision. Adapted from *IES Lighting Handbook*. *Drawing by E.N. Laincz.*

biochemical energy for growth. **For healthy, normal growth, plants need adequate amounts of radiant energy in both the red and the blue regions of the light spectrum.**

Fluorescent Lamps (Tubes)

There are innumerable fluorescents manufactured for plant growth, vision, and for special lighting effects. Since white light contains all the colors of the light spectrum, plants get some red and blue light from any white light source. Plants actually use light of all colors to some degree, except for green light, which they reflect or transmit (this is why plants appear green).

To take advantage of the use of red and blue light by plants, Gro-Lux, Agro-lite, and similar purple-looking "Plant-Gro tubes" were designed to emit primarily red and blue light. Much of the manufacturers' talk of plant growth and tube type (or spectrum) is simply hype. There are several less-expensive regular fluorescents manufactured by many companies that work at least as well as, if not better than, these Gro-tubes. Don't be swayed by manufacturers' claims. In practice, as long as the lamp produces sufficient red and blue light, **the higher overall output (lumens) of white lamps more than compensates for their lesser output in the blue and red regions.** Gro-lamps work well enough, but given the choice, choose those lamps recommended here since they'll work at least as well, are easier to find, last longer, and are usually much cheaper.

Manufacturers use standardized names, such as "Daylight" or "Warm White," to designate a fluorescent tube that has a certain degree of whiteness. Each name corresponds to a tube that emits a particular combination of light in each of the color bands. For example, "Daylight" emits more blue than red light, and appears blue-white. By matching a tube that predominates in blue light with a tube that emits more red light, the tubes complement each other, and produce better plant growth than if either is used alone.

Most of the tubes listed in Table 2.1 are available in HO, VHO, and four and eight-foot lengths. Any of these tubes will grow a good crop, and there will be no noticeable difference in the potency of plants grown under any of these tubes. The only differences will be in slightly faster and more robust growth.

All of these tubes come in four and eight foot lengths from several major U.S. companies including GE and Sylvania, and often are available in five, six and seven foot lengths, and in power twists, efficient use, or high-output type bulbs. It's best to use more red than blue tubes, particularly during flowering. For two-tube gardens, use them one to one; for four-tube gardens use one "blue" to three "red" tubes. For six-tube gardens, use two "red" to each "blue" tube.

Table 2.1
Tubes to use as a single source
(in order of preference)

Vita-Lite*	(Duro-test Corp.)
Natur-escent	(Duro-test Corp.)
White	(many manufacturers)
Agro-Lite	(Westinghouse)
W/S Gro-Lux	(Sylvania)
Gro-Lux	(Sylvania)
Plant-Gro	(General Electric)

*Vita-Lite is better than any of the "gro-tubes" for a single source fluorescent in terms of general growth. Its spectrum closely resembles that of natural daylight. Vita-lites are expensive, but they last from two to four times longer and they're guaranteed for three years. Fluorescents designated "White" perform very well considering their low costs. The combination of Warm White and Cool White listed in Table 2.2 is the best performer overall in terms of good growth versus costs.

Table 2.2 Tubes to use in combinations of "blue" and "red" tubes	
Tubes stronger in blue light	**Tubes stronger in red light**
Cool White	Warm White
Daylight	Soft White
Blue fluorescent	Merchandiser White
	Red fluorescent

An inexpensive yet very effective light system is a combination of one Cool White to each one or two Warm Whites (highest recommendation of all fluorescent systems), Daylight with Soft White, or any other combination of any "blue" to any "red" source listed here. Tubes with the word "Deluxe" in their designation have a more natural light spectrum, but emit considerably less light. For example, preferably buy "Cool White," since it emits up to 50 percent more light than "Cool White Deluxe."

HID's — Metal Halides (MH) and Sodium Lamps (HPS)

Once you decide to use MH or HPS lamps, the next consideration is what bulb to buy. There are some small but noticeable differences in growth when comparing an MH, a super MH, or an HPS. MH bulbs may be coated, diffuse, or clear. The coated bulbs have a slightly more natural light spectrum than clear bulbs, but the coating reduces their output by about five percent. For an MH garden, a **clear, super MH** gives the best overall results because the plants grow slightly faster than under regular, coated, or diffuse bulbs. The light output (total lumens) is far more important to the rate of growth than the particular spectrum.

HPS lamps emit more overall light (lumens) than any other bulb, but most of the energy is in the yellow, orange, and red bands. Despite their unnatural light spectrum, HPS lamps give the best return for electrical and bulb costs. They're also relatively safe to use compared to MH lamps, and the initial set up and the ongoing care of plants is easier under an HPS when compared to fluorescents.

HPS lamps sometimes give inexperienced growers problems when starting seedlings, because the abundance of orange and red light causes seedlings to stretch or elongate toward the light. If this is a problem, position the lamp closer to the seedlings or use a small fluorescent system to start the seedlings, then move them under the HPS after about two to five weeks. **The combination of a small fluorescent system to start seedlings and an HPS for growth and flowering is the best overall light setup you can buy.** HPS bulbs emit about 25 to 50 percent more lumens of light than MH's, promote excellent flowering, **and last about twice as long as MH's.** They also can be mounted in the new horizontal reflectors which increase the light directed to the plant by 20 to 45 percent. Overall, HPS lamps are your best buy and are your best performers except for starting seedlings and rooting clones.

HPS bulbs are less trouble if you are growing in an outbuilding that is susceptible or open to insect invasions. The yellow-orange color of an HPS does not attract night insects, whereas all white lights (all MH's) attract insects in droves.

Growers using several HID bulbs often balance the light spectrum by mixing HPS lamps and MH lamps, or by using HPS lamps only for flowering in rotating gardens. **Preliminary scientific studies in England support this balancing.** During foliar growth, the spectral distribution best for growth decreases in the following order: red, blue, and yellow-green. During flowering, the decreasing order should be red, far-red, blue, and yellow-green. The combination of an HPS with an MH gives additional red and far-red light to the overall light spectrum for flowering.

Table 2.3 lists examples of the recommended HID bulbs. A list of all manufacturers and all bulbs would be tedious, but specifications are similar among all manufacturers, and all of the "safety" bulbs are recommended. North American Phillips (which now includes what was formerly Westinghouse), manufactures the Safety Lifeguard line of bulbs, and other manufacturers have comparable lines of safety bulbs with specifications like those in Table 2.3. Any of these safety-featured lines are recommended because of their built-in safety features.

Table 2.3 Safe HID Bulbs						
Metal Halide (MH)						
Watts 1	Type 2	Position 3	Life 4 Hours	Mean 5 Lumens	Remarks	
General Electric Saf-T-Gard						
325	CL	HOR	15,000	17,350	Watt-Miser	
325	C	HOR	15,000	16,800	Watt-Miser	
400	CL	U	15,000	20,600		
400	C	U	15,000	19,750		
400	CL	VER	20,000	29,900		
400	C	VER	20,000	28,800		
1,000	CL	VER	12,000	83,000		
Sylvania Super Metalarc Safeline						
400	CL	VER	20,000	23,000		
400	C	VER	20,000	21,000		
1,000	CL	VER	12,000	90,000		
1,000	C	VER	12,000	85,000		
Duro-Test Safe-T-Vapor Optimarc 6						
400	CL	U	15,000	34,000		
1,000	CL	U	12,000	90,000		
High Pressure Sodium (HPS) **(many U.S. manufacturers)**						
400	CL	U	24,000+	45,000		
400	D	U	24,000+	42,750		
1,000	C	U	24,000+	126,000		

1. Watts. Rated wattage is power consumed by the bulb alone. Additionally, a ballast typically consumes six to ten percent more in watts, e.g. a 1,000-watt HID and ballast draws 1,060 to 1,100 watts.

2. Cl, clear bulb (commonly, no designation means a clear bulb), **C**, phosphor coated, **D**, diffuse.

3 . Position. Many MH's are manufactured to be positioned in either a vertical or horizontal axis, usually +/- 15 degrees, and they operate **safely and last longest** only in their intended positions. Designations include (**Hor**) for horizontal, (**Ver**) for vertical, **BU** for base up, **BD** for base down, **U** for universal, meaning any position is ok. For example, the designation for a typical vertically mounted bulb might be MH 1,000-BU (1,000-watt Metal Halide operated with base-up). HPS lamps operate in any position.

Some marijuana equipment distributors now offer MH lamps for installation in a horizontal position. When used with an appropriate horizontal reflector, they direct much more light to the plants than vertically suspended lamps, and they have comparable lifetimes. Make sure that the bulb offered to you was manufactured for horizontal positioning. The bulb-ordering abbreviation will end with a "U" for universal (any) burning position or an "HOR" for horizontal burning position. (Hor may also mean a horticultural lamp, e.g., Venture bulbs).

4 . Life hours. A bulb's useful lifetime is based on 10 hours or more per start. The lifetime of fluorescents, MH's and HPS bulbs decreases the more often the bulb is turned on. All of them last the most hours when continuously lit.

Since the lumen output decreases with age, most growers use old bulbs for seedlings and new bulbs for general growth and flowering. Experienced growers often replace MH bulbs every six to nine months, and use old bulbs for raising seedlings and clones. In general, replace MH's for flowering every 12 to 18 months. Replace HPS lamps used for flowering every three years (at 12 hours per day, this is just over half of the rated lifetime, or 13,000 hours of use for a 24,000 hour-rated lifetime).

5 . Mean lumens (a lumen is a unit used for measuring light) is the midpoint of lumens produced in a bulb's lifetime. Initial lumens is the light output for a new bulb, and this is considerably higher than mean lumens. Mean lumens, as listed in Table 2.3, more accurately portray the average amount of lumens a bulb delivers during its useful lifetime. For selling purposes, 'initial lumens' is usually the figure distributors advertise. Mean lumens range from about 60 to 80 percent of the initial lumens, and all bulbs of comparable wattages and types deliver roughly the same amount of light.

6 . Optimarc has the best color-rendering of any HID lamp. The light spectrum closely mimics natural daylight. It should encourage excellent overall plant growth but it might be prohibitively expensive. Use Optimarcs with the HPS ballasts listed. Figures are for initial lumens. Data for mean lumens were not available.

Bulb spectrum and wavelength charts are not included here, nor are charts comparing the spectrum (colors) of bulbs to photosynthesis and chlorosynthesis curves. Growers may draw wrong conclusions from such charts, or become obsessed with the "best bulb spectrum", forgetting that their original intent was to grow good dope. Any differences in plant growth caused by the bulbs listed here are slight, and are mentioned throughout the text.

For example, Plant-Gro fluorescent tubes emit almost all of their energy in the critical blue and red regions of the light spectrum; yet **there are several general lighting white fluorescents that actually foster faster growth.** An HPS produces mostly yellow, orange, and red light with very little blue light; **yet HPS lamps are actually better than any other comparable-wattage MH lamp for general growth after the seedling stage** (despite the MH's "better spectrum"). When comparing any lamps, look at the **total lumen output,** which is usually more important than the break-down of blue, red, or any other particular spectral output. As long as the bulb isn't monochromatic (e.g. low-pressure sodium lamps which emit a single, narrow color-band), and it looks white or is a general "vision" bulb, it'll foster good, healthy growth. Follow the recommendations given here, and you'll do just fine.

An Important Safety Message

MH bulbs emit dangerous levels of UV and particle radiation if the bulb breaks or cracks, or a small hole occurs in the outer protective envelope. A broken bulb may continue to operate without the grower realizing that there is a problem. Exposure to a damaged bulb for even a short time is dangerous and may cause serious eye and skin damage.

All the bulbs in Table 2.3 have safety features which cause the bulb to burn out quickly if the protective envelope or any other part of the bulb becomes damaged. Although their output is slightly less (about 10 percent less) than that of ordinary MH's, this is a small price to pay for this extremely important safety feature. The outer protective envelope of all MH's is tough, and can withstand the typical knocks and bumps of ordinary handling. But remember that the bulb is usually hanging naked, and is not fixed in place or enclosed within a protective fixture. If you bump or drop an ordinary MH, you can't be sure if it's damaged or not, because it will continue to burn apparently normally. Now what do you do? You don't want to risk your eyesight and safety, and you don't want to throw away a good bulb just because of an accidental bump. Also, you may need to spray with water, pesticides, or nutrient solutions, and a tiny droplet of water can cause an unnoticed crack or rupture on a hot bulb.

Table 2.4
Examples of *Unsafe* MH bulbs*

Watts**	Type	Position	Life Hours	Lumens	Remarks
General Electric					
400	CL	Hor	15,000	21,600	
400	C	Hor	15,000	20,700	
950	CL	Ver	12,000	85,600	
Sylvania Super Metalarc Lamps					
400	CI	Ver	20,000	30,500	
400	C	Ver	20,000	28,500	
1000	CL	Ver	12,000	100,000	
Duro-Test Optimarc					
250	C	U	10,000	19,000	S50 HPS
400	C	U	10,000	28,000	S51 HPS

* And similar bulb types by all U.S. manufacturers.
** See footnotes for Table 2.3.

For the convenience of the reader, mail order distributors for complete lighting systems are listed at the back of the book.

Now some of you experienced HID gardeners may think I'm overly cautious, but read what Sylvania says about their Super Metalarc MH, one of the most popular bulbs that hangs naked above many marijuana gardens: "...**must be operated in fixtures which are enclosed in tempered glass or other suitable materials that are capable of withstanding the discharge of hot quartz arc tube particles.**" Sylvania also recently warned that all MH bulbs marked M, MS, MM, and MST be encased in tempered glass fixtures. The hot quartz particles pose a danger of injury and of fire.

Table 2.4 lists typical lamps sold by many distributors of MH's who gear their sales to marijuana growers. Their use is discouraged for safety reasons. If you use these bulbs, be forewarned of their dangers and use appropriate precautions, including using UV goggles and limiting your gardening time when working under these lamps. Notice the small difference in output (about 10 percent in lumens) between the safety bulbs and the regular bulbs in the table.

A few distributors who gear their sales to marijuana growers now offer these bulbs in an enclosed, tempered glass fixture. Look for them and advisedly buy these fixtures or buy the safety bulbs.

Buying Supplies

Standard Fluorescents. One good thing about growing with standard fluorescents is that they're inexpensive. Two-tube, four-foot fixtures including bulbs cost as little as $6.00 at discount stores. You can find old fixtures in dumpsters outside of buildings being renovated or torn down, and in junkyards. Buy new fluorescent tubes, because used bulbs emit much less light. It is also easy to make an effective reflector for any fluorescent fixture from common household materials, such as the cardboard boxes in which the fixtures and bulbs are packaged.

MH and HPS Bulbs and Fixtures. The best place to look for distributors of complete systems (bulb, ballast, and reflector) is in marijuana publications such as *High Times* (subscriptions, P.O. Box 410, Mt. Morris, Il., 61504; office located at 211 E. 43rd St., New York, N.Y. 10017) or *Sinsemilla Tips* (New Moon Pub., P.O. Box 2046, Corvallis, Oregon 97339; 503/757-TIPS). These systems are put together with the idea that you're probably growing marijuana, and

Table 2.5
Prices (approximate retail from lighting supplier)

Item	Price Range
Fluorescent	
Fixture (no reflector)	
4' (two bulbs)	$4 to $10
4' (four bulbs)	$10 to $15
8' (two bulbs)	$12 and up
8' (four bulbs)	$14 and up
Fixture with reflector	
4' (two bulbs)	$6 and up
8' (four bulbs)	$16 and up
8' HO (two bulbs)	$72 and up
8' HO (four bulbs)	$125 and up
8' VHO (two bulbs)	$85 and up
8' VHO (four bulbs)	$140 and up
Fluorescent bulb (tube)*	
4' Standard Cool white	$.88 to $5
6' Standard Cool White	$8 and up
8' HO Cool White	$7 to $10
8' VHO Cool White	$13 to $16
8' HO Gro-Lux	$17 and up
8' VHO Gro-Lux	$19 and up
4' W/S Gro-Lux	$5 to $7
4' Vita-lite (power twist)	$12 to $15
8' Vita-lite (power twist)	$23 to $25

*Tubes are cheaper if bought by the carton, which usually contain six or eight bulbs.

HID's
(HPS and MH bulbs)

HPS (High Pressure Sodium)	
400-watt bulb	$35 to $50
1,000-watt bulb	$85 to $105

400-watt ballast, reflector and bulb	$200 to $230
1,000-watt ballast, reflector and bulb	$275 to $300

MH (Metal Halide)

400-watt bulb	$35 to $60
1,000-watt bulb	$55 to $85
250-watt Optimarc bulb	$168 to $250
400-watt Optimarc bulb	$204 to $300
400-watt ballast, reflector, and MH bulb	$140 to $200
1,000-watt ballast, reflector and MH bulb	$145 to $220
MH and HPS reflectors	$15 to $140

Accessory Equipment

Timers: 10 to 15 amperes	$5 to $18
40 amperes	$30 to $60
Moisture meters	$15 to $70
pH meters	$12 to $100
CO2 generators	$70 to $200
CO2 emitter systems	$150 to $220
Negative-ion generator	$10 to $180
Watering system: a kit including 50 ft. of 1/2" tubing, 25 ft. of 1/8" feeder tubing with clips, connectors, drip emitters, stakes puncture tools, etc, as low as	$15
100 feet of 1/2" tubing	$12.50 and up
Individual emitters (dozen):	$3 to $10
Complete automatic watering systems w/27 outlets, not including pumps & timers = $12 with pumps & timers:	$45 to $250

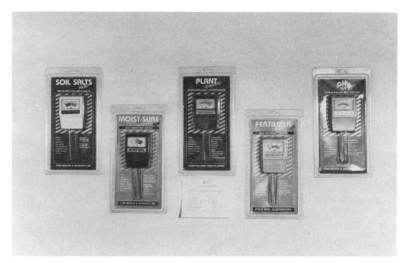

Figure 14. These very easy-to-use meters take much of the guesswork out of gardening.

the systems are constructed with this in mind. Most systems include the bulb and ballast, a reflector, and enough extension wire so that the ballast can be placed on the floor and the wire can reach the bulb hanging from the ceiling. These distributors also sell just about anything else a grower could possibly want, including light balancers, pH meters, moisture meters, CO_2 emitters, soil test kits, hydroponic systems and supplies, and much, much, more (see Chapter 9). Always buy bulbs and ballasts at the same time, because not all are interchangeable.

For information and tips on buying soil, soil amendments, and hydroponic mediums, see Buying Soil and Hydroponic Components in Chapter 9.

Chapter 3

Setting Up an Indoor Growing Room

Setting up a growing room is a simple and straightforward procedure. The larger the garden is to be, the more carefully you must prepare and work out your plans. Modest fluorescent gardens may need no more than the light fixture hanging above some flower pots. A system with two or more HID's needs a large space, and requires exhaust fans or at least an open window for fresh air. You could install a light balancer that moves the HID's slowly around the growing area. You might want to set up a CO_2 dispenser or an automatic watering system. Your garden can be as simple or elaborate as you want it to be.

When deciding where to grow, first consider the garden's safety and security. Is the room secure from outside detection? Can the light be seen from outside or by unexpected visitors? Will the smell of marijuana attract attention? If your room is vented to an outside area or another room, the distinctive fragrance of fresh marijuana is particularly noticeable during flowering (see Negative-Ion generators in Chapter 13). Is there adequate electricity to power your lights? See the section on Electricity and Safety Measures later in this chapter to help you figure your electrical needs.

For a large garden, you need a handy water supply or a strong back, because hauling enough water for a large, maturing garden can become quite a chore, although one that most gardeners don't mind. Kitchen faucets usually have a threaded end to which you can attach a garden hose that will reach the plants or the water holding tank.

There must be enough vertical space to allow the full maturation of your garden. Six feet is the minimum overhead space needed to hang a 1,000 watt HID light system and still have enough vertical space for the plants to grow to a decent size. You can grow a garden in a space only thirty inches high if you use fluorescents, especially if you use clones, and small pots.

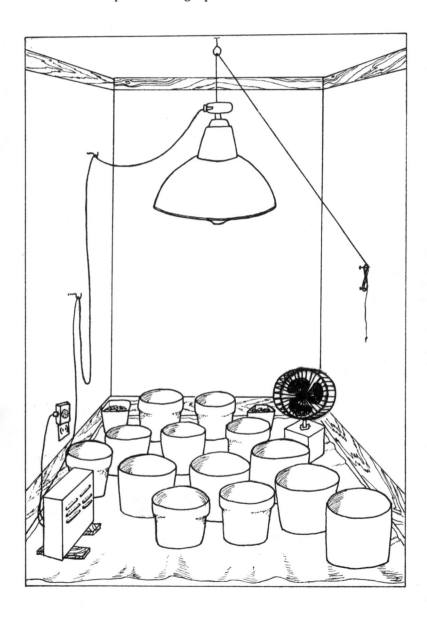

Figure 15. Basic HID garden. A no frills setup. *Drawing by L. P. Kallan.*

You must have enough room to move around the garden comfortably to tend the plants. If you're cramped and can barely maneuver when you start, this discomfort only worsens as the plants get larger, take up more space, and require more frequent attention.

What Size Light System?

When deciding what size light system you want to use, consider how much yield you actually need, and the space and funds you have available to set up your garden. An occasional smoker can supply his or her smoking needs by setting up a system of four four-foot fluorescent tubes, which will consume only 160 watts, an insignificant amount. This is absolutely the smallest light system recommend for growing marijuana, and I would strongly recommend using four eight-foot tubes instead. The eight-foot system yields more than twice as much, because of better plant growth and vigor, for very little additional cost and effort. For the smart shopper, the initial cost might be only $35.00 for the eight-foot fixture and tubes.

Two regular smokers may want to set up a system of at least four eight-foot standard or HO fluorescent tubes (320 or 440 watts), or a 400-watt, or 1,000-watt HID light system. These systems should return at a minimum, from six to sixteen ounces of sinsemilla buds each five months, and at least an equivalent amount in lower grades of shoots and leaves per crop.

Always use the longest tube that can fit in the growing area. For instance, never use two four-foot fluorescents if the area can accommodate an eight-footer, since one eight-foot system is cheaper to buy and run than two four-foot fixtures, and because a single eight-foot tube produces more light for less running costs than two four-foot tubes. The single fixture is easier to set up, and easier to raise and lower, than two four-foot fixtures. Also, always combine fluorescents into one large garden, rather than having separate, smaller gardens. The square foot area will be the same either way, but the effective **depth or cubic area** of the garden increases when the lights are combined (see Figures 16).

A modest inexpensive system that you can buy at any hardware store is one of four eight-foot fluorescent tubes, consuming 320 watts. This system covers an area of 16 square feet (2' X 8') with good results if the plants are maintained properly. Another inexpensive excellent system consists of four four-foot regular fluorescent tubes (160 watts) for nurturing clones, and one 400-watt HPS for growth and flowering. Along with fans and other accessory equipment, this garden might draw only 700 watts; yet the return is excellent, yielding a pound or more of sinsemilla every four months. One 15 ampere household circuit powers the entire garden.

Determining the Garden's Size

The size of your garden is determined by the dimensions and wattage of the light system. Marijuana grows decently with as little as fifteen watts of light per square foot of growing area, but for best results use **a minimum of 20** watts per square foot. In general, to figure total watts needed to illuminate a known area: length times width equals area in square feet; area times 20 watts per square foot equals total watts needed. For example, you have a room 11 feet by 14 feet that you want to fill with plants. The area is 154 square feet [11 ft. X 14 ft. = 154 square feet]. Now at 20 watts per square foot that's 3,080 watts [154 square feet X 20 w/square feet = 3,080 w], or three 1,000-watt HID's.

Another example: a minimum-sized garden could be illuminated by a four-foot fluorescent fixture with four 40-watt tubes, which equals 160 watts. Dividing 160 watts by 20 watts per square foot equals eight square feet of garden space. The garden size then corresponds to a light system that is the length of the fixture (four feet) by two feet in width. A system of four eight-foot HO fluorescents of 110 watts each then works out to be 4 X 110 watts = 440 watts, divided by 20 watts per square foot = 22 square feet, or an area the length of the tube (eight feet), which then tells you the width of the system (22÷8 = 2.75 feet).

In practice, most rooms don't have dimensions that correspond to handy wattages, but this formula is a good general guideline from which to start. Of course, the more light you concentrate on the plants, the faster they'll grow as long as other "growth factors" aren't limiting. Experienced growers often concentrate between 30 and 40 watts of light per square foot, and coupled with supplemental CO_2, the rate of growth dramatically increases. The figure of 20 watts per square foot should only be used as the **minimum concentration** of light necessary to grow a good crop, and as an example to compute maximum garden size with a given amount of light.

Every growing room needs space for the gardener to maneuver when caring for their plants, and fans, storage, etc., may take up some of the area. The preceding example would work well with only two 1,000-watt HID's mounted on a light balancer, with perimeter space for the gardener to work. A setup with four HID's and supplemental CO_2 could easily double the return from the same space. To

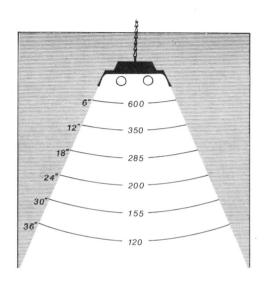

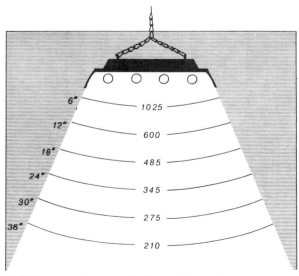

Figure 16. With more tubes, both the width and the effective depth for gardening increase. Light output is in footcandles from 40 watt tubes with reflector. *Drawings by E.N. Laincz.*

figure the size of any garden when you already have the lights: divide total watts by 20 to get area in square feet. For example, if you have two 1,000-watt HID's, the total wattage is 2,000 watts [2 lamps X 1,000 watts/lamp = 2,000 watts] which light a total area of 100 square feet [2,000 w ÷ 20 w/square foot = 100 square feet]. (The use of light balancers increases the garden area or area of effective illumination.)

Using the formula of 20 watts per square foot, the area beneath a 1,000-watt lamp works out to be a circle eight feet across. Use a circle about five feet across for a 400-watt lamp. In multiple 1,000-watt light systems, overlap the circular areas by about two or three feet. A two 1,000-watt bulb HID garden would then have two eight-foot circles overlapping to form an area of light 13 feet long and eight feet wide. A single 1,000-watt bulb on a light balancer illuminates a circle or square about ten feet across. A 400-watt HID on a light balancer effectively illuminates an area at least six feet across.

Hanging the Light System

There are two basic setups to keep the lights close to the plants. The most common is to hang the fixture with chains or rope from hooks attached to the ceiling, from beams, from studs in the wall, or from a frame or shelves constructed for the purpose. The fixture is then raised incrementally to maintain the appropriate distance from the plant tops as the plants grow.

The second, less-common setup has the lights fixed in place with a supporting bed below that carries the plants. The bed or flat is lowered from the light source as the plants grow taller. This second option is commonly used with plants growing under a skylight, with HID lamps that are fixed in place or are on light balancers, or with fluorescent shelf gardens, where it's more convenient to lower a bed rather than to raise a fixture. Put the plants on a table, plywood sheet, or boards on blocks to keep them close to the light source. As the plants grow, remove supporting blocks to lower the bed so that the plants aren't cramped against a skylight, or an electric light source. Use hydroponic mediums, because they're much lighter than soil. The supporting flat also can be suspended by chains from hooks in a frame or an overhead shelf to facilitate easy lowering.

You may not need to raise the fixture at all for HID gardens if you grow a fast-turnover crop where the plants are less than three feet tall when harvested. This is common when the crop is matured under HID's on light balancers after being started under a smaller fluorescent system.

Figure 17. Raising the lights made easy. *Left:* Just move the "S" hook up the links of the chain. *Right:* With rope, loop the rope around a cleat or nails to raise the lights.

Whatever setup you choose, make sure that raising or lowering the fixture or platform is easy, since you'll have to adjust it more often as the plants grow faster and larger with time. A heavy system that's difficult to raise becomes more difficult to manipulate later.

If you hang the light system from the walls or ceiling, locate a stud, and screw strong hooks directly into the stud. Studs are located in every room corner and are spaced 16, 18, or 24 inches apart along the walls, depending on local building codes and requirements. Plaster is too weak to support heavy fixtures, unless you attach a three- to five-foot long wooden strip held by several wingbolts to distribute the weight. Suspend the fixture from a hook at the ends of the wooden strip. Clothes hooks or shelves in closets should be sturdy enough to support a fixture. Anchor gardens under loft beds to the bed's supporting frame or into the bed's mattress platform.

For MH and HPS lamps you could use a pulley, but all you really need is a strong hook imbedded in the overhead (ceiling) over which you run a strong rope attached to the lamp fixture. At the other end, mount a boat cleat, or two strong nails spaced about six inches apart for securing or tying off the rope. By wrapping the line several times around the cleat or two nails, you can tie down the line much more easily than if you try to make a knot around a single anchoring nail or hook while holding the weight of the fixture. Never use electrical wire to hang a fixture. Always use a rope or chain for support and allow the electrical wire to hang free (and off the floor!). Leave at least a six inch space between the ceiling and any HID because the fixture will get very hot.

Several holes for mounting are prepunched in the top surface of all fluorescent fixtures. The easiest procedure for raising fluores-.cents is to slide an "S"-shaped hook through the holes. Make two loops of rope, about four to eight inches long, and attach them to the "S" hook at each end of the fixture. To each loop, attach another "S" hook connected to a chain that's secured above each end of the fixture. When raising the lights, simply move the top "S" hook to a higher link on a chain. Raising the fixture is then easy, and the non-conducting rope loop breaks electrical conductivity between the fixture and you. This helps prevent possible shocks if you raise the fixture when the lights are on. Or just run ropes or strong cords to an "S" hook at both ends of the fixture, then over hooks embedded in the ceiling or frame, and then back down to a convenient place, where the rope is tied off.

Reflectors and Light Balancers for HID Gardens

Always buy a reflector when you purchase an HID. Each company makes its own reflector and some are more effective than others, but it's most important that you buy a reflector rather than not. For vertically mounted HID's, there are broad-cone, deep-cone, and parabolic reflectors. Stationary lights work best with parabolic reflectors. They concentrate the light by about 20 percent more than broad-coned reflectors and increase the effective depth for growing.

Horizontally-mounted HID lamps deliver about 20 percent more light than parabolic reflectors. You must buy an MH bulb intended for horizontal mounting in order to take advantage of the horizontal reflector. HPS lamps mount in any position.

The only good application for a broad-cone or shallow-cone reflector is when using MH with HPS lamps in multiple-bulb gardens. When using a light balancer, position the lights closer to the plant tops. The broad-cone system illuminates all of the garden with a mix of light spectrums continuously since the light radiates to a broader area. Make sure that the garden's perimeter is surrounded with reflective surfaces.

1,000 W Super MH with 45" Vertical Cone Reflector

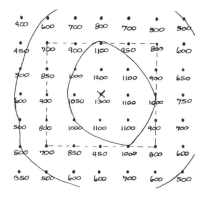

1,000 W HPS with 45" Vertical Cone Reflector

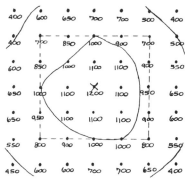

1,000 Watt HPS with 40" Standard Parabolic Reflector

1,000 Watt HPS with Standard Horizontal Reflector

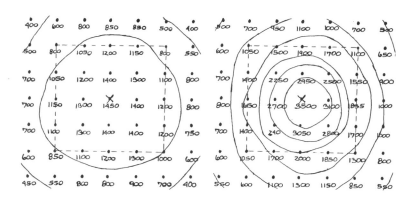

Figure 18. Top: *Left and right:* Comparing the effectiveness (in footcandles) of MH to HPS lamps with vertical cone reflectors. Bottom: *Left and right:* Comparing parabolic and horizontal reflectors using HPS lamps. Notice that horizontal is better than parabolic, and the parabolic is better than the cone reflector in top figure. Area covered is six by six feet. *Study by, and graphs courtesy of Jorge Cervantes.*

Light balancers are what their name implies: they are mechanical arms from which MH or HPS lamps hang; a small motor moves the lamps back and forth slowly across the garden. Light movers distribute the light source evenly, and equally illuminate all parts of the garden. Because the light moves constantly, you can position lamps closer to the tops of the plants without burning them. The constantly moving light eliminates the "pyramiding effects" found under stationary lights, where growth concentrates under the center of the bulb but growth on the periphery of the garden lags behind. For multiple HID gardens either linear or circular light balancers are strongly recommended.

Light balancers are of two types: arc movers rotate around a circular garden; linear movers move back and forth across a rectangular garden. Most light movers take from 40 to 50 minutes to complete one rotation or one back-and-forth movement. Whirlygig, which moves back and forth 180 degrees, covers an eight-foot-wide circle or a 15-foot-wide circle with extenders. The Sun-Circle rotates in a complete circle every 40 minutes. Two lights illuminate a ten-foot-diameter circle. Extension arms and another bulb increase the effectively illuminated area to cover a 15-foot-wide circle. Linear balancers such as the Solar Shuttle cover a room eight feet wide by ten feet long and up to 18 feet long with extenders. One advantage of rotating light movers is that they evenly mix the light spectrum from HPS and MH lamps used in conjunction. For three-bulb flowering gardens, use two HPS's to one MH. Linear balancers keep part of the garden mostly under the MH, and the rest of the garden mostly under the HPS.

In any garden with more than one HID lamp, light balancers are an essential addition to "even out" the light spectrum and overall growth, and to evenly fill the whole garden. They increase the yield of any HID garden at least 20 percent and possibly as much as 40 percent. Retail outlets for light balancers advertise in *High Times* magazine and *Sinsemilla Tips*, in which at least six mail-order houses list light movers in their catalogs.

With two bulb gardens, use an arc light mover with one MH and one HPS lamp. This configuration illuminates the whole garden with strong red and far-red wavelengths, which promote better flowering. Use a wide angle reflector rather than a deep parabolic reflector for better illumination. Parabolic reflectors work best with stationary lights. They concentrate the light and increase the effective depth for growing. Since light balancers allow lights to be placed closer to the plant tops, a broad-coned reflector illuminates all of the garden more evenly throughout the cycle.

If you have a problem with availability or consumption of electricity, install a light balancer instead of another HID bulb. Light balancers usually draw no more than 14 to 24 watts, so the dimensions and yield of your garden increase without any noticeable difference in power consumption. Light balancers have from one to four "arms," each of which holds one MH or HPS bulb and reflector/fixture. If vibrations from your light balancers are a problem, use foam-rubber strips between the ceiling hardware on which you mount the mover to help dampen vibrations.

Fluorescent Setups

For fluorescent gardens, you might prefer to buy the ballasts and end sockets separately or to remove fluorescent ballasts from the fixture, since ballasts make up most of the fixture's weight. Surprisingly, it's often cheaper to remove parts from a whole fixture than to buy the parts separately. Mount the ballasts permanently on a wall or on the shelf's frame, and run the wires to the sockets which you should mount on plywood or a wooden frame. Position the ballasts on a wall or support midway between the lowest and highest positions that the fixture will be, in order to minimize the length of the wire you need to run.

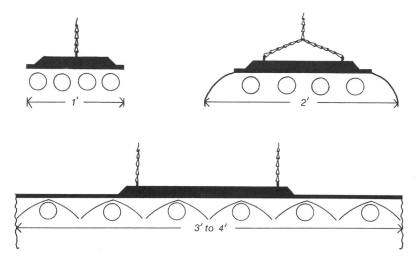

Figure 19. (a) Most fluorescent fixtures come like this. (b) Fixtures with tubes spaced apart are better. (c) Highly recommended: space six to eight tubes on a piece of plywood or wood frame. *Drawing by E.N. Laincz.*

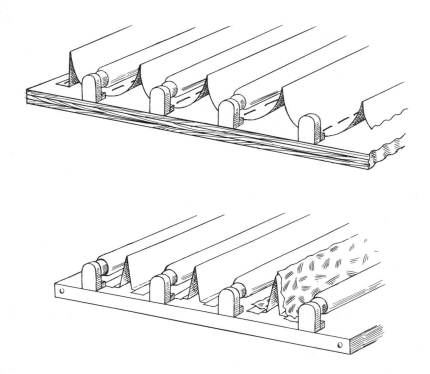

Figure 20. Make reflectors from cardboard or sturdy paper stapled to the wood. You may face them with aluminum foil or white plastic. Don't let the reflectors contact the ends of the tubes. *Drawing by O. Williams.*

There is a schematic on the ballasts to show you how to wire the sockets. Mount the sockets on a frame of one-by-twos or a plywood sheet, and space the sockets evenly across the width of the garden. Or remove the ballasts, but leave the sockets in the fixture. You can space the tubes to distribute the light evenly over all the garden, rather than concentrate it at the center. In typical fixtures, the bulbs are centered close together, and much of the light is kept bouncing around within the reflector or between the bulbs. Spacing the tubes evenly across the width of the garden actually increases the light (by as much as 40 percent!) directed toward the plants. For example, a four-tube, 320-watt, eight-foot-long fluorescent system covers an area about two feet wide. Usually the four bulbs are concentrated in the center eight inches of the fixture. Space the tubes from two to six inches apart. However you mount the sockets, always make individual reflectors for each bulb (see Figures 20 and 21) from heavy-weight construction paper.

Separating the ballasts from the fixture helps, especially with shelf gardens. Once the ballasts are removed, the system is light-weight, easy to raise, and runs cool. There is no problem with the ballasts heating the shelf above.

Mount the end sockets precisely in place, otherwise the tubes may not light consistently. Use a 1 by 2 attached to the plywood or light frame against which you mount the sockets. The wood strip prevents the sockets from flaring out and causing problems with poor electrical contact.

Reflectors for the Room and Lights

Once you've decided upon your growing space, fully prepare it before you start planting. Any household room should have plastic to protect the floor from water damage. Buy white plastic painters' dropcloths from any hardware store for a couple of dollars to reflect light back toward the plants. In greenhouses, use white granite rock, white quartz chips, white sand, or pallets painted white to cover the floor. Anything white or light-colored reflects light, which is especially important in low-light natural-light gardens and in all electric light gardens to help illuminate lower branches.

Whatever setup you choose and whatever lights you buy, reflective materials that surround the garden direct from 20 to 60 percent more light toward the plants. Reflectors contain most of the light

Figure 21. Homemade reflectors separate these "power twist" tubes. Astrolon covers the top and sides of this flowering garden.

within the garden, and more equally distribute light to all of the plants and to their lower branches.

A flat white paint produces a better reflective surface for an even, well distributed reflected light than glossy paints or aluminum foils do. Paint all adjacent surfaces with flat white paint, or cover the surfaces with aluminum foil or another reflective material.

A favorite reflective material for both indoor and outdoor grow rooms is Astrolon, a heavy-duty cloth/plastic material with a reflective, silvered matrix surface. Astrolon doesn't scratch or crinkle, and it lasts for many years. Even when wrinkled, its matrix surface reflects light evenly. Astrolon resists damage from sunlight, physical abuse, extreme swings in temperature, and high winds. Use Astrolon to cover floors and walls, for hanging curtains, or to face overhead reflectors.

Double-layered plastic, black on one side and white on the other, is another excellent reflective material; it works very well as curtains to surround the garden. This double-layered plastic is a heavier gauge than plastic dropcloths; it's a better choice to cover and protect the floor, yet reflect light. Look through any reflective material toward the lights to see if light comes through. Any light coming through is lost. Fold white construction paper or plastic in a double or triple-layer to contain more of the light.

Mylar, which was developed for NASA, has a mirror finish and is very reflective. Mylar is about six percent more reflective than flat

Figure 22. Mylar (on left side of picture) is excellent for covering permanent walls. (Don't use Mylar for curtains.)

white paint. It's an excellent reflecting surface if it's fixed in place and you don't have to move or contact it during growing. You could face all garden walls and not have a better reflective surface unless you used mirrors. There are two problems with Mylar. First, it's electrically conductive; so it's not a good idea to hang Mylar curtains from or near a fixture, since it could conduct a shock to you. Second, if the Mylar has to be moved or repositioned, as when hung as curtains, it scratches and mars easily, which reduces its reflectivity and useful lifetime. For reflective curtains, Astrolon or white plastics are nearly as reflective, and not electrically conductive, so that either is a better choice than Mylar.

If your fluorescent fixtures are not equipped with reflectors, construct them from household materials. Use the cardboard boxes in which the fluorescent tubes and fixtures are packaged. Cut off the end flaps, and about ten inches from one end. Paint the interior flat white, or face it with a reflective material. Position the box over the fixture so that the wide sides form the side reflectors. If the sides won't hold the proper angle after being bent into position, adjust and hold the angle by wedging a wood slat or straightened coat hanger between the sides.

For an MH or HPS light, construct a parabolic or broad, cone-shaped reflector from chicken wire or any sturdy material that's malleable but holds its shape. Face its interior with aluminum foil or Astrolon. Adjust the angle of the cone so that the perimeter of the

Figure 23. Makeshift reflector of aluminum foil on an MH fixture. It's preferable to buy a reflector.

garden is just within the cone of light formed by the reflector when it's hung at the proper distance from the plant tops. It's better to purchase a reflector from a lighting distributor. It will direct more light, more evenly, than any makeshift reflector.

When walls border the garden, paint them with flat white paint or face them with a reflective material. Surround open sides with hanging curtains of Astrolon or white plastic. Or in HID gardens, use cardboard sheets from boxes, and stand them up in a circle around the garden if it's centered in a large room. Staple flaps to the floor or construct a simple frame or stand on which you can lean or attach the cardboard, and cover them with reflecting material. For fluorescent gardens, hang reflective curtains (Astrolon or white plastic) from the long sides of the fixture.

Window gardens also need reflectors; otherwise the backs of the plants get little light. You'll see the obvious increase in light once you've installed reflectors. Surround the backs of the plants with a reflective perimeter and cover the floor with white plastic. For large plants, string a strong cord from which reflective curtains hang to surround the window garden.

Ventilation is very important to the health and growth rate of the crop. Reflectors should not completely encase a garden, thereby cutting off all airflow. Leave open spaces at the ends of fluorescent gardens. Check for heat build-up, and cut holes near the tops of the reflectors to vent excessive heat. For HID's, leave open space above the garden. Read the section on Ventilation in Chapter 13 for information on installing fans.

Additional Preparations

For most indoor growers, the temperature of the floor is not something to worry about. But, if the floor of your prospective growroom is cool (less than 50 degrees), you might have problems with delayed or sporadic germination. Simply raise the pots above the concrete or soil floor, and the cold floor no longer chills the pots. Insulate the floor, or put the pots on boxes or pallets and the germination temperature rises into an acceptable temperature range when warmed by the lights. Where the floor temperature is particularly cold, use heating cables to raise the temperature of the planting mediums (see Chapter 11). Or use a germination box that's separate from the cold growing room to start the seedlings.

A cold floor slows the growth of plants at any stage of their life cycle. A basement floor colder than the air conducts heat out of the pots, which noticeably slows growth (sit on your basement floor for a few minutes, and your rear end will give you an idea of how well a cold floor can cool a bottom). Make a platform of any insulating material such as a plywood sheet raised several inches off of the floor with wooden blocks. Or insulate the floor with fiberglass insulation with aluminum facing for reflectivity, or with white styrofoam squares or sheets.

For pest prevention, a "fogger" insecticide (bug bomb) rids any space of insects (see Chapter 16). Deploy insect foggers before you start any plants, whether or not you have grown plants in the space before.

Disinfecting a growroom to prevent fungal problems may help, but certainly won't preclude microbial problems. You might disinfect the walls and floor with a wash of bleach, ammonia, or whitewash, but fungi are ubiquitous — we live in a "sea" of fungal spores — and it's nearly impossible to raise plants in a sterile environment. Certainly cleaning and disinfecting the room can only help, but fungal spores float everywhere, and fungi naturally degrade any dead or dying tissue, wherever it may be. This is why fruit molds in a refrigerator, why leaves turn to compost, and why everything organic degrades no matter where it is. (If it weren't for fungi, the planet would soon be covered by organic debris.) More effective preventive measures are discussed in Chapters 13 and 16.

Electricity and Safety Measures

While contemplating your prospective garden, you'll want to have a rough idea of what running your lights will cost. Depending on where you live, electrical costs for most homes run between three and eight cents per kilowatt hour (1,000 watts per hour in use). The rate per kilowatt hour appears on your electricity bill. For a fluorescent garden that draws 320 watts (four eight-foot tubes), running your lights for 18 hours a day costs between five and 14 dollars a month, and for twelve hours, roughly three to nine dollars a month — an insignificant cost when compared to the fun of growing or the price of commercial marijuana.

With large systems, say, with two 1,000-watt HID's, the cost of electricity needs to be considered. Two 1,000-watt HID's actually draw about 2,120 watts, plus the current for fans and perhaps a light mover for a total of about 2,400 watts. A garden illuminated for 18 hours a day would cost about $40 to $100 per month, and for twelve-hours a day, from $25 to $70 dollars a month. (For a single 1,000-watt HID garden, the costs would be half these figures.) Gardens grown under 24 hours of light a day do grow faster than those under 18 hours of daily light; but for many growers the cost for electricity outweighs the increase in the rate of growth. Other growers reason that, considering the cost of marijuana, who cares about electrical costs? If electricity costs are of concern to you, 18 hour light cycles are your best choice. Also, a daily "rest-period" for the lights is a safety measure, since the electric lines and fixtures have less chance to overheat.

Next, does your prospective grow room have enough electricity to safely power your lights? For any system other than HID's, this should never be a problem. The least amount of power for living spaces is in old apartments, which have only two 15-ampere electrical circuits. Fluorescent systems are not much more than adding a TV. For any 1,000-watt HID garden, you'll need to find out how much power (wattage) you have at your disposal.

Before you buy any large light system, find out how much current is available in your prospective grow room. Most outlets for normal house current are on either 15- or 20-ampere circuits. New homes may have 30-ampere circuits. Go to your fusebox and read the amperage off the fuses or the circuit breakers. Circuits with amperage higher than 20- or 30-amperes are often for stoves, heavy appliances, or machine tools and they might combine two circuits into one that doubles the voltage to 220 volts. These 220 volt circuits are fine for grow rooms, but you may need an electrician's help to

Figure 24. An HPS garden with foil on the wall (left), ventilation fan (back), and white plastic covering the entrance (right). Using curtains of white plastic to cover the entrance reduces the chance of electrical shocks.

set up all of your equipment, although most mail-order houses provide instructions for both 110- and 220-volt light installations. Next you need to find out which circuits power your grow room, and what other rooms are on the same circuit.

To find out which outlets are served by a particular fuse or circuit breaker, get a friend to help you. Have your friend plug a lamp into an outlet while you remove fuses or shut breakers off one at a time, until the light goes off. Once the light goes off, you know that this fuse or circuit breaker services the room. Turn all other breakers back on. Move the lamp from outlet to outlet until you find all the outlets that are on this circuit (it's still off, and the lamp won't light unless it's on another circuit). If you have to do it alone, use a radio with the volume turned up so that you can hear it from the fuse box. A large room or basement may have two or three circuits for all the outlets. A typical bedroom has one or two 15- or 20-ampere circuits for that room alone. In typically wired homes, that limits you to one or two 1,000-watt HID's and accessory equipment in normal household rooms.

Does your prospective grow room have enough electrical power to safely run the lights and equipment? To figure wattage, multiply the amperage (current), read off the fuse or circuit breaker, times the voltage (standard voltage in the U.S. is 110 to 120 volts): watts equals total amperage times volts, [W = I (amps) X E (volts)]. A 15-ampere fuse indicates that if no other rooms are on this circuit, you have 1,650 watts of power [15 amperes X 110 volts = 1,650 watts]. Two 15-ampere circuit breakers for a basement mean that you have [15 + 15 = 30 amperes], and multiplied by 110 volts = 3,300 watts, enough to power two 1,000-watt HID's and accessory equipment. In practice, always leave a safety margin of at least 20 percent, because some power is lost through heat and resistance of electrical runs; so the maximum power a 15-ampere circuit can provide is actually 1,320 watts, or a single HID, a fan, and a light mover. For safety reasons, figure one 1,000-watt HID for each 15-ampere circuit. Old apartments may be wired for as little as 30 amperes, but most modern homes have from 60 to 200 available amperes. If the room does not have enough current, have new circuits run by an electrician before you purchase any equipment.

For large commercial gardens and gardens in remote areas without electricity, consider using a generator. Diesel and gasoline generators are satisfactory if they operate outside where the poisonous exhausts (deadly carbon monoxide, among others) are safely vented. However, they are very noisy. Installing the generator in a hole in the ground helps dampen noise and keeps the equipment in better shape. If you're mechanically handy, adapt an automobile muffler to reduce noise. Before purchasing any generator, ask for a demonstration and choose the quietest.

Propane generators are much safer for inside installation. Propane generators burn cleanly when the flame is blue. The exhaust is CO_2 which increases growth in the garden. Gasoline generators can be adapted to run on propane, and adaptor kits for generators may be available for conversion.

Wiring the Lights

Fluorescent light fixtures usually come prewired, and you need only hang the fixture and plug in the cord. Sometimes the insides of the fixture need to be wired. All the wires are present, along with a schematic glued to the ballast, that identifies the wires by their color. Anyone without previous knowledge of electricity can wire the fixture. Just attach the wires to the lamp sockets as shown in the diagram. New fixtures have terminals into which the bare end of a wire is pushed; the terminal automatically makes and holds electrical contact. Older-type lamp sockets have conventional screw terminals.

When you get your HID, inspect the top of the fixture where the cord enters to connect to the bulb. There should be a protective

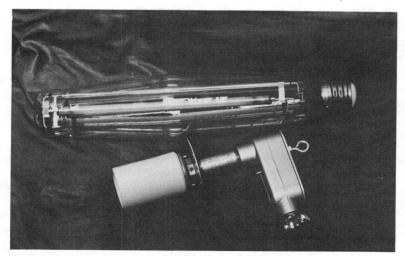

Figure 25. Reputable distributors install protective housings to shield the wires entering an HID fixture. Also shown is a 1,000-watt HPS lamp.

sheath of heavy insulation or metal tubing. If the cord has no additional protection, wrap several layers of electrician's tape around the last six inches of cord that enter the fixture. Inspect the connection every month because short circuits and shocks may occur if the insulation breaks down because of heat. Many of the mail order companies that sell HID lights now install a protective sheath to prevent the occurrence of any such problem.

If an extension cord is necessary, make sure you buy one rated for 20 amperes (#12 gauge wire) or 15 amperes (#14 gauge wire). The typical extension cords from a supermarket (#16 or #18 wire are rated for, respectively, 13 and 10 amperes) won't safely conduct the current that your system draws. Electricity follows the "weakest link" adage. Always use extension cords or wires that are rated equal to or higher than the required current. You'll never go wrong unless one "link" or wire in your system conducts less than the maximum amperage that your garden requires. Test any cord for safety by simply feeling how hot it is after a few hours of operation. Replace any extension wire that feels more than mildly warm with a heavier gauge extension cord.

For any household wiring, red or black wires are hot wires, that is, they conduct the current to feed the equipment. The other conductor in any circuit is the white wire. In any properly wired house the white wires are the grounded wires. The white wires

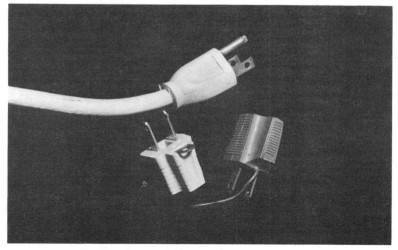

Figure 26. Use heavy gauge extension cords with three-prong plugs (top). Use an adapter plug for two-prong outlets (bottom).

Figure 27. For two-prong outlets, connect the terminal (*top left*) or wire (*top right*) from the adapter plug to the screw that holds the cover plate. This converts the plug to three wires which grounds the system.

conduct electricity, but are connected to the metallic parts of your house and ultimately routed to ground. You can touch a bare white wire while it conducts electricity and not experience a shock, because the grounded system is a better conductor to ground than you are, and electricity will take the path of least resistance. In a properly wired house the screw-in part of a lamp (shell) is grounded when used with the new polarized plugs (which fit in one direction only); this is why you don't get a shock when you change a light bulb and accidentally touch the shell.

A green wire is a grounding wire. The grounding wire does not normally carry electricity — it's a safety conductor that carries electricity to ground in the event of a malfunction. All safety-conscious growers want to install the grounding wire in their systems. The grounding wire is the third contact on a three-pronged plug or outlet. If your fixture, whether HID or fluorescent, comes with a three-prong plug, plug it into a three-prong outlet, and you need to do nothing more. If your fixture comes with a three-wire plug, but your outlet receptacle has only two slots, then buy a three wire adapter plug from any hardware store. The three-wire adapter has a third wire or terminal that you must connect to the outlet box. Connect the third terminal or green wire of the adapter to the center screw that holds the cover plate on the outlet box. If your light system has only a two-wire cord, connect a single #14 or #12 gauge wire from any bare metal screw on the fixture housing (a mechanical screw, not an electrical terminal) to a bare, mechanical screw on any metal part on the housing of the outlet box. Whether you install an HID or a fluorescent, always use a three-wire system to assure your safety.

Safety First

With electric-light gardens, there is an inherent danger from electrical shocks and short circuits, because water and electricity in close proximity always present a risk. You will be in a garden where there are lights, fixtures, reflectors, and water in the pots and possibly on the floor, all of which can conduct electricity. This can be a dangerous situation, particularly with larger systems, such as HID's, which draw considerable current. Danger from electrical shocks can be eliminated or at least reduced to non-dangerous proportions with the three-wire (prong) grounding system described above. After grounding your equipment, follow the precautions described here for daily care, and you should never have a problem.

Whenever you care for your plants, be aware that water and electricity are a dangerous combination. Always turn off all electricity in the garden while watering, and never care for your plants when the floor is wet or moist. Few of you will shut the lights off every time you water. But make sure that you never touch a fixture or a reflector while you're watering or caring for your garden.

An electrician's adage is to use only one hand. That is, don't ever touch two conductors at the same time, whether fixture, floor, or reflector. The most dangerous situation is when you are the bridge between a potential electrical source and ground. In a growing room this means touching an electrical fixture with one hand while your other hand touches a reflector, or your feet are on a good electrical ground such as a moist or wet floor. You are placing yourself as a conductor between source current and an electrical ground.

For safe gardening, never touch the fixture unless the electricity is shut off. Never raise the fixture with the lights on if your fixture is hung with chains or wires or any other electrical conductor. Keep all electrical cords raised off the floor and away from water. Any ballast on a damp floor is very dangerous. Put the ballast on a brick or block of wood to raise it off the floor. Third, if you have aluminum foil or other metallic reflectors, don't touch them while standing on a wet floor or handling the fixture.

Don't fool around with electricity. You could be seriously burned or killed. This is serious. Don't take chances or become lax after a

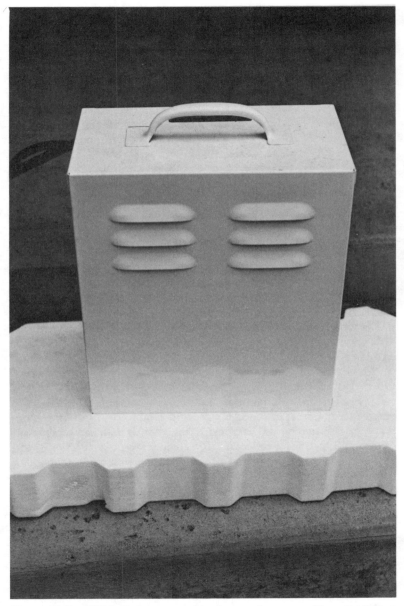

Figure 28. An HID ballast on a wet floor is very dangerous. Place the ballast on an insulator such as styrofoam (shown), wood, or a plastic flowerpot.

few months of easy care has made you complacent about caring for your plants with the lights on. My electrical teacher used to say, "The thing about electricity is that it gives you one chance, and that could be your last chance. You may never have the opportunity to learn from your first mistake."

General Safety Measures

When you spray your plants, whether the spray is an insecticide, nutrient, or plain water, take a few necessary precautions. All sprays work best if you thoroughly spray the undersides of the leaves. This means that you'll direct the spray upwards toward the lights. Lights that are on (hot) will implode when they contact water. Incandescent or HID bulbs implode forcefully when hit by a single droplet of water; obviously, the resulting spray of glass fragments is dangerous. Always turn off the lights and wait until they cool before you spray the garden. Raise the light system above the spray, and wipe bulbs dry before relighting. If an HID lamp cracks or breaks, don't look at it! Avert your eyes and pull the plug. Wait for the bulb to cool before you handle it. Fluorescents might not implode, because they operate at cooler temperatures, but why take a chance?

You'll want to periodically clean your lamps, since they'll collect dust and grime from static electricity, which cuts down their usable light output. Hot bulbs may implode from pressure or from being cleaned with wet solutions. You'll also need to change old bulbs. Always turn off the lights and allow them to cool to room temperatures before you clean or change them. **When HID lamps are turned off, they require about a 15-minute wait before they'll relight.**

It's a good idea to wear UV screening sunglasses when working in any garden, especially with HID lamps. The small glasses (the lenses you can see through) which just cover the eyes for people in tanning parlors are very effective in screening out any UV rays from your lights. Any good pair of sunglasses should screen most UV rays. A painter's mask is a must for any grower who is mixing soil or soil amendments, or spraying with any insecticide. These few, inexpensive, and easy to employ measures are more than cautious, they're required of all safety-conscious growers.

Chapter 4

Photoperiod

The most important plant/environment interaction for the marijuana grower to fully understand is the influence of the photoperiod. The **photoperiod** is the daily number of hours of day (light) versus night (darkness). Under natural-light conditions, the longer nights of autumn signal the marijuana plant that winter is coming, and that it's time to flower and produce seeds for the next generation. As long as the **daylength** (hours of light) remains long, the plants continue to grow vegetatively and if any flowers appear, they will be few, and they won't form the large clusters or buds that are the desired harvest. Marijuana plants constantly produce a flowering hormone called **phytochrome**. Phytochrome initiates flowering, but if phytochrome is exposed to even a flash of light, it's rendered inactive. To initiate flowering, marijuana plants need a long and **uninterrupted** period of constant darkness each night for about two weeks. When the dark period is long enough, phytochrome levels rise within the plant to a level that promotes flowering rather than leaf growth.

The natural photoperiod changes throughout the year. Daylength in the northern hemisphere is longest on June 21 and gradually decreases to its shortest duration on December 22. On March 21, the spring equinox (which means "equal night"), the daylength and night period are equal; both are 12 hours in duration. Daylength increases until June 21 and then decreases until September 21, the fall equinox, when the daylength and night period are again equal. (All dates reverse six months in the southern hemisphere.)

The actual length of daylight depends on local conditions, such as cloud cover, terrain, and altitude. On a flat midwestern plain, the effective daylength is about 30 minutes longer than sunrise to sunset. *Cannabis* **generally needs about eight days to two weeks**

of uninterrupted and successive long nights to initiate flowering. Varieties from temperate areas (Afghani) may need nights of only ten to 11 hours duration to initiate flowering. Tropical varieties may need nights of 12 or 13 hours duration to initiate a strong flowering response.

The flowering response regulated by light gives marijuana growers two basic situations: long, uninterrupted periods of darkness initiate flowering; long periods of light, or interrupting dark periods with light, maintains vegetative growth and prevents flowering. These two options offer marijuana growers innumerable possibilities for modifying growing to fit unique growing situations.

Long days do not influence male flowering as much as they do the female plants. Male plants often flower even under long days of 18 hours of light. Older female plants may also flower under long days but the flowers will be sparse.

The farther from the equator a variety originated, the less obligated by the photoperiod it is. For instance, *ruderalis*, and some South African and Afghani plants might flower after a continuous photoperiod (24 hours of daily light) is reduced to 16 hours of light even though they normally would need a shorter light cycle to flower if they were started under 18 hours of daily light. Many *ruderalis* varieties flower almost immediately, no matter how long the photoperiod is, although they won't form good buds. The influence of the photoperiod allows marijuana growers several important options and a number of creative possibilities:

1. **Forcing flowering in normal crops.** Anytime you want the plants to flower, simply reduce the photoperiod (light hours) to produce the number of dark hours recommended here, and within two weeks the plants will respond by forming flowers. Usually, if you turn the light hours down to 12 hours or less, most marijuana varieties begin flowering within eight to 14 days.

2. **Preventing flowering for off-season crops.** If you wish to prevent flowering — for example, when you are growing in the wintertime with natural light, the short natural photoperiod of winter normally causes the plants to flower prematurely, yielding undersized plants and a small harvest of buds — simply lengthen the natural photoperiod to at least 16 hours of light by using electric lights. This keeps the plants growing vegetatively for as long as you wish before they flower. Interrupting the dark period with light forces the plants to grow to a decent size before they flower. To keep plants growing vegetatively, expose the plants to a flash of light each night.

The mature plants are then much larger, and yield a satisfactory amount of mature buds when you want them to flower.

3. **Double harvests and regeneration.** You have grown a normal crop and are about to harvest. Whether the plants are growing indoors or outdoors, you have the option of regenerating the females for a second crop. If you extend the photoperiod to at least 16 hours duration, any plant that is left with some healthy leaves and shoots responds within a week or two with new growth. From now on, growth is faster than if you restarted from seed, because the plant has a mature root system and stem that supports the new growth. Under lights, keep the light cycle at 18 to 24 hours of daily light for about three to eight weeks. Once the leaves and branches start to fill the space, shorten the light cycle for flowering, and harvest a second crop in about two months. This double-harvest procedure saves time and work; no time is wasted starting seeds in new pots, and no space is wasted on any males.

With regenerated plants, you know the plant's sex and have had the time to evaluate (by smoking) the plant's potency before the second harvest. Besides knowing each plant's sex and potency, you can evaluate appearance and growth habit (when it flowers, size, disease resistance, etc.) so you know which plant will be the best mother for the next generation of seeds or clones. Regenerated plants afford growers the rare opportunity to benefit from hindsight, since they still can pollinate and propagate the mother plant that has turned out to be the best. (See Chapters 20 and 22.)

4. **Clone gardening.** You have just taken cuttings or cloned a number of plants: keep the photoperiod long (18 to 24 hours of light) for about four to eight weeks, at which time the clones should be growing well. Now cut the photoperiod to 12 hours, and within two weeks the flowering cycle begins anew (see Chapters 5 and 19).

Whatever your situation, keep in mind that once you turn the light cycle down to initiate a flowering regimen (usually about 11 or 12 hours of daily darkness), it takes about eight to 14 days for the plants to begin flowering. Full maturation of the crop then takes a minimum of five weeks, and it takes up to 14 weeks for sinsemilla to ripen and be ready to harvest. Hence you should plan on at least seven and up to 16 weeks of growing after turning down the light cycle before you can harvest the plants. About nine or ten weeks is most common.

Marijuana varieties differ in the number of hours of darkness necessary to initiate flowering. As a general rule, the closer to the equator the stock originated, the longer the dark period must be to initiate flowering. For example, Colombian plants originate from very near the equator, (where the daylength is nearly constant at about 12.5 hours of daily light.) When growing under artificial light, any photoperiod of 15 hours or more light prevents the plants from flowering. Any dark period longer than 11.5 hours initiates flowering. The dark period must not be interrupted by any (even a flash of) light. Equatorial varieties such as Colombian, Thai, Cambodian, Nigerian, Congolese, Sumatran, Indonesian, or any other varieties that originate from near the equator will respond to the following regimen: at least 15 (16 or more is safer) hours of light keeps the plants growing vegetatively and prevents flowering. About 12 to 14 hours of uninterrupted nightly darkness initiates and continues the flowering stage. For example, you are growing Colombian: start the plants under 18 hours of light. After ten weeks of growth, shorten the light cycle to about 11.5 hours of light. The plants should be ready to harvest in about ten to 13 weeks.

Suppose you are growing a variety from a temperate zone, say, Afghani. When you want the plants to flower, reduce the light period to about 12 to 13 hours duration. This should be enough to cause the plants to flower. If all of the plants haven't responded by flowering within two weeks, cut the light period one more hour to 11 or 12 hours, and the plants definitely will respond by flowering.

Figure 29. Various timers. A timer is essential to regulate the photoperiod (on and off light cycle).

You don't want the duration of the light period during flowering to be excessively short. If the light cycle is too short, plants respond by less overall growth, and sometimes hermaphroditic or abnormal flowers develop just prior to full ripeness. Neither of these responses is desirable, and the quantity and the quality of the finished harvest diminishes. You always want to set the light cycle just below the minimum amount of hours necessary for a strong flowering response. You don't want to turn down the light cycle to nine hours for an Afghani crop which would respond to 13 hours; not only might this initiate abnormal or hermaphroditic flowers, but you'll have a shorter daily growing time for bud growth. This short photoperiod is why many indoor sinsemilla growers find male flower parts forming on their female buds later in life. For best results **set the photoperiod one hour less than the minimum length necessary to induce strong flowering on all of the plants of that variety.**

A shorter than necessary photoperiod lessens the time necessary to complete maturation. A Colombian under eight hours of light may take only eight weeks until harvest, but under 12 hours of light, the same plant may need 12 weeks to ripen. An Afghani under eight hours of light may take only six weeks until harvest, but under 13 hours it may need nine or ten weeks before reaching peak potency.

You may choose to hasten maturation by using a shorter than necessary photoperiod if for some reason you can't wait, but you'll harvest a somewhat smaller crop. Let me repeat that the best way to find how many hours of light a specific variety needs for the flowering regimen is to have the light period short enough to cause **all the plants** of that variety to **flower profusely.** If a few plants have not flowered or are flowering weakly or slowly, shorten the light cycle by another hour. This procedure maximizes the yield and encourages the best development of buds.

Chapter 5

Electric Light
Garden Strategies

Electric lights offer growers innumerable possibilities for raising marijuana: with a little planning, the seeds may be started and mature plants harvested at any time the grower chooses. Let's go through a few scenarios to give you some ideas of the possibilities.

1. **Vegetative gardens** are the simplest; but don't opt for vegetative gardens unless you're an occasional smoker who doesn't want to spend much time, energy, or expense in gardening. Marijuana "light-weights" might set up a few pots in a sunny window or under a small, fluorescent fixture in a closet or the corner of a room. Keep the light cycle on for a **minimum of 16-hours** of daily light. Randomly harvest leaves and shoots to satisfy your occasional smoking.

All vegetative gardeners should use seeds from the most potent grass that they can find, since bud characteristics and maturation need not be considered. The potency of the leaves and shoots is all that counts. Males and females don't need to be identified, and the grower needs only to maintain continuous healthy growth (see Chapter 22 for the best time to harvest).

In continuously growing vegetative gardens, some plants may grow for up to three years before they need to be replaced by new plants. For the best return in vegetative gardens, continuously start and maintain plants of different ages and sizes. Replace older plants when they're harvested with new seedlings. Place new seedlings on boxes or shelves to keep them close to the light system, while they grow alongside taller, older plants.

A continuously growing vegetative garden is very easy to care for, since there should be no problem with rot, no concern about flowering, and no need to harvest the entire crop. Anytime you want to start anew, change the photoperiod to 12 hours of daily light, which directs the plants into the flowering regimen. Vegetative gardens are strictly

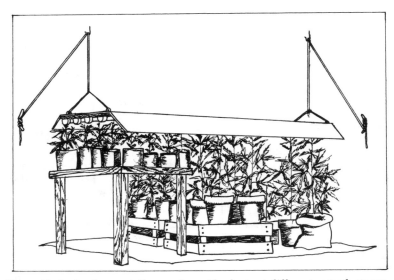

Figure 30. A simple vegetative garden with plants at different growth stages. *Drawing by L.P. Kallan.*

for occasional smokers who enjoy growing plants, smoke infrequently, and don't want to associate with dealers or spend exorbitant amounts of money on marijuana.

2. **Harvest gardens** are the most popular. Growers start, raise, and mature gardens under one light system. The plants may be any age from eight weeks to a year old when harvested. Usually gardens are from 11 to 26 weeks old by harvest; 13 to 20 weeks seems to produce the best yield and turnover.

Work backward from desired harvest date to decide when to plant. Varieties take anywhere from five to 14 weeks to ripen, once flowers start to form. Another six to 14 days is necessary to initiate flowering. Seedlings should be a minimum of four weeks old before flowering is initiated by a decreased photoperiod. (You'll get a better return if the plants are six to 10 weeks old before flowering is initiated.) Start seedlings in small pots, and transplant into larger pots once you know their gender (see Chapter 17). This guarantees that only females will eventually fill all the garden space.

3. **Multiple-light system gardens (or rotating gardens)** are one good option for maximizing the yield in a given space and using electricity

efficiently. After you've grown a crop or two, you'll realize that putting seedlings under an HID fixture wastes much space, light, and electricity, since much more room is necessary to mature the seedlings. It's more efficient to start seedlings under a small light system, and then move the female seedlings to a larger "flowering" system, where the plants grow and fill a larger area. While the plants mature under the large light system, start another group of seedlings under the small fixture. When the first crop is harvested, move the second group of seedlings to the large light system for flowering.

The advantage to this setup is that you increase your return from a given amount of electricity. You can start seedlings and clones under a 320-watt fluorescent system, flower the plants under a 1,000-watt HPS, and have enough reserve electricity to run fans, pumps, etc., all on a single 20-ampere circuit. It's possible, particularly with clones, to harvest four to eight crops a year without an elaborate system or a great deal of work.

One popular and very productive procedure is to set up separate gardens: one for clones, seedlings, and vegetative growth, and the other for flowering. You can carry rotating to the extreme with three systems: the first for germinating and growing for five weeks; the second for raising plants to ten weeks old; the third for ten weeks of flowering.

To start a rotating system, use a simple two-system garden. Find out how long your plants take to mature after reducing the photoperiod, and how much room the maturing plants need in a given number of weeks. Once you learn, for example, that the plants need ten weeks to complete maturation under a 12-hour photoperiod, work backward and plan a corresponding ten-week vegetative garden. You might start seeds or clones in a germination bed for three weeks, move them to a growth garden for seven to ten weeks, then put them in the maturation garden for the final ten weeks. This garden then operates on a 20-week cycle, but you harvest a new crop every ten weeks. With hindsight, estimate the amount of room each stage needs, and adjust the number of seedlings and the amount of space each stage needs to maximize the return from the total growing area.

Two Room Gardens: Simple and Efficient Gardening

One important advantage of using separate rooms or areas, one with constant light for growth and the other with a dark period for flowering, is that it's very easy to maintain a continuously productive garden. When you try to use a rotating system with three or more gardens, it's a full-time operation. These multiple-system gardens work well only when you already have found out precisely the optimum rotating procedure for the specific variety that you're raising, including the optimum space and time needed for each stage of growing.

Some growers envision that they'll root clones under one light system, grow them for another month under a larger system, then force flowering under another system, and finally ripen the garden under yet another system. These imaginary gardens may look fine on paper, but in practice they're very difficult and time-consuming to make work. Theory is in the mind — practice is in the hands and sweat of your effort. Plants are living organisms that may not adhere to your paper projections. Such gardens are possible, but only after the variety's growing habits are intimately known. In most cases, multiple-room gardens are much work and a source of considerable frustration.

For almost all serious growers, a two-room (or two-area) rotating garden is the best option. Use one room for seedlings, rooting clones, and vegetative growth; use the second room exclusively for flowering. This setup drastically simplifies the operation, and makes continuous gardens practical in both time and space. You can keep the "growth" garden on 18 hours of light (or constant light), and the "flowering" garden on 12 hours of light.

Now it becomes easy to grow many different varieties and sizes of plants of different ages. There's no pressure to transplant or move a batch of plants at a specific time, or to harvest an entire crop, or to take cuttings at a specific time, since only two gardens serve all purposes. Start seedlings and clones anytime, move plants to the flowering area whenever they're large enough, or harvest whenever a particular plant is deemed ripe. The whole process is continuously maintained, but it's done at a leisurely pace, and no specific timing or adjustments have to be made for any given plant or variety.

I strongly recommend that you start with a two-room (or two-area) setup before trying to grow with multiple rooms. In fact, for almost everyone, don't bother with more complicated systems, because they're usually much more trouble than they're worth.

You could start with a four-tube eight-foot fluorescent that's on constantly. Start 80 to 140 seedlings, and root clones continuously. If you are growing in one room, use opaque curtains or a light-tight barrier to separate the constant-light garden from the flowering area. Move the seedlings into your flowering garden whenever clones or seedlings are considered large enough for flowering.

The following examples are based on 20 watts of light per square foot of garden space. Increase the light to between 30 and 40 watts per square foot to get the most out of a garden using supplemental CO_2. With strong ventilation and adequate nutrients, most gardens grow much faster with 30 watts of light per square foot even without supplemental CO_2.

Table 5.1
Examples of Multi-System Gardens

Type of Light system	Square Feet of Garden	# of Weeks of Growing	# Hours of Light Cycle
Example 1: one 20-amp circuit			
1. 320w 8' fluorescent	16	6	18 to 24
2. 1,000w HID	50+	12	12
Example 2: two 15-amp circuits			
1. six 8' fluorescents (480w)	24	10	18 to 24
2. 1,000w MH and 1,000w HPS	100+	10	12
Example 3: two 20-amp circuits			
1. 8' fluorescent (320 w)	16	4	18 to 24
2. 1,000w MH	50	6	18 to 24
3. 1,000w MH and 1,000w HPS	100+	10	12

For example 1, each plant is about 18 weeks old at harvest. Start 80 or more seedlings in four-inch pots, and maintain about 40 to 50 ripening females. Use the fluorescent to root clones and raise seedlings. Replenish the flowering system with fresh plants as the plants are harvested.

For example 2, start 140 to 200 seedlings, and harvest 70 to 100 females. Take cuttings for the second crop to reduce crowding under the fluorescent. Use a two-lamp light balancer for the flowering room to increase the amount of growing space.

For example 3, root and grow about 100 to 140 clones under system #1. Move the clones to system #2 for four to six weeks of growth. Use this system to raise some plants as mothers of clones for the next garden. Flower the clones under system #3 for ten or more weeks. Use a light balancer to increase the growing area. You should be able to harvest about 100 good-sized females every ten weeks.

Your first crop will be successful, but fine-tune succeeding crops to take special circumstances and the properties of your variety into account. You may add a week or two for vegetative growth, or subtract a week from flowering; you might add another couple of fluorescent tubes to increase the number of seedlings, clones, and prospective females; you might set up four four-foot fluorescent tubes in the corner of the room to root clones or germinate seeds.

Shelf Gardening

The following paragraphs are some of the most important in this book for commercial gardeners. Skim these at first reading, because much of the information you'll need to know is detailed in later chapters.

Large MH and HPS lamps have replaced fluorescents in most indoor electric-light gardens. These high-intensity lamps foster plants larger and more robust than those grown under fluorescents. But the wave of the future is a return to fluorescent-light gardens and smaller HPS's with all the advantages of clone gardening by using the **shelf method.**

To use these techniques successfully you need experience and some fundamental knowledge of growing, which you'll learn from this book. You must also have a satisfactory working stock with which you're familiar; you must know how many weeks your variety needs to ripen; you need to have selected females to provide clones; you need to master cloning procedures, and you must know how to maximize the use of space when setting up the light systems.

Growing clones by the shelf method takes advantage of the efficiency and moderate expense of running fluorescents, and of the small stature of the matured clones. A growing "factory" can fit in a relatively small space: a half-basement or attic, or in one small room. Fluorescents can't support the large, robust plants that can grow under HID's. However, if the entire growing process keeps all of the growth between one and three feet tall, fluorescents and small HPS's become particularly advantageous.

You can buy fluorescents at any hardware or lighting store; you don't need to mail order for them. The advantages of fluorescent gardening with clones are that it: reduces the height necessary for maturing gardens and allows growing by shelf method; drastically reduces costs of electricity and bulbs; greatly increases yield for the space available. Overall, **this method yields the highest return for a given space and use of electricity.**

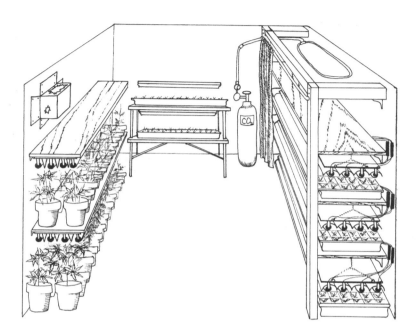

Figure 31. Fluorescent shelf garden. *Left:* Clone mothers and a light trap box enclosing a vent fan. *Back:* Clones being rooted. *Right:* Flowering section separated by curtain has CO2 emitter. Notice tubes are mounted on plywood. Ballasts are on wall to reduce heat beneath plants and lessen the systems' weight. *Drawing by L.P. Kallan.*

The beauty of shelf gardening is that the whole operation fits into a small space. Fluorescent shelf gardens enable you to stack fluorescent systems one on top of the other. In rooms ten or more feet high, three or four systems — each only a few feet high — stack comfortably along each wall. To figure your possibilities, start with the room and the amount of power it has. Let's consider four examples of typically wired rooms starting with the smallest:

Garden example #1. One 15-ampere circuit = 1,650 watts. Subtracting 20 percent for a safety margin = 1,320 usable watts. Two shelves for flowering are illuminated by 320 watts each (four 80-watt, eight-foot fluorescent tubes). Use another 2' X 8'= 16 sq. ft. garden illuminated by 320 watts to grow mother plants for taking cuttings. Use four 40-watt, four-foot tubes (or two eight-foot tubes) to root the clones. Once the operation is going, you'll have from 60 to 90 plants flowering at all times. This entire garden comfortably fits into a room only 6' X 9' X 8' high. Place the four-foot clone system along one wall above the mother system. Position the two flowering shelves on the opposite wall, starting on the floor. Total power being used is 1,120 watts. There are 200 watts left to run accessory equipment.

Garden example #2. One 20-ampere circuit = 2,200 watts, with 1,760 watts of safely used power. You have two four-tube, 320-watt systems for mothers and clones. Keep at least 16 mothers growing at all times. Each mother provides about 25 clones within 12 weeks. Root at least 100 clones under the second system. Use three four-tube, 320-watt systems for flowering. These systems cover 2' X 8', and each system supports from 20 to 50 maturing plants. Two six-tube, 480-watt systems cover the same area. Total power used is 1,600 watts, with enough current left for an exhaust fan and CO_2 emitter.

Garden example #3. Two 15-ampere circuits = 3,300 watts (2,640 watts of usable power). Use three systems of 320 watts (four 80-watt, eight-foot fluorescents) to support the mothers and root the clones, and three 480-watt, six-tube, eight-foot gardens for maturation. This garden easily fits in a room only 10' X 10'. Stack the three flowering systems on one side of the room. They cover shelves three-feet wide by eight-feet long. Stack the three mother/clone gardens on the opposite wall. Hang a curtain of black plastic or Astrolon to screen any light on the clone side from the flowering side. The electrical consumption for this garden is about 2,400 watts. There is enough power left to run a fan, negative-ion generator, and CO_2 system, or hydroponic pump system.

Garden example #4. Two 20-ampere circuits = 4,400 watts, or about 3,520 usable watts. Four 110-watt HO fluorescents are roughly equal to six 80-watt regular output fluorescents in terms of output and power consumed. Figure on using about 3,000 watts for the lights. You could have seven four-tube HO systems, or six 6-tube regular output systems that are 8' X 3' wide, or nine four-tube systems that are 8' X 2'. Because shelf gardens are kept short, they work well enough with a little less than the usual 20 watts per sq. ft. of light for the clones and mothers. This garden also fits in a room as small as 10' X 10'. Stack three gardens on each of three walls.

General Considerations on Lighting

Visualize a growing factory with shelves of plants along each wall. A shelf garden could have anywhere from two to twenty shelves in one small room. There are many possibilities but the idea is what I want to communicate. You can gradually modify your growing situation as you learn how to grow in the most productive manner. It usually takes a few trial crops to efficiently allocate all of the available room. Since all the growth is under fluorescents, you need only move a few bulbs from one side to another before you've found the arrangement that maximizes the use of the space. (See Chapter 3 on how to hang the lights and reflectors.)

For most gardens, use only standard fluorescents; they're inexpensive and interchangeable. Use new bulbs for flowering; use the older, weaker bulbs to raise the clones. HO fixtures are much more expensive than standard fixtures, but the replacement tubes are relatively cheap. If you believe that the matured plants could have better buds, try HO tubes; their higher intensity penetrates deeper along the plant. If you keep the plants short, there should be little difference. Any hardware or lighting store stocks standard Cool White and Warm White bulbs, and they cost only $.88 to $3.00 each. Look for "energy efficient" tubes to reduce electrical consumption (see Chapter 2).

One new innovation is the use of low-output HPS lamps of 150 watts in horizontal fixtures. The unit is completely self-contained with a built-in ballast. It's only six inches high, and illuminates an area at least 2' by 2' at a distance of one foot. These mini-HPS units encourage excellent flowering, take up little vertical space, and draw about 165 watts. The horizontal fixture directs up to 50 percent more light toward the plants than conventional vertical bulb units with reflectors.

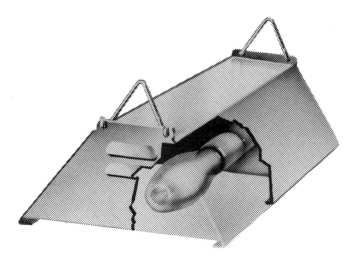

Figure 32. A mini-horizontal HID in a self-contained (ballast built-in) fixture. *Courtesy Applied Hydroponics.*

These are perfect for shelf gardens in closets or small rooms. Considering their long lifetime and the strong flowering they promote, they're very economical for mini-shelf farms. **If cost is no object, use 400 watt HPS lamps in horizontal fixtures.** Mount them fixed in place to illuminate a flowering chamber; there is no need to raise the lamps. With these HPS lamps and CO_2, a garage or basement becomes a true factory in terms of production.

Pointers on Setup and Care

The main problem with fast-turnover clone gardens is having enough mother plants to continuously supply enough clones. The mothers take up a lot of space. Fortunately, you can grow mothers elsewhere, in windows or in another room under a small fluorescent if necessary. Pinch each mother's top shoot after the plant has four sets of leaves. Later, take cuttings from the branch shoots (now there are eight). Soon you'll have more than sixteen shoots for the taking. Keep taking shoots until the new shoots are too small for good rooting or the plant's vigor wanes. Fertilize mothers with nitrogen immediately after taking cuttings to encourage fast foliar growth, but don't fertilize just prior to taking cuttings, because cuttings root more slowly after storing nitrogen.

Shelf gardens work best when continuously operated — you don't suddenly start all new mothers, and you don't have to move all your clones at once. Take cuttings constantly and replace old mothers with a cutting whenever needed. Each time you harvest a plant, replace it with another clone. Move clones to the flowering room once they're forming new leaves. Maintain strong flowering growth by keeping all the plant tops close to the lights (see Chapter 15).

In shelf gardens you're growing top colas, not full-sized plants. Each plant is basically a flowering shoot and usually it forms one good cola along much of its length. Fully matured plants will be only one to two feet tall at harvest. Most plants are from 8 to 14 weeks old from the time you take a cutting until it's harvested. It takes some time to get the operation going at full capacity, but the system is well worth the time once it's fully operational.

At normal room temperatures, use the top shelf for rooting clones; they'll root faster with the warmer temperatures nearer the ceiling. Clones root well with as little as 15 watts per square foot of growing area. A shelf for rooting clones may be only 12" high. You can have six to eight shelves for clones along one ten-foot-high wall.

Flowering plants benefit from the lower temperatures nearer the floor. High temperatures lower potency. Flowering gardens need to be **no higher** than two to a maximum of three feet from shelf to shelf. Position the clone mother shelf anywhere on the constant-light side that's convenient. Mother gardens should be, **at most**, three feet high. Make shelves along a wall no wider than four-feet. Wider shelves make caring for the plants a hassle.

Don't feel that each shelf must be used only for one purpose. You might find that you've allocated too much space for clones and not enough for mothers. Raise clones up on boxes to keep them close to the light under a "mother" shelf. Clones take up so little room that you might set up all of the 18-hour light (or constant-light) shelves for mothers, and use part of each for rooting clones. This way you'll soon figure out just how much space each part of the operation requires.

Use hydroponic mediums, since in smaller pots growth is faster than with soil. Rockwool cubes and slabs make the entire operation — rooting, transplanting, and growing on slabs — very convenient. Instead of transplanting, you insert the one-inch block holding the rooted clone directly in a larger, four-inch block, or onto rockwool slabs. Rockwool slabs take up only a few inches of vertical space; yet they can support larger plants than you'll be growing. Or you can root clones with vermiculite in small paper cups and insert the rooted clones directly in hydroponic mediums.

Because there is a premium on fast growth, you should supplement the room with additional CO_2. Since the room is packed with plants within a confined area, and the plants are kept short and saturated with light, CO_2 enhancement increases growth in shelf gardens, whereas ordinarily CO_2 is not worthwhile in small fluorescent gardens. Install a CO_2 emitter, especially if venting the room is a problem. In the flowering chamber, increase the concentration of light to 30 to 40 watts per square foot. Experienced growers often install additional fluorescents along the sides of the shelves. The increase of light to 30 or more watts per square foot, coupled with suppplemental CO_2, may double the total yield of buds in a given amount of time.

With either HPS's or fluorescents, clone shelf systems provide the best return relative to setup costs, running costs, and manpower input. Shelf gardens are the wave of the future, and for many growers, the future is now.

Chapter 6

Natural Light Gardens

Sunlight is free. Many growers raise superior marijuana (as they have for thousands of years) without a Herculean effort or great expense. Gardeners raise large, potent crops inexpensively under skylights or in a sunporch. In the simplest case, plant seeds in the spring in flower pots positioned in a bright sunny window, porch, or backyard garden.

It is beyond the scope of this book to describe outdoor gardening, or guerrilla and field farming in detail (see the *Marijuana Grower's Guide Complete Edition* from Red Eye Press, 1989). The chapters on preparing soil mixtures also apply to gardening outdoors and most of the information provided herein is useful or adaptable to all outdoor growing. There are several options and growing methods described that you can adjust to fit your outdoor situations. An inexpensive, yet successful indoor or outdoor natural light garden is within the reach of almost everybody, whether you rent or own the land, whether you live in California, Florida, Maine, or Alaska.

The main difference between gardening with electric lights versus gardening under natural light is that natural-light gardens work best when they follow the rhythms of the natural growing season. Starting at times other than spring or early summer usually means that you'll need supplemental lighting and/or shades to manipulate the photoperiod to control flowering and the time of harvest.

A second difference is that under sunlight the light is equally strong at the bottom and the top of the plant. Sunlight strongly illuminates lower branches so there is no need to keep a light system close to the plants' tops. Rather than pruning or bending plants to keep equal heights, you need only turn potted plants occasionally so that they grow symmetrically. Spread the plants apart, or prune and train tops to fill all of the garden space.

The most important criterion for successful natural-light gardening is an understanding of the photoperiod and how it affects the outcome of all crops, year-round. The two fundamental ways to control the photoperiod under natural light are: (1) use supplemental electric lights to **extend the photoperiod, which prevents flowering and keeps the plants growing vigorously** when the photo-period is naturally short such as during winter months; (2) **block the natural light during part of the day to shorten the photoperiod and force the plants to flower** when you want them to flower, e.g. during the long days of spring or summer.

In the simplest case, start your crop at the same time that outdoor growers would start their crop, after the last spring frost. This crop would then be harvested in the fall, as would any crop grown outdoors. Since you can use either shades or electric lights to modify the natural photoperiod, your possibilities increase to four basic situations, listed in Table 6.1

Table 6.1
Basic natural-light growing situations

Start	Harvest	Light/Shade
1. Spring	Fall	(only natural light)
2. Summer	Fall/Winter	(only natural light)
3. Winter	Spring	(supplemental lights & shades)
4. Anytime	Anytime	(supplemental lights & shades)

Start in spring when frosts are past.

Figure 33. The simplest case: start in the spring and grow in a sunny window. Notice that string holds the branches out of view below the window. *Plant by Marianne.*

Every natural-light gardener has these four basic options when growing indoors or in heated greenhouses. Outdoors, local frosts limit the growing season and your possibilities.

1. The **natural garden.** Start the crop in the spring and harvest in the fall, following the natural rhythm of outdoor crops. A common problem that occurs with window gardens started in the spring is that by fall, when the plants are flowering, the light is weakening, and only a fraction of each plant might be sunlit. A large plant left with little bright light consequently develops small, puny buds. It's better to have smaller plants that are covered with light and perhaps supplemented with a spotlight. You're left with smaller but more vigorous plants that have sufficient light to produce larger, better-formed buds. Large plants growing in windows also may be hard to hide. It's easier to obscure smaller plants from the line of sight from outside.

Outdoors, sow the seeds after the last spring frost. When you should sow depends on where you live: in Minnesota, you may not be able to start until early June; in most of California you could start as early as February or March. The most important consideration, next to subterfuge and security, is to be sure the plants ripen fully before fall frosts. In northern areas, find the earliest maturing variety you can, such as a South African or an early Afghani that ripens by September or before the onset of local frosts. If you start a tropical variety, you'll harvest only leaves (see Chapter 10). Marijuana withstands mild frosts with little damage, but if temperatures drop below about 25 degrees, or if a mild frost lasts several days, the plants will die.

2. **Late-start gardens** are for growers cultivating small plants for subterfuge or hidden breeding programs, or because circumstances dictate that they must start later than usual. Start plants in late June through August. Late starts are useful for tropical varieties that may not mature until November or December. Window crops may outgrow the windows if the plants are started in the spring. If you start in July, plants are of manageable size during flowering. For example, by starting Afghani plants at the beginning of July, growers hide marijuana amongst their outdoor garden plants. See the accompanying photographs for some ideas.

3. **Growers of winter starts with spring harvests** cultivate crops year round or start breeding programs for seed crops for their summer crop. Winter starts are perfect for greenhouses (see Chapter 7). For example, start the plants at the end of December or the beginning of January. Raise the seedlings indoors exclusively with electric lights, or grow them with supplemental electric light in greenhouses to **lengthen the photoperiod** to at least 16 hours duration. At the end of February, use the supplemental lights only to increase the **amount** of light at the time of day of weakest light. The short natural daylength (less than 12 hours) initiates flowering. Don't **extend** the photoperiod at this time with electric lights, but use them only to bolster the weak natural daylight. Set the timer to be "off" when the plants naturally would be in the dark **or to maintain a photoperiod of no longer than 10 to 12 hours.** Buds should be ready to harvest in May.

This system works well enough without supplemental lighting, but if you supplement the natural daylight with a few hours of strong light to strengthen natural daylight, and if you make sure that the plants get only 10 to 12 hours of light each day, the plants respond by maintaining flowering and the buds ripen completely and more naturally. Once the plants flower, shade the plants during April (block natural light to make the photoperiod no more than 12 hours per day), and buds form better than if left on their own.

Figure 34. A simple way to grow year-round. Supplement natural light with floodlights and surround the garden with opaque reflective curtains. *Drawing by O. Williams.*

4. **Starting anytime** of the year requires the use of either **supplemental lights** to lengthen the photoperiod, **opaque curtains** to reduce the photoperiod for flowering, or both. Use opaque shades in the spring or summer to shorten the photoperiod. Supplement the natural photoperiod with electric lights anytime to extend the photoperiod, so that you can grow seedlings or flowering plants year-round.

Set up opaque curtains to cut off the light and reduce the photoperiod (or move the plants to a darkened room) to force the plants to flower. For most of the year, you need only three weeks of artificial darkening for a strong flowering response. Only if the plants are maturing during the middle of the summer (when the natural daylength is long) will plants revert to vegetative growth after a discontinuation of the darkened period.

If it's easy to darken a room, start seedlings in early spring, and you can have strong summer sunlight during maturation. In any growing situation, buds form faster and fuller when the light is strong during flowering. For example, darken the room each morning or afternoon (whichever is easiest) during July to reduce the photoperiod to ten or 11 hours of light. Once the buds are forming well, discontinue the darkening, because the weakening light at this time won't reverse the flowering response.

General Considerations for Indoor Sunlit Gardens

Windows get more or less sunlight at different times of the year because the sun's position constantly changes. You want to set up your garden **where it will get the longest duration of sunlight (or the brightest indirect light)** while the plants are flowering. If you expect your variety to be harvested in October, look to see where the sunlight hits during March and April. Whichever windows or area is best lit during these months will also be brightest during September and October: for November harvests, find the windows of brightest light

Figure 35. *Left:* Little Colombians flowering in April. Sprouts had photoperiod lengthened with incandescents. Grower moved the pot indoors each night to maintain 11 hour photoperiod during April. *Right:* Little Nigerian formed excellent cola.

during March; for December harvests look at the prospective garden
area during February.

Skylights are bright all year round. Even if sunlight doesn't
directly strike the skylight, the bright light under skylights is usually
strong enough to support good growth. Take advantage of any skylight for an inexpensive garden with a worthwhile return. Make a
platform to hold the pots and keep the plants close to the skylight.
Gradually lower the platform as the plants grow taller.

Individual pots are always more versatile than planting beds or
troughs. You might move pots to a secure room if you have visitors.
Move individual pots to a darkened room to force flowering. Rotate
individual pots periodically into the strongest light to maintain
uniform growth.

Always surround window gardens with foil or other reflective
curtains to reflect light toward the plants. Along with supplemental
electric lights, reflectors make a major difference in the amount of
high-quality buds a garden yields. String strong twine between walls
and hang aluminum foil or Astrolon behind the plants, or cut open
cardboard boxes to stand free, and cover them with aluminum foil or
paint them a flat white.

Curtains that are both opaque and reflective serve a dual purpose:
during the day, Astrolon curtains reflect light when positioned behind
the plants; during evening light, cover the windows with Astrolon
curtains to block light and maintain a reduced 12 hour photoperiod
for flowering. Protect floors with white plastic or with white paper on
plastic dropcloths.

Venetian blinds opened upward obscure the inside of the house to
the outside yet allow most of the light into the garden. By closing
blinds each evening, gardeners have easy control of the photoperiod.

Chapter 7

Greenhouses and Outdoor Plots

Greenhouses and outdoor plots can be the most inexpensive and productive ways to grow marijuana. Electric companies haven't yet figured out how to charge you for sunlight. In a greenhouse or outdoor plot plants are weighed in pounds rather than in ounces. Unlike electric light, sunlight illuminates plant bottoms as strongly as plant tops. Lower branches develop much better buds under sunlight than under electric light.

A greenhouse also is a permanent investment for a homeowner, who may opt to grow flowers or vegetables at any time without losing the value of his or her initial investment. Sunlight supports excellent growth of any marijuana variety, including hard-to-grow varieties, such as Thai or Central African, which may not grow well under electric lights. The disadvantage of greenhouses or backyard plots is that sometimes they're in view of whomever has access to your property. Also, if you wish to grow crops year round, you must use supplemental lighting or shading to control the photoperiod.

Setting Up a Greenhouse

Ideally, and if growing grass were legal everywhere, you would want to construct your greenhouse or set up your outdoor plot in full, day-long sunlight. Subterfuge is more important than total sunlight, not only because of legal problems, but also because theft is more of a problem for most growers than the law. When the plants get bright, indirect light, all they need for good growth is about three or four hours of daily sunlight. The more sunlight, the faster and larger the plants will grow. The figures for THC in Table 10.2 are for plants grown with only four hours of daily sunlight. Because of the necessity for subterfuge, a prudent choice for an outdoor plot may be next to a fence, or beneath madrona trees (California), ohia trees

Figure 36. Greenhouse and outdoor plants may be weighed in pounds rather than ounces.

(Hawaii), or any other moderately shading trees. A hidden pathway between a fence or hedge and the side of a house might be the safest place to cultivate.

Rooftop gardens that are not visible to neighbors, and are not beneath routes of helicopters and low-flying aircraft, are another option. One gardener in New Jersey had a rooftop greenhouse that

Figure 37. Marijuana hidden in the Sierra foothills beneath madrona and oak trees.

Figure 38. A rooftop garden in New York on the Fourth of July.

couldn't be seen from adjacent buildings. He covered the greenhouse roof with plywood, and enclosed the four sides with see-through plastic. The garden got plenty of morning and afternoon sunlight; yet the plants weren't visible to overflying aircraft.

City gardeners often construct simple, inexpensive rooftop greenhouses. Construct the greenhouse with a 2 x 4 frame covered with polyethylene plastic or rigid plastic panels. Leave a few spaces along the top of the walls or at the peak of the roof for ventilation.

Greenhouses benefit when reflective materials cover any opaque interior walls and the floor. For a dirt-floor greenhouse, brighten the floor by spreading white gravel or rock quartz chips, or light-colored sand. For rooftop gardens, raise the plant pots on pallets covered with white plastic. (Raise rooftop pots because the tarred roof might get too hot during the heat of summer.)

Reflectors even out the light throughout the greenhouse, and all of the space becomes effective for growing, rather than just those areas illuminated by direct sunlight. Astrolon is probably the best reflective material for facing interior walls.

There are several brands of inexpensive rigid plastic panels manufactured for greenhouses. Usually they come in six- and 12-foot lengths and are two feet wide. Panels may be flat or corrugated,

Figure 39: *Left:* In full sunlight, marijuana will completely fill your greenhouse. *Right:* In low-light greenhouses, make sure to cover the floor with reflective material (white gravel shown).

and transparent or translucent. Filon is one brand that has several desirable features: the panels are cheap, about $10 for a 2 x 12 foot length; the faceted panels allow light in, but the plants can't be identified by anyone looking inside from the outside; the facets disperse the light in an even "glow" throughout the greenhouse, even when sunlight hits only a small portion of the panels; there is a minimum of shading in the greenhouse, so that all of the space supports good growth; side panels or windows aren't necessary, because sunlight diffuses when it hits the overhead panels; the panels are very easy to install, are cheap, and last for many years. By using faceted, diffusing panels, a grower can build a greenhouse that from the ground, doesn't look like a greenhouse. The greenhouse sides can be made of wood, and only the roof, which is out of sight from the ground, needs to be covered with plastic panels.

To construct a greenhouse in a cold-weather area, use a double layer of siding: an outer layer of Filon and an inner layer of 8-mil polyethylene plastic works very well. To insulate against both heat and cold, leave a four-inch space between panels and plastic. This double layer of dissimilar materials makes a good insulator, which keeps summer temperatures lower and conserves heat in the winter.

Examples of Greenhouses

Figure 40 shows a greenhouse in San Francisco, California. This old shed is 12 x 15 ft. (180 square feet) and eight feet tall at the highest point. The roof was removed and covered with corrugated Filon, but a perimeter of the old roof was left intact around the edges to maintain the "old shed" look. Recycled, frosted bathroom windows still in their frames were picked up from a glass recycling yard for a dollar or two each, and installed in two walls. These windows not only obscured the greenhouse's contents, they diffused sunlight, which greatly brightened the lower reaches of the garden.

The beauty of this greenhouse is that even in a high-traffic area, frequented by neighborhood kids, no one has ever suspected that it is a greenhouse. The roof slopes away from the path of general traffic and cannnot be seen from the ground. This greenhouse has yielded about 16 pounds of buds a year in two crops, during each of the last six years. The point here is that you may have a situation where you can alter an outbuilding or construct a modest, inexpensive, and unobtrusive greenhouse with a little creative thought. It cost only $200 to convert this shed into a greenhouse with Filon panels and reclaimed windows.

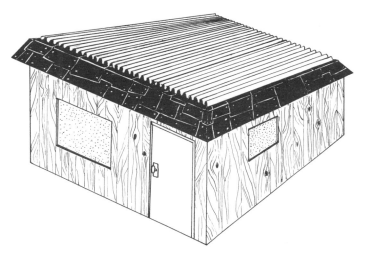

Figure 40. An inexpensive, unobtrusive homemade greenhouse. *Drawing by L. P. Kallan*

Figure 41. Homemade greenhouse. Whitewash helps hide contents.

Figure **41** is in a remote area of California. It's constructed with a 2 x 4 frame faced with a transparent, rigid plastic. Dimensions are eight x ten feet, and 12 feet high at the apex. Materials cost about $300, and this greenhouse has yielded about seven lbs. of pure bud each summer.

Figure **42** shows a professionally constructed greenhouse. This greenhouse is 25 feet wide, 48 feet long (1,240 square feet), and 11 feet high. It's constructed with a tubular frame covered with eight-mil double layered plastic. The cost is about $3,500 for materials, and total cost is from $10,000 to $12,000 including installation. Construction costs for greenhouses generally run about 1/3 for materials, 2/3 for labor. This greenhouse in Vermont yielded about 60 lbs. of buds, 20 lbs. of shake, and about 30 lbs. of leaf from the summer crop for first-time, novice growers.

A greenhouse in New York, 16 ft. x 25 ft., built on the same plan, and equipped with fans, vents, electric heat, and new electric wiring from a source 100 ft. distant, cost $13,000 for the entire installation. Because this greenhouse is heated, two crops return about 40 lbs. of pure bud each year.

Both of these greenhouses are expensive, but you can construct much cheaper greenhouses quite easily, or the same greenhouses for about 1/3 the cost if you provide the labor. If you're handy, a 2 x 4 frame covered with a Filon roof and plywood sides is inexpensive, unobtrusive, and surprisingly productive.

Figure 42. Professionally-constructed greenhouse in Vermont. Intake and exhaust fans are necessary at opposite ends. See back cover for interior.

For any greenhouse, ventilation is very important. Good ventilation lowers temperatures and humidity, discourages mites, and helps prevent fungi from gaining a foothold. A drafty shed with a translucent roof may need no fans since ventilation from cracks in the walls may be enough to circulate the air. Fans are essential to any greenhouse completely enclosed in plastic. Install exhaust fans, and cover both intake and outlet holes with a fine mesh cloth to prevent insects from being drawn into the greenhouse. Exhaust fans work better than intake fans for ventilation, and **they're a must for any large greenhouse or any greenhouse tightly enclosed in plastic.** In general, install an intake and an exhaust fan at opposite ends of any large greenhouse.

Controlling the plant's height is important if the height of the greenhouse is limiting. Bury transplants up to their first set of leaves. Prune seedlings after they have at least four pairs of leaves. Train plants to grow along a greenhouse's walls, or train tops as described in the section in Chapter 15 on Training. It may take a couple of crops before you find the ideal time for planting and the best method for training to completely fill your greenhouse with colas.

Keep records of planting times and how you control height. Records help you to develop the "perfect procedure" for your growing situation. Never keep these records in your house or greenhouse. Hide them in a secure place outdoors, preferably off your

Figure 43. You may need no fans in a small, loosely-constructed greenhouse. But make an opening for ventilation near the top of the greenhouse.

property. Records are always helpful, but especially to law enforcers when the prosecution develops a case against you for a history of growing. Never, never grow a few plants in your house or backyard at the same time that you keep a record of a large plot growing elsewhere. You might be busted for those few plants and after a search, you'll be busted for the large plot.

Outdoor Plots

Outdoor plants rooted in the ground usually grow larger than plants restricted by a pot. However, pots make a plant mobile. If a landlord pays a visit, or sends workers to care for the property, you can move potted plants to a safe place.

For potted plants, use a soil mixture as described in Chapter 9. For good-size plants, use a pot with a capacity of at least five gallons. **For plants growing in the ground, prepare the soil as you would for corn.** Most important is that the soil be loose and well-aerated, and does not have too much clay. Mix in humus, composts, or manures to increase fertility and loosen the soil. Add sand or perlite if the soil is particularly dense, compact, or rich in clay. Make sure to add lime if the soil tests acid or add gypsum if the soil tests alkaline (see Chapter 9).

The easiest way to prepare the ground is to make planting holes or beds rather than to prepare an entire plot. You could prepare individual holes, but you'll save time and energy by making larger holes that can accommodate a half-dozen sprouts and several mature females. Make the holes about 18-inches deep and at least three feet in diameter. It's better to make the holes wider rather than deeper. Start about eight to 12 seedlings per hole, and you should end up with four or more females in each hole by the season's end. After removing the males, spread the females apart by staking and tying the stems away from each other. This opens up the center, and greatly increases the light shining on each plant, and hence the yield from each hole. Spreading the plants apart makes a **major difference in yield,** but this simple act is often overlooked by even experienced growers. Adjust the plants' positions throughout the season, always reducing the shading and maximizing the light and room for each plant. Tie a cloth loop around each stem, and tie rope from the loop to a stake. Without a protective cloth loop, rope or cord gradually cuts into the stem, injuring the plant.

Figure 44. Backyard plants can outgrow your yard if given full sunlight and room to grow.

Maximizing Yield

One question outdoor and greenhouse growers debate is whether to grow fewer large plants or many small plants. **In sunlit gardens, whether in a greenhouse or a backyard plot, the best yields come from gardens with large plants that fill all of the space.** It's possible to grow up to eight females per square foot, and then harvest the top colas. But experience has shown that one large plant that fills a nine- to 16-square-foot area yields up to three times as much grass as the same area packed with crowded plants. Also, more females develop when the seedlings have room to grow.

Outdoor growing is different from growing under lights. You can pack the space under a light system, harvest fast turn-over plants, and get a better return per space and time, than if you grow fewer, larger plants that take more time to mature. Outdoors the natural season determines when a particular variety will ripen. Outdoor plots that are crowded with plants return more stems than good colas. As with plants under light, it's the cubic area of good buds that determines the worthwhile yield.

A plant develops large, worthwhile colas from its bottom to its top, if given access to light and space; crowded plants have only one good top cola — the rest of the plant is so shielded from sunlight and restricted in space that it's almost entirely bare stem. It's better to grow ten large, female plants that fill a greenhouse from top to bottom with good colas, than to have a hundred skinny plants with only top colas. Fewer, larger plants also allow you a better evaluation of an individual's yield; they're easier to manicure; and the buds tend to be larger, tighter, and better developed overall. A dozen large plants are also easier to care for than a jungle of a hundred smaller plants.

When growing for the largest plants, start when spring frosts are past. Start plants indoors under lights if you live in a short-season locale such as Maine or Michigan. Use black plastic or a thick mulch to cover and warm the soil if the ground is cold. Cold soil can stunt a plant's growth, and it may never fully recover. Bury the stem up to the first set of leaves directly in the ground. Burying the stem saves height when the greenhouse overhead is low or limiting.

Prepare the soil 18 to 24 inches deep, and enrich the soil with fertilizers, or use pots of a minimum of eight gallons and up to one bushel in size. The sooner the plants are in the ground, the larger they might be by the season's end. You can "pump" plants to maximize growth by applying water and fertilizer almost continuously but only

Figure 45. A jungle of crowded plants produces empty stems and yields much less worthwhile marijuana than plants left with room to grow.

if you know what you're doing from experience. Be careful not to poison the plants with too much fertilizer (see Chapter 14).

To grow for large size, it's imperative that you water deeply. Don't give a little water each day; water until the ground is **saturated each time you water.** This is very important for maximizing yield in arid areas. Cover the ground with mulch to conserve water. A mulch of cocoa bean hulls is near in color to the red/brown soils of California and therefore less conspicuous to aircraft.

Plant Only Females

One way to maximize the use of space is to plant only females. You could develop "female seeds" (Chapter 20), or you might "key" for sex before moving the plants to a greenhouse for transplanting into the ground (Chapter 17). To key for sex, set up a fluorescent fixture about one month before you plan to transplant the seedlings to the greenhouse. Germinate seeds in February, March, or April, and transplant respectively in March, April, or May. The light system doesn't need to be large; a system of four four-foot or eight-foot fluorescent tubes is adequate. Start from 70 to 140 seedlings in four-inch pots under an eight-foot, 320-watt fixture. Grow the plants for about two weeks under constant light. Then cut the photoperiod to 12 hours of light. When the plants flower in about two weeks, eliminate

Figure 46. Outdoor growers start the plants under lights to get a head start on the growing season in cold winter areas. See Figure 47.

the males. Now transplant and fill your outdoor plot or greenhouse with exclusively female seedlings. Females gradually respond to the lengthening daylight of spring and revert to vegetative growth (see Chapter 23).

Staggered Starts to Maximize Yield

In warm winter areas or with heated greenhouses, growers may start early maturing varieties (such as Afghani) in the spring, and harvest them during September or by early October. Tropical varieties, such as Thai or Colombian, are started in June or July, and harvested in November and December. If you start the plants at different times, the tropical plants grow alongside the early-maturing variety but don't take up much room. When the "early" plants are harvested, garden space is opened up so that the tropical plants have plenty of room to fill out while they're flowering.

Experienced growers in warm winter areas may carry this staggered start/staggered harvest procedure to the extreme. Some South Africans are ready to harvest in early August; an Afghani might be ready by the end of September; Mexican or Nepalese by the end of October; Colombian by the end of November; and Thai and Nigerian by the end of December. Each successive harvest opens up the greenhouse, and gives the next group plenty of room

Figure 47. Plants started under lights (*left*) have head start on seedlings started outdoors (*right*) in this upstate New York garden. Transplant after last spring frost. Notice the plastic planting bags.

and light for development during its maturation. Once given more room and light, these small plants take off and fill out quickly.

Spring Crops for Greenhouses and Outdoors

Warm area or heated greenhouse growers usually grow two crops: one for spring and one for fall harvests. Start the spring harvest plants in December or early January in the greenhouse, with supplemental lights that are on for several hours each day (electric lights extend the photoperiod, prevent premature flowering, and intensify the natural light); or grow the plants indoors for the first four to ten weeks, solely under electric lights. Depending on the variety and locale, the best results are achieved when plants are placed outdoors during late February to the first week in March. The short natural daylength initiates flowering, and the plants ripen for harvest by early to late May. If you have the facilities, use electric lights to supplement the natural light, and extend the photoperiod to 12 hours for the first few weeks. Turn the lights on during the morning or evening, whenever the natural light is weakest. When using supplemental lights to regulate a 12-hour photoperiod, move the plants to the greenhouse during the third or fourth week of February.

Figure 48: *Left:* Started in February under lights, these plants are ripe in May. Small plants (*left: Afghani; right: Colombian*) are hidden next to irises. *Right:* Late-start Colombian is still small and hidden while ripening in October.

Some varieties form much better spring buds than others do, and you should experiment with several varieties the first year. Plants might revert to vegetative growth, because the natural photoperiod is lengthening while the buds are maturing. Short season varieties usually respond better than tropical varieties. The best response seems to be from hybrids of short/medium plants, such as Afghani crossed with Mexican. If you can, set up opaque shades and from mid-March through mid-April lower the shades each night to cut off all light and maintain a 12-hour photoperiod. Shades negate the effects of increasing daylength and the buds will form perfectly. For tropical varieties, maintain a ten- to 11-hour flowering cycle.

Even when the buds aren't the best formed, you'll have an excellent start on the fall harvest. Harvest only buds and leave some growing shoots and healthy leaves on each stem. Water and fertilize the plants with a nitrogen rich fertilizer, such as fish emulsion or Ra-Pid-Gro, to encourage a renewal of rapid leaf growth.

After the spring harvest, you already know that these plants are female. Also, because the root and stem are strongly developed, by autumn these plants may be larger than spring seed starts. Because the buds have been cut, many strong, new growing shoots have the entire summer in which to develop. The resulting plants have a very bushy profile with numerous strong branches laden with large buds. You'll also have a good idea of which plants responded the best and which plants yielded the most potent grass (since you'll have smoked them during the summer) well before autumn. Watch for individuals that are rot- and disease-resistant. Breed the best of these and you'll be well on your way to developing a potent variety perfectly suited to your growing situation.

Forcing Early Flowering Outdoors

To force plants to ripen before they would naturally, shorten the photoperiod by moving potted plants to a darkened shed or room. You might move potted plants into a darkened basement each afternoon for two weeks, and move them back into the daylight each morning. Move them back and forth to maintain about a ten- to 12-hour period of daily light. When this is done toward summer's end, two weeks of artificially shortening the photoperiod causes almost all varieties to flower normally. At summer's end, discontinue moving the plants **once flower clusters begin to form**. The dwindling natural photoperiod is not enough to reverse the flowering cycle. By forcing the plants to flower earlier in the season, you can cause tropical varieties to ripen fully even in northern latitudes. Any variety flowers better under the stronger sunlight of late summer than that of late autumn. Also, plants which ripen before late season rainy weather escape problems with rot or slow growth. Start the two-week darkening period 12 weeks before you plan to harvest. In the north, this may be as early as late July. Continue to move or cover the plants until flower clusters begin to form. A local Farmer's Almanac or guide can tell you when to expect the first serious fall frosts. Plan to have the plants ripen just before the frost date. Cover small plants with large cardboard cartons, or opaque tarps or covers if this is easier.

Subterfuge

Late starts may be your best option for subterfuge, since even mature plants are small and easily hidden. Figure 49 shows a group of late start potted plants that are between a house and a line of bushes demarcating property lines. When started in July, these plants never grew over four feet tall, and they remained hidden by

Figure 49. Late-start plants in pots are easily hidden among bushes. Plants in pots can be moved into darkness to force them to flower early in the season.

bushes all season. Even though this garden was grown near down-town Berkeley, there was never a problem of discovery by the law or by roving potheads.

Outdoor growers have the best situation to exploit pruning tech-niques. You might train plants on a trellis along the side of a fence, house, or out-of-the-way alley. One of the most ingenious subter-fuges I ever saw was by a grower in Santa Monica, California. She grew only three females, which were planted about one foot from the side of her house. She trained them throughout the season to grow on a trellis that had been used for roses against a side of her house. The plants were so unobtrusive that even when she had cookouts, her family never asked what the plants were.

One gardener in Massachusetts grew only a few females each summer. His only worry came from his next-door neighbor. Along a five foot fence separating their yards, he planted females from indoors after he had pinched their tops. As each branch grew, he tied the branch down to a stake in the ground. When the branches grew upward, he tied them down again close to the ground. His plants developed six to eight long, snakelike branches that never got higher than a foot or two above the ground. Each mature plant looked like an octopus or a pinwheel of snakes. Each branch grew up, then down, repeating the up-and-down profile in soft "S"-shaped curves along the length of each branch. Despite their low stature, each plant yielded from four to nine ounces of bud per plant. His neighbor has never suspected or said anything about his "unusual" plants after four summers of growing. (See Pruning in Chapter 15, and for much, much more on growing outdoors, look for the *Marijuana Grower's Guide Complete Edition*, Red Eye Press, 1989.)

Part III
Soil and
Hydroponic Mixtures

Chapter 8

Pots and Containers

In its natural state, marijuana grows an extensive root system, a fibrous network of fine, lateral roots that branch off a main, carrot-shaped tap root. Small pots or dry soils restrict the development of an extensive root system. Although one published report claimed that a marijuana plant in San Diego County had a tap root over six feet long, I've never seen one more than about 18-inches long and this was on an 18-foot tall plant. Usually the tap root grows no more than four to ten inches deep, even on the largest of plants. By watering and fertilizing as needed, you could grow a six-foot plant in a four-inch pot or in a three-foot layer of soil; however neither of these extremes is desirable or practical. (Pots are measured by diameter across the top of the pot.)

Small Pots and Containers for Starting Plants

Fit as many pots as you can within the garden's perimeter or lighted area, to make the most efficient use of space. Many growers prefer to start plants in smaller pots, and transplant into larger pots when the root systems get pot-bound.

Seedlings take up much less room than mature plants; so while the plants are smaller, place them closer together, and many more plants can fit under the light system. Once the plants begin to crowd each other, harvest the less vigorous plants (or the males) for smoking and transplant the more vigorous plants (or the females) into larger containers. This procedure assures that the garden is filled with plants throughout growth, and during flowering the space is filled with females. None of the garden is wasted on empty space or unwanted males later in growth. Also, if the plants are to be carried and transplanted in another growing area, the pots weigh considerably less and are easier to transport.

Although planting trays are often recommended for starting plants, their shallow depth restricts the seedlings' roots. When the seed germinates, the tap root grows to a depth of about four inches within a couple of days. In a shallow pot or tray, the root curls or circles within the confines of the space, which delays the plant's development. The roots recover after transplanting, but for best results always start plants in a container at least four inches deep.

Compressed fiber pots are often used to start seedlings. Most garden shops carry them in several sizes, but growers should use a four or six-inch pot. Compressed fiber peat pots are supposed to break down in the soil, but marijuana's delicate lateral roots may not be able to penetrate the sides unless you break or score the sides while transplanting. You'll get better results if you use the other pots that are recommended here.

Don't confuse compressed fiber pots with peat pots (or discs) that are encased in nylon-mesh. **These nylon mesh peat pots and expandable discs are excellent for starting seeds.** Jiffy-7 is one brand that works very well. The smallest discs (which expand to about two inches deep) should be buried directly in the soil surface when you sow the seeds. Marijuana roots easily penetrate all expandable peat pellets and peat pots encased in nylon mesh. All of them should be planted, pot and all, directly in the soil.

Figure 50. The disks *(center)* expand when wetted into peat pellets *(left)*. Peat pots *(right)* work best outdoors.

Wax paper, plastic or styrofoam cups (six to eight ounces) or one-quart milk containers, cut in half, and filled with a soil mixture, work very well, and are cheaper than compressed-fiber, plastic or clay flower pots. You can use small plastic or clay flower pots, tin cans, or small plastic bags for the first few weeks of growth. Puncture the bottom of all containers so that excess water can drain out. Use a drill to make holes through a stack of plastic pots; don't try to punch holes individually, since you'll only crack the bottoms.

Large Containers for Mature Plants

According to scientific tests, growing a fully mature marijuana plant under the best of conditions in a pot smaller than 16 inches in diameter and less than eight inches deep results in a smaller plant. A five-gallon container measures approximately 12-inches in diameter and is about ten-inches deep. A five-gallon container is roughly the capacity necessary for a fully grown indoor plant with no restriction of growth due to an undersized pot.

You could buy costly, large clay flower pots but this is an unnecessary expense. Experienced growers use their ingenuity to

Figure 51. Milk containers are an alternative to regular pots for starting seeds.

find suitable, inexpensive substitutes. Any container that holds an adequate amount of soil, does not disintegrate from repeated waterings, contains no toxics, and is at least as wide at the top as at the bottom will suffice.

Many garden shops sell used plastic containers at a reduced cost. Wholesalers sell plastic pots by the carton at a considerable discount. Ice-cream outlets discard or sell sturdy cardboard and plastic containers for a few cents each. Supermarkets and food outlets regularly discard five-gallon metal or plastic food containers.

Tubs, bushel baskets, or half barrels serve as good large containers for greenhouse growing. Boxes or troughs made from wood work well. Redwood containers are the best since they resist damage by termites, weather, or repeated waterings. Cedar containers work almost as well as redwood and cedar also repels termites. Start at least six seedlings in each large container so that you'll have several females growing in each container by the season's end.

An inexpensive alternative to large containers is plastic trash bags. They're cheap and lightweight, but they must be handled carefully to avoid shifting the soil and damaging fragile roots. The capacity of the bag should be no more than twice as many gallons as the amount of soil used. For example, for four gallons of soil, the bag should be of at least a five-gallon size, but not more than an eight-gallon size; otherwise, the bag settles into a shapeless mass rather than forming a cylinder. Punch holes in the bottom for drainage, and use masking or duct tape to repair any tears.

Better than trash bags are plastic bags manufactured as plant containers. They're sold in many sizes, from three-inch starter bags to twelve gallons in capacity. These planting bags form a cylinder or a square base when filled, and usually come with drainage holes prepunched. Guerrilla growers prefer planting bags because they are cheap, lightweight, space-saving, and easily transported. These horticultural planting bags are of a thicker mil than plastic trash bags; they're much tougher and more durable, and in fact can be reused many times. They're highly recommended. (See Figure 47.)

Chapter 9

Soil and Hydroponic Mixtures

Soil

The soil or growing medium is a source of water, air, and nutrients; it nourishes the plant and anchors the roots. Marijuana grows extremely fast, and it has higher water and nutritive needs than houseplants, flowers, or vegetables grown indoors. Your garden's success depends on you to provide the plants with a root medium that supplies the plant's "soil needs" without creating toxic conditions of too much water, fertilizer, poor texture, or an extreme pH.

There is no such thing as the perfect soil for marijuana. Each variety can grow in a wide range of soil conditions. For healthy, full growth, marijuana prefers a soil that is fertile, is not tight or compact but rather loose and well-aerated, and is near a neutral (7.0) pH. These ideal conditions result from the interaction of a complex set of physical, chemical, and biological factors. To simplify, they are reduced to three: (1) texture, which affects aeration and drainage; (2) nutrients or fertility; (3) pH, or the sourness or bitterness of the soil.

Most marijuana growers who work indoors buy the soil from which they prepare their soil mixture. These commercial mixes are usually sterilized or pasteurized, and have good general soil properties. Since they seldom list the contents, pH, or nutrients, do some of the simple tests described here to get some idea of the properties of your soil. Whether you buy the soil or dig for it, once you know your soil's general characteristics, you can modify and adjust the soil to meet the plants' needs.

Soil Texture

Texture describes the soil's physical properties or consistency. Soil texture determines water-holding capacity, drainage properties, air or oxygen retention, the ability of the roots to penetrate and grow healthily, and through a complex set of interactions, the ability of the plant to absorb water, air, and nutrients from the soil.

Marijuana must have a well-drained soil for healthy growth. **The primary prerequisite for the soil is that it drains well and consequently has oxygen available to the roots.** Plants can be cultivated in soil that has low fertility and a pH that is not ideal, and the grower still can manage to raise a healthy plant; but if the soil texture is too tight and suffocates the roots or inhibits their development, no amount of good care can remedy this situation. It is imperative to start with a soil that has good texture.

Find out what the texture of your soil is from its appearance and feel. Dry soil should not cake or crack, or form impenetrable crusts. Dry soil that feels spongy or light-weight and has a lot of fibrous material tends to hold a lot of water when wetted. Mix these soils with materials that loosen the soil and lessen water-holding capacity, such as perlite, sand, lava-rock, aggregates, or even kitty litter.

Soil that feels heavy, is sandy or gritty, and looks or feels dense benefits by being loosened and lightened with fibrous materials such as vermiculite, sphagnum moss, humus, or Jiffy-mix. Even the best of soils tend to compact in a pot over time, and may become too dense for roots to penetrate. Add some of the soil conditioners listed here to improve drainage if you are growing in containers.

Moist soil should not be sticky, and should remain spongy or loose when wet. Take a handful of moist soil and squeeze it into a ball; the soil should retain a porous, lightweight quality, or easily separate when poked. Your main concern is that the soil retains some water, yet drains excess water. If wet soil is too dense, compact, or sticky, the roots will not be able to penetrate and will not absorb necessary oxygen, and the plants will die or grow very poorly.

If you dig for your soil, look in well-kept fields, in ditches or depressions, along fences or hedges, or in other areas where leaves and plant debris tend to collect and degrade to form a rich, natural humus. Screen the soil to remove undecayed matter and rocks. Sterilize the soil by adding chemical preparations sold for the purpose such as formaldehyde. Or sterilize soil in a pressure cooker at 15-lbs. pressure for 15 minutes, or by baking soil in an oven at 200 degrees for 30 to 40 minutes. Be advised that baking soil releases some formidable odors. You're better off buying sterilized soil.

Figure 52. Common soil conditioners: perlite, vermiculite, peat moss.

Soil Conditioners to Improve Texture

Perlite and Sand. Perlite (expanded sand or volcanic glass) is a practically weightless substitute for sand. Sand and perlite are inert, contribute no nutrients of their own to the soil mixture, and do not affect soil pH. They hold water, air, and nutrients from the soil on their irregular surfaces. They are particularly good at improving drainage and aerating the soil by keeping it porous. Because the texture of perlite and sand is so good, it's actually possible to grow marijuana in pots filled with only perlite or sand hydroponically by adding soluble fertilizers while watering.

Sand (not beach sand, which contains poisonous concentrations of salt) is an excellent soil conditioner. The only disadvantage to sand used indoors is its heavy weight. This heaviness is advantageous with outdoor plants, because it stabilizes the pots in strong winds. Use perlite indoors to keep the pots lightweight.

Lava rock or red lava (or aggregates) are similar to perlite, but the individual particles are much larger (about 1/4 to 1/2 inch in diameter) and considerably heavier than perlite. Lava rock or aggregates hold air, water, and nutrients much like sand and perlite, and they work well as an aerating additive or as the sole medium.

Kitty litter can be used if none of the above conditioners for loosening the soil is available. It works well enough but if you are planting more than a couple of pots, take the time to find one of the above-mentioned soil conditioners.

Vermiculite (an expanded micaceous material) contributes some nutrients, and is near neutral in pH. Vermiculite holds water, air, and nutrients in its fiber, and it improves the texture and water-holding capacity of fast-draining and sandy soils. Vermiculite holds three to four times its weight in water, and should not be compressed when filling a pot. It also has good buffering properties and a high cation exchange capacity (CEC), which means that vermiculite reduces the problems associated with an extreme pH and can hold nutrients for a time, and release them to the soil and plant when the nutrients are needed.

Considerable amounts of potassium and magnesium irons are present in raw vermiculite. Vermiculite has excellent rewetting properties, and even the driest of mixtures readily absorbs water.

Sphagnum and peat moss are fibrous plant materials that hold about ten to 40 percent of their weight in water. Sphagnum has a pH of about 3.5, and peat moss, which has at least five different sources and forms, is about 4.0 to 4.5 in pH. Because of their acidity they can be helpful in lowering the pH and in buffering the alkaline water and soils in the West or arid areas. Eastern growers prefer Jiffy-mix or vermiculite to sphagnum and peat moss. If the water in your area is alkaline (hard), sphagnum or peat moss will work better for your soil than vermiculite. If your water is soft (acidic), then avoid sphagnum and peat moss, and use vermiculite and perlite to condition your soil. In many wet areas of the country, the water is "soft".

Jiffy-mix, Ortho-mix, or similar commercial mixes are made of mostly ground vermiculite and sphagnum moss. They are fortified with small amounts of all the necessary nutrients, and are intended to be used to germinate seeds or to start cuttings. They are available at a neutral pH, are good general soil conditioners for improving both drainage and aeration, and are excellent planting mediums for starting seedlings.

Rockwool is a processed product that may be made of rock, or a mixture of rock, limestone, and coke: it looks and feels like fiberglass insulation. Rockwool is made in three forms: loose bulk or granulate, planting blocks, and slabs. Always wet any rockwool when handling, especially loose bulk, granulated, or bailed rockwool. During handling, **you could inhale fibers** which surely would be unhealthy, and the fibers may cause an allergic reaction.

Blocks or slabs of rockwool for hydroponic gardens are strongly recommended. Use one or two-inch blocks for rooting clones, transplant to four-inch blocks, and later, place on slabs. The advantage of rockwool blocks and slabs is that the roots grow out of the blocks, so that a smaller block can be placed in a larger block, and any block can

Figure 53. Rockwool. The one-inch blocks fit into the holes of four inch blocks, and four inch blocks are placed on the slabs. All transplanting is simple, clean and problem-free.

be placed on a slab, where roots then grow into the new rockwool without the need for transplanting. Use slabs as the bottom medium; set plants rooted in rockwool blocks on slabs, and the nutrient solution is fed to the plants through the slabs. This encourages roots to grow through the blocks, and eventually root directly in the slabs.

Rockwool in granular form increases both the aeration of the medium and its water holding capacity, but remember to wet rockwool before handling or mixing. Overall, rockwools are excellent planting mediums. You could grow hydroponically in pure rockwool, or use granular rockwool in place of vermiculite, perlite, or lava rock.

Synthetic polymer soil conditioners eliminate crusting of hard soils, reduce the stickiness of clay soils, and improve drainage in any soil. These conditioners last for years, and have the advantage of being extremely lightweight. A few pounds of polymer condition soil as much as hundreds of pounds of humus or compost; they are an important aid to guerrilla farmers, because they transport easily to the growing area. Polymer also helps the homegrower, because it is lightweight and reusable.

Fertility or Nutrients

The fertility of a soil refers to the soil's ability to provide essential minerals to the plant for healthy, normal growth. Most essential minerals are needed in very small amounts, and any good soil supplies the plant's needs for most of the nutrients. However, even the most fertile of potted soils seldom can supply the total quantity of the major nutrients that a vigorous, fast-growing marijuana plant can use.

The primary or **major** nutrients necessary for healthy growth are **nitrogen (N), phosphorus (P), and potassium (K). These three nutrients correspond to the three numbers or percentages, in that order, that appear on all fertilizer or manure packages, and they give the percentages of each nutrient in the mixture.** For example, a "rose food" might be 12-6-6 which means it has 12 percent N (nitrogen), six percent P (phosphorus, actually P_2O_5), and six percent K (potassium, K_2O). Any fertilizer that contains some of each of these three major nutrients is called a "complete" fertilizer.

Nitrogen (N) is by far the most commonly depleted of all nutrients in potted plants, and you should anticipate the need to fertilize the plant with a soluble fertilizer containing nitrogen several times during growth (see Chapter 14). However, it's possible to prepare a soil mixture that provides most of the nutrients that a plant might need, and certainly a well-prepared, very fertile soil can at least sustain healthy growth during most of a plant's life.

Organic Composts and Manures

Many growers enrich their soil by adding organic fertilizers such as sterilized manure or humus, or chemical fertilizers, while initially mixing their soil. Organic fertilizers work very well, and many contain a good balance of the three major nutrients. Organics such as humus, manure, or compost also condition the texture of the soil mixture by loosening the soil and holding water in their fiber. Don't use too much manure, compost, or humus in your soil, particularly if you have added peat or sphagnum. In excess they cause drainage problems, make the mix too acidic, attract insects, promote molds, and encourage other pests to grow. A good mixture is one part compost, humus, or manure to five to eight parts basic soil mixture. In large pots (four or more gallons), these mixes may provide all of the nutrients the plant will ever need.

You should use commercially prepared organic manures and composts, which are sterilized or pasteurized. Home-made manures and composts may, and usually do, contain insect eggs, nematodes, or other organisms that may, with time, cause considerable problems with potted plants; it is best not to use them indoors.

Leaf mold consists of partially decayed maple, oak, elm, and sycamore leaves, and it's acidic. Despite some growers' recommendations, don't use leaf mold in indoor soils because it takes from 12 to 18 months to break down and release nutrients to the soil. By this time you will have harvested.

Worm castings are the collections of soil that have passed through worms when they burrow (or eat) through soil. Worms and other small soil animals recycle, break down, and condition soil and organic debris. The processing of soil that they accomplish is extremely important to the development and health of natural soils. The pH is usually between 6.0 and 6.5. Worm castings are such a good, natural, and fertile soil base that you could grow plants in pure worm castings although it's not recommended. For best results, use no more than about one-third of worm castings by volume in your mixture. Worm castings are probably the best natural fertilizer that you can use, because they're conditioned by the worm's gut, are balanced for all major nutrients, and contain some of all of the micronutrients. A mixture of two parts worm castings mixed with one part bat guano is an excellent nutrient additive for anyone growing organically.

Bat guano is made from the droppings of bats. It's collected from caves where millions of bats contribute to a deep layer of guano. Guano is an excellent natural fertilizer. It's particularly rich in phosphorus, which many growers value for enhancing flower production. My only reservation about bat guano is that some scientists have expressed concern that guano may harbor some disease-causing viruses. However, this connection has yet to be confirmed, so don't worry about it. Use bat guano to enrich any soil with phosphorus and some nitrogen.

Processed Organic Fertilizers

Table 9.1 lists some of the processed or prepared organic fertilizers that can be mixed with your soil. They differ considerably in the concentration and ratios of available nutrients, and they may be low or missing one or more of the major nutrients. Mix them together so that the mix has some of each nutrient, or use them with manures or composts, which are complete fertilizers (that is, contain an adequate amount of all three major nutrients, N, P, and K).

When adding fertilizers, remember that organic fertilizers break down at different rates. Use combinations such as cow manure with blood meal. This way, nutrients are released over the course of the plant's life. Also, fertilizers work best when their nutrient compositions complement each other, to provide a balance of the three major nutrients (e.g., bat guano and wood ashes together provide a good balance of all three major nutrients).

A good idea when mixing any fertilizer into your soil is to fill your pots with a mixture of fertilizer and soil and then add a 2" layer of pure soil to cover the mixture. This helps discourage molds and insects from invading your pots, and reduces the chance of "fertilizer burn" from fertilizers on germinating seeds. Not included in Table 9.1 are organics such as greensand and granite dust, because they break down too slowly to be worthwhile in potted marijuana gardens. Organics such as cottonseed meal are only worthwhile with crops that stay in their pots at least four months.

Table 9.1
Prepared Organic Fertilizers

Type of Fertilizer	Percentage by Weight of			Availability to Plant
	N	P	K	
Bat guano	5.0	8.0	0.3	Rapid
Blood meal	13.0	0	0	Rapid/medium
Blood/Bone meal	6.0	7.0	0	Medium/slow
Cow Manure*	0.25	0.15	0.25	Medium
(concentrated)*	1.5	1.0	1.5	Medium
Chicken Manure*	1.5	1.0	0.5	Medium/fast
(concentrated)*	6.0	4.0	2.5	Fast/medium
Cottonseed meal	6.0	2.0	1.0	Slow/medium
Fish meal	8.0	0	0	Slow/medium
Rock phosphate	0	34.0	0	Gradual/steady
Wood ash (fine)	0	1.5	3 to 7.0	Rapid/medium
Worm castings	3.5	1.0	1.0	Rapid

*Manures come in various concentrations, depending on their source and the amount of water they contain. The figures given are approximate concentrations; low concentrations mean high water content, and vice versa. Most packaged brand name manures will be closer to the higher concentration figures.

Soil Mixtures

Table 9.2 gives examples of soil mixtures combined after you've decided whether your soil is gritty or fibrous, and whether your water is acidic or alkaline. Most likely your soil texture and pH will fall between these extremes, and you should use your common sense to reach a happy medium.

Table 9.2
Examples of Soil Mixtures*

Gritty Soil	Fibrous Soil	Acidic Water	Alkaline Water
5 soil	5 soil	3 topsoil	3 topsoil
3 vermiculite	5 perlite	1 sand	2 perlite
2 humus	1 humus	2 vermiculite	2 peat moss
1 cow manure	1 worm castings	1 worm castings	1 humus
1/2 bat guano	1 cow manure	1/2 wood ash	1/2 bat guano

*Figures are by volume or parts. Use any container to measure the recommended parts or units.

Humus, worm castings, manures, and composts are good sources of all three major nutrients; do not use too much of them in your soil mixture, because they tend to hold water and make the mixture soggy or too acidic with time.

Chemical Fertilizers

Chemical fertilizers are made in practically every conceivable combination and concentration. Growers select "complete" (contain a good amount of all three major nutrients) fertilizers. For example, rose foods might be 12-12-12 or 20-20-20, and both work very well for marijuana. Others are Vigoro 18-4-5, and Ortho 12-6-6. The higher the numbers, the more concentrated the mix is, and consequently the more nutrients are available.

Indoor growers may also use "time" or "slow release" fertilizers which come in capsules, pellets, or sticks. These gradual release fertilizers do not work as well indoors as do standard organic and chemical fertilizers. In backyard plots or fields they work very well.

Chemical fertilizers don't appreciably affect the soil's texture, but don't use them in concentrations higher than what is recommended here or by the fertilizer's manufacturer. In higher concentrations, chemical fertilizers can "burn" plants, particularly seedlings.

Fertilizer packages may not list the amount to mix per pot. Estimate the amount to add per pot from the instructions given for the amount to use per square foot. Use that amount for each 1/4 cubic foot of soil mixture. One cubic foot equals approximately four-gallons; if directions are given at one cup per square foot, use 1/4 cup for each gallon of soil mixture. Be careful not to get your fertilizer wet. Chemical fertilizers absorb moisture and then harden, making them difficult to use, if not useless.

Recently, fertilizer manufacturers have added micronutrients, particularly chelated forms of iron (Fe), manganese (Mn), and zinc (Zn) to their mixtures to counteract problems associated with alkaline water and soil. Two popular fertilizers are Bandini and Ortho rose foods, which have respectively, 6-12-6 and 8-12-4, along with chelated micronutrients.

Many growers add no nutrients when they make their mixture of soil, perlite, vermiculite, etc; they rely on watering with soluble fertilizers. Soluble fertilizers and their application are discussed in Chapter 14. If you have any doubts about adding fertilizers to your soil mixture, then don't add any, or add only a small amount of a general organic fertilizer, such as cow manure. Read Chapter 14, and there shouldn't be any problem you can't rectify.

Table 9.3 Standard Mixtures		
#1	**#2**	**#3**
4 soil	3 soil	4 soil
3 perlite	1 lava rock	2 sand
2 humus	1 vermiculite	1 humus
1 chicken manure	1 worm castings	1/4 rose food
1/2 wood ash	1/2 cow manure	

For more information on buying a good soil, see the section Buying Soil at the end of this chapter.

pH (Acidity or Alkalinity)

The pH is a measure of the acidity or alkalinity of the soil. It is another way of expressing whether the soil is sour (acid) or bitter (alkaline). The pH is measured on a logarithmic scale of zero to 14. The mid-point 7.0 is neutral; soil is acid below 7.0, alkaline above 7.0.

You can think of the pH as a measure of the overall "chemical charge" of the soil. The pH affects whether nutrients dissolve to chemical forms available to the plant or into forms the plant can't absorb, and the nutrients remain locked in the soil.

Marijuana responds best to a soil mixture that is slightly acidic to neutral in pH. **Ideally, for soil-based mixtures the pH should be from 6.3 to 7.0,** although in a fertile, well-draining soil, marijuana might grow well in a pH from about 5.8 to 7.5. The pH of a hydroponic solution is tested after the fertilizers are dissolved, because fertilizers will affect the final pH. **The ideal pH for hydroponic solutions should be from 6.2 to 6.8.**

There are several ways to measure the pH to see whether it is generally acidic or alkaline, and various test kits and meters will tell you precisely the number value of the pH. There are litmus papers (from drug stores) which indicate only whether the soil is acidic or alkaline, and nitrazine tape (from gardening stores) which gives you an approximate number value for pH when mixed with a wetted soil sample. Much better are pH meters, which test the pH of both soil and water: they are very simple to use, are accurate, last a long time, and can be purchased through mail order, greenhouses, and nurseries for between $12 to $100. Along with an automatic timer, an accurate pH meter is the wisest investment any marijuana grower can make, and it's a must for hydroponic cultivation.

Adjusting the pH of Soil

To test soil pH, mix and wet the soil, wait an hour, then test. If the pH is lower than the ideal range of 6.3 to 7.0, add **fine** dolomite lime and retest. Repeat, adding more dolomite lime until the pH is at least 6.3. Dolomite lime acts slowly and continuously, and hydrated lime acts almost instantly. Use hydrated lime instead of dolomite lime for faster results, but don't use too much; you can create toxicity problems, which won't arise with dolomite lime, by using too much hydrated lime. Always use fine dolomite lime, since coarser grades take years to have a substantial effect.

For soil-based mixtures, the best procedure is to adjust the pH while you're mixing the soil. In general, for eastern growers, or others who know their soil is acidic, mix one cup of hydrated lime or agricultural limestone, or two cups of fine wood ash to each 50 lbs. or six gallons of soil before mixing in amendments such as perlite or vermiculite. If you don't have a pH tester, this procedure should work well for most growers in the East and other high rainfall areas.

In general, one cup of hydrated lime raises the pH of a 50 lb. (six-gallon) bag of soil roughly one point (most commercial soil does not have an extreme pH). To be exact, use a pH meter. To adjust the pH for a large quantity of soil, thoroughly moisten a one-gallon sample of soil, then test the pH. Let's say the pH has tested at 5.7. Add either two or three tablespoons of hydrated lime to a gallon of dry soil. Mix thoroughly, wet, wait an hour, and retest. The pH should now be within the optimum range of 6.3 to 7.0. **There are 16 level tablespoons to a cup.** By using one gallon of soil and adding tablespoons of hydrated or dolomite lime, you can figure out with simple arithmetic how many cups of lime to add to your large bags of soil. This is much easier than trying to mix and remix 50-lb. bags of soil each time you need to test. Mix soil, sphagnum and peat moss, humus, manures, and fertilizers together before checking the pH. Perlite, sand, lava rock, vermiculite, and Jiffy-mix are neutral in pH, and may be added after the basic soil mixture is adjusted.

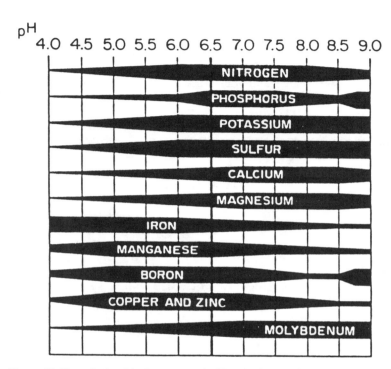

Figure 54. The relationship between soil pH and relative plant nutrient availability. The wider the bar, the more the availability. This chart is for soil types recommended in this book.

If the starting soil tested alkaline, mix one cup of gypsum (from garden stores) to each 50 lb. bag of soil. Wet a sample, wait, and retest. Add correspondingly more gypsum if the soil is still too alkaline. One cup of gypsum per 50 lbs. of soil should be more than adequate for any commercial alkaline soil. Iron sulphate and other sulfur compounds available in garden shops also lower the pH. Follow package directions and test after each addition. Bulk topsoils shouldn't be too alkaline for healthy growth. Any soil that initially tests above 7.5 should not be used, or else you'll certainly see nutrient deficiencies (Fe, Zn, Mn among others). Add acidic amendments such as peat and sphagnum, humus, or manures to fertilize and improve the texture of alkaline soils. All of these help lower the pH, and they work continuously during the growing season.

The pH of your water supply also influences the availability of nutrients. Pure or distilled water is neutral, 7.0. Generally in the East, water is acidic (soft), and your starting soil must not be lower than 6.3 for long-term good results. In dry regions such as the West, water is often alkaline (hard), and your soil should be slightly acidic, from 6.3 to 6.8 for best results.

Adjusting pH During Growth. If you discover that your soil is too acidic during growth, dissolve a teaspoon of hydrated lime in each gallon of water. Water as usual. Retest the soil's pH after a couple of days, and repeat the application if the soil still tests too acidic.

Hydroponics

Hydroponics is growing plants without soil. There are innumerable hydroponic systems, some of which use only water, but most of which use an inert growing medium such as sand or gravel to support the plants. Hydroponic gardeners have used a myriad of growing mediums, including gravel, marbles, sand, rubber, foam, rockwool, perlite, vermiculite, straw, wood chips, sawdust, sponge, peat and sphagnum moss, plastic beads, styrofoam, and broken brick or records, to name some.

Many hydroponic systems geared to the marijuana grower include pots, growing mediums, and nutrient formulas, and they sometimes include a watering system with pumps and timers. Manufacturers sometimes claim that their "magic formula" grows the most potent plants or the largest plants. Trust me on this: **there is no magic formula that will make any obvious or even detectable difference in the potency of your plants, and growth will vary only if the plants don't receive enough of any critical mineral (fertilizer).** Most commercial hydroponic solutions should work quite well. Follow their instructions, check the sections here on fertilizing and deficiencies, and you should be able to get fast and healthy growth from any commercial solution.

There are four key points that universally apply in hydroponics, and these points are more important than any particular ratio of nitrogen to phosphorus or whatever, no matter which system or nutrient solution you choose.

The foremost criterion is the pH. The pH depends on the water you are using and the nutrient solution you dissolve in the water. The resulting pH determines which nutrients will be absorbed, and how easily each is absorbed by the plants. If the **final** pH is within the recommended parameters (6.2 to 6.8), you should have few problems with nutrients.

Second is aeration. A medium that is too tight (only with organics, such as manures or sphagnum), or a system that is constantly saturated or standing in stagnant water suffocates the roots. Roots need oxygen, and without air (oxygen) they suffocate or actually drown, and consequently the health and growth of the plant suffers. Suffocated roots are difficult to rehabilitate without setting the development of the plants back; you must dry and loosen the medium, and you may have to transplant to a new medium. If you use any of the mixtures listed here, this won't ever be a problem, as long as the plants aren't kept standing in an uncirculated, watery medium.

Third is salt buildup. This won't be a problem in most gardens, but if it does appear it can be a pain. Excess salt buildup causes numerous "deficiency signs" or may lead to toxic conditions (see Overfertilization in Chapter 14). To remedy, you must flood the pots over and over with pure water, hopefully flushing the toxic salts out of the growing medium. Don't ever try to force growth by fertilizing with higher concentrations or more frequently than recommended.

Reusing growing mediums for a second crop is also discouraged because of salt buildup. Always start anew, unless you use an inert, fast draining medium, such as gravel, aggregates, or plastic beads. Even these reusable mediums should be flooded several times with fresh water before you restart. Hydroponic mediums are cheap and easy enough to mix. Don't try to save a couple of dollars by recycling because you could run into serious problems later in growth.

Fourth is the ratio of nitrogen to potassium. The duration and intensity of light affects the absorption and utilization of both elements. Under high intensity light, such as in a greenhouse during the summer, plants need about twice as much nitrogen as potassium. During winter or under low light (fluorescent systems), they need about equal amounts of nitrogen and potassium.

It's possible to buy each nutrient separately and mix your solutions (Sudbury is the most commonly available brand of these individual nutrient packages), but you must know what amounts to mix, and sometimes mixtures of mineral compounds don't dissolve into forms that the plants can use. If you're inexperienced, use a premixed commercial hydroponic mixture.

Hydroponic Nutrient Formulas

There are many possible formulas, but the chemical compounds in the following formulas are easy to find (or you might talk a pharmacist into selling you weighed amounts of each compound). The compounds in Table 9.4 should be mixed in the order listed; otherwise there may be precipitation or antagonism between compounds. It is a good idea to have your water analyzed to tell you the concentration of elements (measured in **parts per million** or **ppm**). For example, if you find a high concentration of iron in your water, lessen the amount of Fe in the micronutrient formula accordingly after looking at the ranges for Fe given in Table 9.6. Most of you will buy premixed, commercial formulas but for you horticultural enthusiasts, here are two micronutrient formulas, two general· formulas for parts per million (ppm), one formula for compounds that you can find and mix yourself, and one set of instructions that allows you to easily mix and formulate your own solution according to the concentrations or parts per million you decide on.

Table 9.4
Micronutrient Formula #1

Compound	Element	Milligrams/gal.	Grams/100 gal.
Boric acid	(B)	2.0	0.2
Zinc sulphate	(Zn)	0.2	0.02
Ferrous sulphate	(Fe)	5.0	0.5
Manganese sulphate	(Mn)	2.0	0.2
Copper sulphate	(Cu)	0.2	0.02
Molybdic acid	(Mo)	0.1	0.01

Add one tablespoon of Formula #1 to each gallon of your nutrient solution once a month.

Table 9.5
Micronutrient Formula #2

Compound	Element	Teaspoons/gallon
Part 1		
Manganese chloride	(Mn)	1/2
Fe 330, iron chelate	(Fe)	2
Boric Acid	(B)	1 and 1/4
Part 2		
Zinc sulphate	(Zn)	1/2
Copper sulphate	(Cu)	1/4

*Because of compatibility, formula #2 is mixed and stored in two separate parts. Dissolve the compounds listed in Part 1 in one-gallon of water. Add one ounce (about 1/8 cup) of this solution to each two-gallons of your nutrient solution each time you make a new solution. Dissolve the compounds in Part 2 in one-gallon of water, and add two drops of this concentrate to each two-gallons of your nutrient solution.

Nutrient Solutions for the Major Nutrients

Most nutrient formulas are tested in a laboratory with distilled water. Your solution will be different, because household water contains dissolved salts and nutrients in concentrations that depend on the local water supply. In practice, almost all fertilizer grades of compounds used to make nutrient solutions also have impurities which often contain micronutrients. Don't worry about being extremely precise (e.g. 100 vs. 110 ppm), because you actually have much latitude in preparing or selecting nutrient solutions. Also, plants seem able to adjust themselves to various conditions. The two most important points for homemade preparations are: first, be sure the solution is balanced; second, be sure that concentrations fall within the limits shown in Table 9.6.

Table 9.6
Acceptable Concentrations of Nutrients

		Parts per million (ppm) in solution	
Element	Symbol	Limits (range)	Average
Nitrogen	(N)	150-1,000	300
Phosphorus	(P)	50-100	80
Potassium	(K)	100-400	250
Magnesium	(Mg)	50-100	75
Sulfur	(S)	200-1,000	400
Calcium	(Ca)	300-500	400
Iron	(Fe)	2-10	5
Boron	(B)	0.5-5	2
Manganese	(Mn)	0.5-5	2
Zinc	(Zn)	0.5-1	0.5
Molybdenum	(Mo)	0.001-0.002	0.001

The best results occur when you use formulas that are close to the average in Table 9.6, not when you try to force the issue by having ppm near the high end of the range. Look at the recommended formulas in Table 9.7. Formula #1 is for strong light (sunlight and 1,000-watt HID's). Formula #2 is for moderately lit gardens (fluorescents) and winter natural-light gardens. Be particularly careful with nitrogen. Even though an acceptable limit is 1,000 ppm, keep nitrogen below 400 ppm.

Table 9.7
Recommended Formulas in ppm

	N	P	K	Mg
Formula #1 for strong light gardens				
First two weeks	60-100	30-50	80-150	30-50
Growth	250-350	70-90	150-250	50-80
Flowering	40-100	70-100	100-200	30-60
Formula #2 for moderate light gardens				
First two weeks	40-80	30-50	100-180	30-50
Growth	150-250	60-80	250-350	50-80
Flowering	40-100	70-90	120-220	30-50

During flowering for sinsemilla make your formula nearer the low end of these ranges. For seed crops, make the solution nearer the high end of the given ranges.

Table 9.8 gives an easy-to-mix general formula for the primary
and secondary nutrients. The compounds are weighed in ounces and
mixed into ten gallons of water to make the nutrient solution.

Table 9.8
Easy-to-mix General Formula

Compound	Element	Ounces/ 10 gallons	ppm
Calcium nitrate	(N)	1	74
Sodium nitrate	(N)	1	97
Ammonium sulphate	(N)	1/2	75
Potassium sulphate	(K)	1	250
Superphosphate (single)	(P)	2	75
Epsom salts	(Mg)	1	58

This general formula works out to approximately the following
ppm: N, 236; P, 75; K, 250; Mg, 58.

During flowering, eliminate sodium nitrate and ammonium
sulphate. Cut the amount of potassium sulphate and epsom salts in
half. The formula now has the following ppm: N, 74; P, 75; K, 125; Mg,
29. During the first two weeks of growth cut all nutrients by one half
(or dissolve the same amount in 20 gallons of water). These formulas
are adjusted for more nitrogen than you might commonly see in
greenhouse formulas, because marijuana is a nitrophile ("nitrogen
lover") and requires more nitrogen to sustain its fast growth than
other crops grown hydroponically.

Many growers want to make their own formulas, but lack the
necessary training. The fact that the U.S.A. still uses the English
system of weights and measures rather than converting to the metric
system merely adds to the difficulty of creating nutrient formulas.
Table 9.9 is included so that with a little basic arithmetic, you can
figure concentrations for your own solutions for ppm and experiment
with whatever ideas you might have.

Table 9.9
Guide for the Preparation of Nutrient Solutions

Compound	Fraction of ounce per 100 gallons of water to get 1 ppm of element
Sodium nitrate	0.103 N
Calcium nitrate	0.135 N (and 1.4 ppm Ca)
Ammonium sulphate	0.076 N
Potassium nitrate (for N)	0.122 N (and 2.8 ppm K)
Potassium nitrate (for K)	0.044 K (and 0.36 ppm N)
Potassium sulphate	0.040 K
Potassium chloride (muriate)	0.033 K
Superphosphate (16% P_2O_5)	0.268 P (and 3.8 ppm Ca)
Triple superphosphate	0.089 P
Monocalcium phosphate	0.076 P (and 0.6 ppm Ca)
Monopotassium phosphate	0.07 P (and 0.056 ppm K)
Magnesium sulphate (epsom)	0.172 Mg
Magnesium nitrate	0.13 Mg
Ferrous sulphate	0.089 Fe
Ferric ammonium citrate	0.138 Fe
Calcium sulphate (gypsum)	0.076 Ca
Manganese sulphate	0.065 Mn
Boric acid	0.090 B

For example, to make a solution that has 150 ppm of N from ammonium sulphate, 0.076 X 150 = 11.4 ounces for 100 gallons of water. For 10 gallons, 11.4 + 10 = 1.14 ounces of compound dissolved in water.

If you keep your plants healthy, then ratios among nutrients will not make a noticeable difference in the potency of your crop. Mail-order houses may advertise their "secret formula" for superpotent plants: don't believe it. On the other hand, over the years mail-order houses that gear their sales to marijuana growers have gotten very good at what they do, and most formulas that you see in *High Times* or *Sinsemilla Tips* work very well.

The uptake of nutrients depends on the individual plant, the variety, and all growth factors such as light intensity, humidity, and temperature. That you have a certain ratio of N to P doesn't tell you what the plant actually absorbs. If you provide a balanced formula with adequate (but not excessive) amounts of nutrients, you will have done all you can for the nutritional health and potency of your crop. In this case, your plants and nature make the final decisions.

There are some important generalizations worth emphasizing. Experiments in England have shown that successful hydroponic nutrient formulas have this in common: in summer (strong light) plants respond best with formulas that provide up to twice as much nitrogen as potassium, and in winter (weaker light) up to twice as much potassium as nitrogen. The temperature also affects the utilization of N; when the weather is very hot (90 degrees and up), cut the amount of nitrogen by about 20 percent.

During flowering, marijuana's need for phosphorus is higher, although the plant can draw on stored phosphorus for the formation of flowers and seeds. Make sure that any nutrient formula you use during flowering has a good amount of P.

Anytime you rely exclusively on a nutrient formula, watch for signs of nitrogen deficiency. If such occurs, increase your nutrient solution from 50 to 100 ppm of N during the growth stage. During flowering only increase nitrogen if the leaves are **rapidly yellowing**. A **gradual** yellowing of the **lower leaves** during maturation is normal, and in fact is desirable, so that the grass won't taste "metallic or green" from the richness of chlorophyll. If there is too much yellowing (a severe N deficiency), buds won't fill out to their full potential size, and dying leaves encourage the growth of bud rot. You may prefer not to fertilize your plants at all (or only mildly) during the last few weeks before harvesting. But if you've had problems with fungus or rot, keep the plants a healthy green. Rot is part of the natural decomposition process; it first attacks yellow or dying leaves. Often, the infection of a bud began on a single dying leaf within the bud.

For greenhouse growers, **during the summer a weaker nutrient solution given more often works best, because of rapid evaporation. During winter or cool weather, a more concentrated solution applied less often works best** because the beds will stay wet for a long time.

The most important single factor is that your pH must be within an acceptable range (6.2 to 6.8; try for about 6.5) **after** you've dissolved all of the nutrients. When the pH is right, there should be few if any problems with nutrients.

Adjusting pH for Hydroponics

When you purchase a hydroponic nutrient solution it usually includes a pH adjuster. Use the manufacturer's adjuster and follow the enclosed directions. For homemade hydroponics, to lower the pH add either nitric or sulfuric acid to your nutrient solution one drop at a time (obtained from greenhouses or mail-order hydroponic suppliers). For lowering the pH, ascorbic acid (vitamin C in crystal form from health-food stores or pharmacies) works well, or try white distilled vinegar, which is added one-eighth teaspoon at a time.

You'll often find that the pH suddenly drops dramatically on, for example, the fourth drop of nitric acid, when after three drops the pH had barely moved (titration principles for you chemists). **Test the pH of the solution after each addition.**

Whatever pH adjuster you decide upon, add it very slowly and minutely. Pay attention to the total you finally add and after a few times standardize the procedure for quick mixing. However, always check your final pH because the starting pH of your water supply may change as the season goes on. By the end of the summer, shrinking reservoirs concentrate salts, and can raise the pH of your water supply. Also, if the pH rises, check your holding basin because salts may have accumulated on the container's sides, and they'll affect the final pH. Wash the container thoroughly if salts have accumulated (you'll see mineral deposits or a ring around the basin), and renew the nutrient solution.

To raise the pH of acidic nutrient solutions, use bicarbonate of soda (baking soda from supermarkets and pharmacies), hydrated lime (hardware stores), or fine wood ashes. Add these half a teaspoon or less at a time per gallon, until you have a good idea of how much to use. Standardize the amount for a fast adjustment throughout the life of the growing crop.

When the pH is correct, there should be few problems except for an occasional N or Mg deficiency. Deficiencies are easily recognized by the pictures and text in Chapter 14, Nutrient Deficiencies.

Home-made Nutrient Solutions

Even though hydroponics has been used for more than 300 years, specialty sources for marijuana growers are fairly new. Yet 20 years ago, hydroponic growers grew excellent marijuana with standard fertilizers available at any supermarket. Although simple to do, you should have some experience; you must be familiar with healthy growth and be able to recognize nutrient deficiencies. Reading this procedure will provide you with some insight into common nutrient deficiencies, and home-made hydroponics is cheap and simple, and it gives excellent results. There are many complete hydroponic nutrient formulas available now that simplify the entire process.

Best early results came from a combination of hydroponics and soil-based culture. By mixing a fifth to an eighth part of soil, humus, or manure, into a medium of 1 part perlite to 1 part vermiculite, most of the micronutrients were provided by the soil. Garden shops and nurseries sell micronutrient packages that are either mixed into the rooting medium or applied when watering. For organic growers, seaweed solutions are an excellent source of all the micronutrients.

Many micronutrients are needed in such minuscule amounts that the impurities in fertilizers or in tap water supply the plants with adequate amounts. Deficiencies of Fe, Mn, Zn, and Mo weren't seen, probably because they were part of the soil and general fertilizers. The remaining necessary elements (sulfur, calcium, etc.) were supplied by the water or were part of the chemical compounds of the fertilizers, e.g. NO_2SO_4 or $CaNO_3$, which supply, respectively, sulfur and calcium along with nitrogen. To supply magnesium (Mg), water with a solution of one tablespoon of epsom salts per gallon of water when the plants are two weeks old. Water with this solution about twice each month.

For the major nutrients (N,P,K), use a general high N fertilizer such as Ra-Pid-Gro (23-19-17) or Miracid (30-10-10) during early growth, after diluting as directed on the back of the container. Apply the fertilizer every week or two (instead of once a month as the instructions say). During midgrowth you might use fish emulsion (organic 5-1-1) or Miracle-Gro for tomatoes (which contains almost every element necessary for growth) about once a week at half strength for safe fertilizing. Once the light cycle is turned down for flowering, use a high phosphorus fertilizer, such as Miracle-Gro (15-30-15).

Most organic or natural fertilizers contain trace elements along with the listed major nutrients; so they are excellent to use during midgrowth. With organic fertilizers there is much less chance of over-fertilizing than with chemical fertilizers. Between regular fertilizations, if the plants are growing well and are a healthy green, water with pure water, or with a dilute concentration of organic fertilizer, to lessen the chance of overfertilizing.

Adding one tablespoon of agricultural or dolomite lime per pot helps to supply Ca and Mg as well as trace elements. Micronutrients such as molybdenum (Mo) are needed in such small amounts (one part or less per 100 million) that it's actually difficult to create such deficiencies without using stringent laboratory conditions and distilled water. There are many general fertilizers such as Ra-Pid-Gro that now include the trace elements Fe, B, Mn, Zn, and Cu; so the only element that the plants might need is Mg which can be added with an epsom salt solution several times during growth.

Many pre-packaged hydroponic formulas use one formula (fertilizer) or a series of formulas — one for seedlings, another for general growth, and the last for flowering — and they simplify the whole process of supplying nutrients because the formulas are balanced and contain every element necessary for growth. Twenty years ago none of these products were available for home-growing. Today, the hand water procedure is nearly foolproof when used with a good commercial hydroponic fertilizer program.

Passive Hydroponic Systems

Hand Water System. I like the hand water method. Other systems work well, but with this method the setup is simple and relatively problem-free, and it's easy to learn and use. Other than a completely automatic system, what more could a grower want? Hand watering also keeps the grower in close and frequent contact with his or her plants which is important. **The most successful gardeners are those who take the time to consistently observe and care for their plants.**

The hand-water system means watering periodically, just as you would do for pots filled with soil. The only difference is that you water with a nutrient solution into a soilless medium. If you take a short vacation, place the pots in trays filled with nutrient solution; this temporarily converts the garden into a reservoir system.

Water with your solution when the first two or three inches of the potting medium is dry. Every other time you water, use pure water to prevent overfertilization. In fact, if the plants are a healthy dark green, water with a dilute nutrient solution every third time that you water. As soon as the plants need additional fertilization, you'll see pale or yellow leaves at the bottom of the plant (N deficiency). Just fertilize with your nutrient solution. Healthy growth resumes in a couple of days. Fertilize more frequently now that you know the plants can use more fertilizer. This procedure takes some observation and common sense, but it's easy to learn. When in doubt, use half-strength concentrations of your hydroponic solution. Or use a mild solution of an organic fertilizer, such as fish emulsion, or an organic "tea" made by mixing manure, worm castings, or bat guano at the rate of one tablespoon per gallon of water. Let the solution stand overnight after a vigorous shaking. Use a fine mesh strainer or cheesecloth to remove large, undissolved particles while watering. If bottom leaves continue to yellow, fertilize with your nutrient solution every time you water. Foliar feed (see page 218) the plants to give them additional nutrients. Use pots from two to four gallons for the hand water system.

There are many good manufacturers: formulas from Applied Hydroponics, Eco-Grow, Dyna-Gro, Hydrofarm, Hydrolife, and many others, offer complete nutrient packages that supply all the nutrients your plants need. Look in *High Times* or *Sinsemilla Tips* for telephone numbers and addresses of many companies that offer free catalogs which will help you make your decisions. Originally, many of the mail-order advertisers in *High Times* offered products that were troublesome at best. In the past few years, almost all of them progressed to the point that they offer excellent hydroponic mediums, solutions, lights, and accessory equipment.

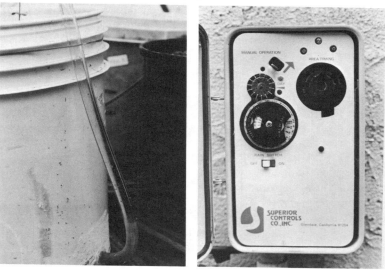

Figure 55. *Left:* Reservoir system with one container fitted into another. You can use a tube or plastic "window" to see the level of water in the reservoir. *Right:* Timers like this precisely control several water lines simultaneously. Very useful for drip systems.

Reservoir System. The reservoir system consists of individual pots that sit in a tray with a reservoir of nutrient solution. The solution is passively drawn into the medium by absorption and capillary action. Each pot may have its own reservoir, or several pots may sit in one large basin or "kiddie" pool. Fill the reservoir deep enough so the lower few inches of the pots are immersed in the solution. The drainage holes in the bottom of the pots act as absorption holes.

Discarded plastic food or ice cream containers can be cut in half to serve as inexpensive, individual reservoirs. Clear plastic plant saucers of 12" diameter and 4" depth cost about $1.00 each. Kitty-litter trays hold three one-gallon pots. Strong cardboard or wooden boxes or trays can be lined with double layers of plastic bags or polyethylene plastic to construct large makeshift water-holding basins.

You could use a single large tub with holes in the bottom placed in a large holding tray. But you may find that most of the males are at one end of the tub, and the females are at the other, which leaves you with a garden of empty space and crowded females, and you must transplant to best utilize the space. Individual pots make better use of space, and the garden is more easily cared for.

The reservoir system encourages roots to concentrate at the bottom of the container and to grow out of the drainage holes. Often the top half of the pots are devoid of any roots and the growing medium tends to become soggy at the bottom of the pot. Because of this, use the wick system in preference to the reservoir system.

Wick System. The wick system is an improved variation on the reservoir system. One or more wicks run through the planting medium out of holes punched in the bottom of each pot. Wicks are submerged in a reservoir of nutrient solution which is passively drawn up the wicks and distributed to the growing medium.

Professionals use glass wool or braided cloth wicks manufactured for the purpose, but nylon rope from any hardware store will do quite well (cotton rope will disintegrate). **Splay or shred the ends of the wick and arrange the strands evenly throughout the pot when you fill it with the growing medium.** This distributes the nutrient solution evenly and encourages the root system to fill the entire pot. Test one pot with one wick and allow one day with the wick sitting in water to see if it's enough to moisten all of the growing medium. If not, add another wick, and repeat the test until you determine how many wicks work best in your medium. In general, two wicks per gallon of medium suffice. You might find that two glass-wool wicks satisfactorily saturate a three-gallon pot, or you might need five nylon wicks to

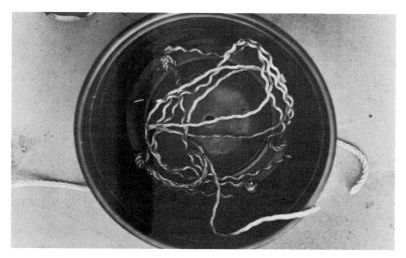

Figure 56. To keep all of the medium evenly moist, separate and distribute the ends of the wick throughout the container.

saturate the same pot. Take a few days to find out how many wicks you need per pot, and the rest of the growing season will work out much better. Use more rather than fewer wicks.

Place each pot on a brick, piece of 2 X 4, boards on props, etc., to raise the bottoms of the pots above the reservoir solution. Make the wicks long enough to curl at the bottom of the reservoir. You could use individual trays, a pot with wicks within a pot that has no drainage holes, a few reservoirs to supply several plants each, or one reservoir to supply the whole garden. The easiest setup is to span several large reservoirs with heavy screens or chain-link fencing. The number of pots sitting on the screens is limited only by the space the plants need to grow.

The wick system doesn't saturate the bottom of the growing medium like the reservoir system does, and it allows more air to migrate into the medium. Also, if you separate and evenly spread the strands throughout the medium, the whole pot becomes filled with roots. The plants are steadier, sturdier, and more firmly rooted. The wick system requires less frequent watering than the hand-water system, since the reservoir can be made as large as you want, and you don't need to worry about overwatering, since the wicks regulate a slow but constant flow of solution to the plants.

Active Hydroponic Systems

Flood System, or Ebb and Flow System. Flood systems are what the name implies, and they can be automated or done by hand (flood systems are now commonly referred to as "ebb and flow" systems). The principle is that periodically a nutrient solution is released and floods the pots. Drainage tubes or runoff troughs catch the excess solution that drains from the pots, and the solution is then recycled during the next flooding, thus the term "ebb and flow".

On the simplest level, use a pot that has a single drainage hole connected to a piece of tubing that leads to a collecting container positioned below the planted pot. Flood the growing medium with solution, and the excess drains to the collecting tank, from which it is reused. Flood systems work best with mediums that drain well, such as gravel, lava rock (also called "red lava"), aggregates, perlite, and sand. Don't use automated flood systems with vermiculite, peat moss, or other fibrous materials.

Automated flood systems do basically the same thing, except that the recycling and release of the nutrient solution is automated. Place pots on or above a gradually sloping trough that drains excess solution to a holding basin. A pump then raises the solution from the holding basin back up to a feeder holding tank, which is raised above the pots. Periodically, a timer releases the solution from the feeder tank and the solution feeds by gravity or is pumped to the plants.

The easiest setup for an automated watering system is to run a central tube from the feeding tank to emitters that run from the tube to each pot. Set the pots on corrugated plastic raised on props, and sloped toward your holding tank. Empty the holding tank into the feeder tank by hand and release a stopcock or spigot from the bottom of the feeder tank to flood the beds. For complete automation, a sump pump on a timer raises the water to the feeding tank and a sprinkler valve on another timer releases the solution.

Some commercial systems use a strong pump to flood the pots from a feeder hose in the bottom of the pots or bed. The nutrient solution fills the pots and the pump turns off. The nutrient solution drains away to a holding tank from which the solution is again, periodically pumped into the medium to flood the pots or basins. As long as your commercial system uses a well-draining medium, and the solution completely saturates the pots or bed often enough to maintain moistness without constantly being saturated, it should work very well. Hydrofarm from Applied Hydroponics is one "ebb and flow" system with a good record of performance and reliability.

Figure 57. This ebb and flow system uses a strong pump to automatically flood the medium from below.

For home setups, the trick is to experiment with the timing of the feeding until you reach a median between oversaturating and under-watering the pots. Usually one to three floodings a day work better than flooding four or five times a day. Periodically check your holding tank and add fresh water to maintain the original level, or else the nutrient solution will tend to concentrate because of evaporation.

For a single bed setup, have the release from the nutrient solution at the high end of a gradually sloping bed. For two or more beds, use a watering system with a central tube that forks into a single outlet at the high point of each bed. Slope the beds very gradually, and install the holding tank at the low end of the lowest bed to collect runoff.

A system popular in greenhouses is the tiered bed system. Here you have several beds, and each successive bed is lower than the preceding one. After the initial flood fills the first bed, the solution gravity-feeds to flood the next lower bed, and so on.

You can plant directly in the medium or bury pots in each bed. Transplanting with pots is as easy as replacing a space from a male plant with a pot holding a female, until the whole garden is evenly filled with female plants. If you use pots, bury pots about eight inches tall in a bed at least 10 inches deep. Fill the beds with the same medium that is used in the pots, so that a two- to four-inch layer covers the pots. Start two or three plants per pot to assure enough females to fill the garden. When planting directly in the bed, start at least four plants per square foot to assure at least one female per square foot. By using Jiffy-7 peat pellets or pockets of vermiculite, you can fill the space with females without using any pots. (Chapter 11).

To set up the tiered-bed system, where each bed drains into the next lower bed, each successive drainage hole should be smaller than the preceding hole. For example, the hole from the feeder tank is two inches. The drainage hole from the first bed is one inch; the second bed's is half an inch; the third bed has a drainage hole of 1/4 inch. Progressively smaller holes keep the preceding bed filled with nutrient solution before it drains to fill the next bed. A problem with the tiered bed system is that roots may grow into the drainage hole. Insert a short length of plastic drainage pipe after punching it with numerous pin-sized drainage holes. If roots gravitate and clog the pipe, it's easy to remove the plug pipe and clean any roots that are clogging the holes.

Professional greenhouse growers use the tiered system with solenoid valves that release the solution to the next lower bed after the preceding bed has filled with solution. The progressively smaller outlet method works well. It's is simple and cheap to set up and maintain.

Some commercial systems connect one inch tubing to the bottoms of small beds. Periodically a strong pump fills the bed with solution from below. After the beds are filled with solution an outlet valve opens and the solution passively returns to the feeder tank. A small (1/4 inch) outlet hole eliminates the need for an active outlet valve.

Whichever system you choose, if you have a number of plants growing in a single large bed, spread the plants apart to maximize the amount of light and space each plant has. Tie a cloth loop around each plant and attach a rope to the loop. Tie the other end of the rope to stakes, uprights, or some other sturdy anchor. Spreading the plants apart dramatically increases the yield in any garden.

Flood System by Hand. This system is very simply set up without automation and requires less frequent flooding. By using about 1/3 vermiculite in the planting medium, you need to flood the system only once every one to three days, depending on pot size (use two- to four-gallon containers). Just empty the catch basin into your feeder holding tank, and release the solution to run to the pots. The release from your feeder basin may be as simple as removing a cork from a drainage hole or tube in the bottom of the feeder tank, which may be an old sink or bathtub. For large gardens, this system allows you to water all your plants in about 5 minutes.

The simplest and easiest setup is to use a central tube from which individual feeders run to each pot. The central hose is 1/2" to 1" tubing. Cut lengths of 1/4" feeder hose to fit your garden's configuration. Feeder hose can be bought along with central tubing as part of a complete watering system from almost any garden supply store. Complete watering systems are very inexpensive, and for 25 pots it should cost you no more than $30.00, including all necessary fittings, filters, stakes, punch tool, etc.

Pure sand or perlite may show some flocculation (precipitation and lumping of minerals), and doesn't work as well as pea or construction gravel or lava rock and aggregates in flood systems. In any system, spill or splash the solution into the feeder tank to aerate the solution: this infuses oxygen into the solution, and a well oxygenated solution is crucial to healthy growth.

Drip System. This system is set up like the flood system, but the rate of flow is different, and the excess solution is not usually recycled. The drip system conserves water, doesn't leach nutrients from the growing medium, and soil moisture can be regulated so that the pots are neither waterlogged or underwatered. You could set up any number of inexpensive commercial drip systems, and they'll work very well for years. Drip systems may use central tubing from

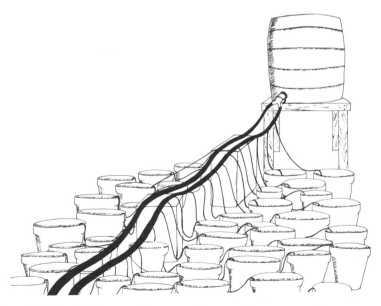

Figure 58. A simple, low-cost drip system. You can also automate drip systems very inexpensively. *Drawing by L.P. Kallan.*

which individual spaghetti emitters (very small tubing, 1/8") drip a nutrient solution slowly and frequently into each pot; or a feeder tube may be run over a line of pots, with emitters installed along its length to irrigate each pot. The rate of flow, and its duration, is adjusted so that the pots are constantly moist, but little or no excess water runs out of the pots. You need to adjust the flow rate several times until the medium maintains moistness but stops seeping from the pots. Later you'll need to increase the flow rate as the plants grow larger.

Complete systems including stopcocks (which allow you to regulate or stop the flow to each plant) are inexpensive. They're available through mail-order, greenhouse and nursery suppliers. One system at Sears had 27 emitters and all necessary plastic hardware for only $15.00. Systems that use timers and valves to turn on and off the flow from a holding tank or a spigot are also reasonably priced.

Use self-cleaning emitters, so that they don't clog with salts from the nutrient solution. Don't use this system if your water is high in iron (Fe), which will clog lines and emitters. Before starting up a drip system that recycles run-off, it's a good idea to flush the pots with water to rid the medium of any particles or sediment. Pour water repeatedly over the pots until there is little sediment left to clog the lines. The drip system works best with fast-draining materials, (gravel, sand, aggregates, and lava rock) mixed with about 1/3 part of water-holding components (vermiculite and sphagnum). To recycle your nutrient solution in an automated system using drip emitters, use aggregates, gravel (pea gravel or construction gravel), or lava rock, or mix either one with 1/3 part of sand. Fibrous materials and vermiculite clog emitters when the solution is recycled. Although inexpensive in-line filters are available to prevent this problem, you'll need to clean the filters almost daily.

You can buy an automatic drip control unit at almost any garden shop or large hardware store for as little as $15. The unit connects to a hose or faucet, runs on batteries, and often includes a moisture probe. The control unit automatically releases water through the distribution tubing when the pots or beds are dry. The controller has a range of settings. It'll cover practically any situation. Adjust the controls to release water until the pots are sufficiently saturated. They'll turn on as often as needed when signaled by the moisture probe. Automated drip systems can be the simplest to set up, cheapest, yet the most **efficient and trouble-free automated systems that you can find, especially for large, commercial gardens.**

Aeration Systems. In aeration systems plants grow in pots filled with a hydroponic medium that is set in a basin holding nutrient solution. Aquarium bubblers pump air into the solution to replenish oxygen. Aeration systems today are much superior to those sold ten years ago. These systems can be very successful: simple to set up; easy to maintain. Cost is minimal for start-up and for electricity--under 5 watts per bubbler. A typical basin is about 3' square, 6" deep. Use six or eight inch pots. Punch holes in the bottom and make slits in sides of the pots up to the depth of the nutrient solution. Use aggregate hydroponic mediums such as lava rock; not peat moss, vermiculite, soil or any medium that tends to compact. A good quality bubbler is critical, better, buy two, the second as a back-up. Plants endure for a while in solution without aeration, but take no chance on breakdowns since cost of a back-up aerator is nominal. The back-up also gives peace-of-mind when your garden is unattended. You can't over-aerate the medium, so you might always use two bubblers per basin. An excellent set up uses two basins, one to start seeds or clones under four-foot fluorescents and the second for flowering under a 400 watt HID. **For personal gardens, it's a productive, great working system.**

Table 9.10
Suggested Hydroponic or Soilless Mixtures

Flood system:

1	2	3
1 part gravel*	1 part lava rock	2 parts aggregate
1 part lava rock	1 part perlite	1 part vermiculite

Drip system: (systems which recycle use mixture #1 or #2)

4	5	6
1 part lava rock	3 parts aggregate	1 part gravel
1 part coarse sand	1 part perlite	2 parts perlite
1 part vermiculte	2 parts Jiffy-mix	1 part vermiculite

Hand water system:

7	8	9
4 parts perlite	4 parts sand	3 parts aggregate
2 parts vermiculite	2 parts vermiculite	2 parts Jiffy-mix
1 part worm casting	1 part humus	1 part soil

Alkaline Water Supply:

10	11
4 parts aggregate	4 parts perlite
1 part vermiculite	2 parts sphagnum or peat moss
1 part peat moss	1 part humus

Use mixture 10 for drip or mixture 11 for hand water systems. Use either mixture if your water supply is naturally alkaline (hard).

*You can substitute aggregate mediums for either gravel or lava rock.

Don't use styrofoam or plastic beads, neither of which actually holds water or exchanges minerals as well as the materials recommended here. Don't use straw, wood chips, or other organics; they become soggy and encourage the growth of molds, insects, and other diseases.

Although hydroponic gardens grow well in pure vermiculite or perlite, these components are very lightweight. Once the plants are larger, you may easily knock pots over. Plants grown in pure gravel, aggregates or lava rock tend not to be firmly rooted in the medium. You can easily knock these plants down, separating the root system from the medium.

In either situation you may find yourself spending a lot of time propping up your plants with supports; hence in general, use one heavy component (lava rock, gravel, sand, or aggregates) to stabilize the pots, mixed with a root holding component such as perlite, vermiculite, sphagnum, or sand. (See Supports in Chapter 15.)

Buying Soil or Hydroponic Components

All the soil amendments mentioned in this book are available at farm or garden stores, and nurseries. Many suburban supermarkets sell large bags of soil, humus, and peat moss. Whichever soil or soil components you buy, always buy them in the largest units you can use. The markup on soil, perlite, etc., is enormous for smaller units, and in the long run the large bags (four cubic feet) save considerable money. Large bags of soil and humus come in 50-lb. bags (which fill six to eight gallons) or in one- to four-cubic-foot bags. Perlite, vermiculite, and Jiffy-mix come in four-cubic-foot bags and in progressively smaller sizes. There are about eight gallons in a cubic foot, and about 32 gallons in a four-cubic-foot bag. Most wholesale gardening and nursery supply companies will sell you cartons of pots and large bags of soil conditioners if you buy the whole carton or unit. A carton of 50 one-gallon pots from a New York wholesaler costs $12.00. Take a walk through the Yellow Pages to find local wholesalers.

Perlite and vermiculite come in three grades: coarse, medium, and fine. All work very well, but if you have a choice, choose coarse. Sand is expensive if you buy horticultural sand from a gardening store. A much cheaper alternative is to buy sand from lumber yards or hardware stores, where it is sold for cement work. This is the same sand you see piled at construction sites. It's free of salts (the cement would crumble if the sand contained salt such as in beach sand), costs less than 1/100th as much as gardening or horticultural sand, and works very well for growing plants.

Buying Soil

In eastern and midwestern states and anywhere else there is good rainfall, the local commercial soils usually are very good because these soils are dug from fertile topsoil beds and then processed and conditioned to make good, well-balanced, basic starting soils. Swiss Farms' potting **soil** (not potting mix) is an example of an excellent commercial soil available in the East.

In drier areas of the country, soils often are manufactured completely from wood byproducts, conditioners, composts, etc., because large quantities of good natural topsoil are harder to come by. Unfortunately, these manufactured soils, common in the West, are usually very poor starting mixtures. Salt levels may be very high, and nutrient concentrations are often unbalanced. On the West Coast, the only commercial soil tested and recommended is Super Soil, but even Super Soil needs frequent fertilization with N after a month or two of growth. Also, Black Gold, which is produced in Oregon, worked very well in one garden. Most of the other packaged soils will cause innumerable problems. Typically, these manufactured "soils" are much too high in several or all of the following; K, Mg, S, Fe, Mn, Cl, Na, and NH_3 or ammonia, any of which can cause imbalances, toxicities and other problems. It took me a few years after moving to the West Coast from the East to test and find out why Western growers had so many soil problems compared to growers back East. A better alternative is to buy real topsoil.

Bulk Topsoil

Bulk topsoils generally are the best starting soil you can get, and are extremely economical compared to bagged soil mixtures from nurseries or greenhouses. There are about 216 gallons of soil in a cubic yard, and the cost may be as little as $12.00 including delivery.

The Yellow Pages lists under "Soils" the local companies that sell and deliver topsoil. Topsoil is natural soil that is screened of debris and sometimes sterilized and bolstered with humus. The minimum amount that most companies will deliver is one cubic yard. The soil is not packaged, but arrives loose via truck, and is unceremoniously dumped wherever you say. In other words, you need a yard to accommodate the pile, or you need to be able to move the soil indoors if the deliveryperson dumps the soil on the sidewalk or street.

Calculating the Amount of Soil or
Hydroponic Components

To calculate the total amount of components you need, multiply the capacity of the pots by the number of pots you can fit beneath your light system. Let's consider two examples. Example 1 is a soil-based garden under a four-tube, eight-foot standard fluorescent system: [4 X 80 watts = 320 watts + 20 watts/square feet = 16 square feet]. About 18 three-gallon pots can fit in 16 square feet, so you'll need 54 gallons total [3 X 18]. Table 9.11 lists the supplies needed.

Table 9.11
Calculating Supplies

Buy	Component	Amount (in gallons)
Example #1		
Three 50-lb (6-plus gal ea.)	bags of soil	18
Two 1-cubic foot	bags of perlite	16
One 1-cubic foot	bag of vermiculite	8
One 1-cubic foot	bag of humus	8
10 lbs of	chicken manure	2
One bag of	dolomite lime	–
	Total 52 gallons	
Example #2		
Three 4-cubic foot	bags of vermiculite	96
One 4-cubic foot	bag of perlite	32
Two 4-cubic foot	bags of lava rock	64
	Total 192 gallons	

The actual amount you use will be slightly less than the total capacity of the pots — you must leave a couple of inches of space at the top of the pot to make watering easier.

Example 1 is a soil-based garden. Example 2 is a hydroponic garden under an HID lamp: 1,000 watts divided by 20 w/square feet = 50 square feet. About 50 four-gallon containers (200 gallons) can fit into a circle of 50 square feet.

Mixing and Potting the Growing Medium

Mixing. To mix your components together, use a large basin or bathtub or the floor (after spreading plastic sheets). To make any of the potting mixtures, simply use any smaller container to measure out parts by volume. Use a painter's mask or handkerchief over your nose and mouth, because mixing dry soil and perlite raises clouds of fine dust. You can also make your mixtures outdoors. The fibers in rockwool are much like fiberglass insulation, and are unhealthy if inhaled. Wet mediums such as rockwool before you handle them to prevent the fibers from becoming airborne.

Potting. Place a piece of window screen or several pieces of newspaper in the pot to cover the pot's drainage holes and keep the mixture from running out. Cover this with a one-inch deep layer of perlite, lava rock or gravel to assure drainage. Fill the pots to within an inch or two of the top of the pot. This top inch of space holds a pool of water and makes watering faster and easier. If you've added manures or composts, cover the last inch or two of mixture with a layer of pure soil or sand. This helps prevent flies, gnats, molds, and other pests from being attracted to and establishing a foothold in the mixture.

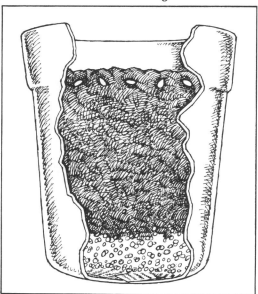

Figure 59. Potting for soil mixture. *Drawing by O. Williams.*

Press spongy soils firmly but not tightly to allow more soil in each pot; otherwise, after a period of watering, soil settles, and the pot isn't being used to its capacity.

Water the pots and let them sit for a while until the soil is evenly moist. Probe to the bottom of one pot to make sure that all the soil is moist. Don't plant in soil while the lower levels are dry. The surface tension of water may prevent moisture from penetrating very dry soil, and the bottom reaches of the pot may never become moist. This is a pain to correct after the plant is growing. Water from the top, and submerge the pots in a few inches of water in trays or in a bathtub. By the next day all of the soil should be evenly moist, and ready for planting. (See Chapter 12 for more tips on moistening dry soil.) Once the soil has initially been moistened, the soil should absorb water easily in subsequent waterings.

Part IV
Starting the All Important Seed

Previous page: A Mexican plant with the classic Christmas-tree shape. The plant was about 19 feet tall and still growing when photographed in California. It yielded seven pounds of sinsemilla at harvest.

Chapter 10

Selecting A Variety
To Grow

Cannabis: Are They Species or Varieties?

Since the early 1970's, much work has been done on taxonomy (ordering and naming) of the previously neglected genus *Cannabis*. Besides the need to clarify the genus for botanical reasons, a need to answer the question of species within the genus *Cannabis* was important for legal reasons. During the 1970's, botanists who were sympathetic to the marijuana growers' plight offered to dispute marijuana growers' arrests on botanical grounds, which became known as the "species defense". The prosecution's contention was that the accused were growing *C. sativa*. The growers' defense counsel argued that there were several species within the genus *Cannabis*, notably *C. indica* and *C. ruderalis*. Since the law specified *C. sativa* as the illegal plant, the law was not applicable to their clients, who were growing species other than *C. sativa*.

A number of researchers examined *Cannabis*, and after numerous experiments and studies on structure, anatomy, cross-breeding and chemistry, they concluded, after some argument, that *Cannabis* is indeed a single species, *Cannabis sativa* L. Although the species *Cannabis* is quite variable in overall appearance, growth habit, ecology, cannabinoid chemistry, etc., the innumerable variations are due to human intervention, predominantly the breeding for specific characteristics, and the transport of the plant to new environments, rather than due to natural evolution (natural evolution or speciation is a prerequisite for true species status).

The species defense was made moot in California courts when an appeals court ruled in favor of the prosecution by deciding that, although there might be a botanical question, the law's intent was clear whether or not there was more than one species.

Among the many possible species that have been proposed in scientific literature are the following:

(1) *C. sativa*	(9) *C. rupulus*
(2) *C. folliisdigtatsis*	(10) *C. macrosperma*
(3) *C. erratica*	(11) *C. americana*
(4) *C. mas*	(12) *C. generalis*
(5) *C. femina*	(13) *C. gigantea*
(6) *C. chinensis*	(14) *C. ruderalis*
(7) *C. foetens*	(15) *C. interstitia*
(8) *C. indica*	

A modern scheme now generally agreed upon for classifying *Cannabis* is shown in Table 10.1.

Table 10.1

Divisio—Tracheophyta
Subdivision–Pteropsida
Class–Angiospermae
Subclass–Dicotyledoneae
Order–Utricales
Family–Cannabaceae
Genus–*Cannabis*
Species–*sativa Linné*

Many growers familiar with the variability of *Cannabis* and with the different names growers use for their *Cannabis* (most commonly *C. indica* and *C. ruderalis)* might argue that they have grown more than one different "kind" of *Cannabis*; that they look quite different, have different growth habits, fragrances, tastes, and potencies, and thus must be different species. But simply looking different, or having different properties, does not a species make.

Human selection for particularly desirable traits can powerfully alter plants. Six vegetables — cabbage, cauliflower, brussel sprouts, broccoli, kale, and kohlrabi (cruciferous vegetables) — are descended from a single species of mustard herb, *Brassica oleracea*. All six are still considered one species, since cultivation for certain characteristics such as flower buds (broccoli) or buds (cabbage) resulted from human selection for the desired traits. However, **natural evolution (or speciation)** is a prerequisite for true species status.

Cannabis has been cultivated for at least six millennia and is now cultivated around the world. *Cannabis* may be grown for hemp fiber, seeds and seed oil, marijuana, or medicines derived from the root, leaves, or flowers. It is the diversity of environments and the results of selective breeding for specific traits that has led to the numerous varieties of *Cannabis* we see today. We should be thankful for this variability. Every grower can hope to find desirable characteristics in a few populations or in certain individuals, and then breed them so that future generations express the desirable characteristics. With a little time and observation, every grower can develop his or her own variety suited to individual tastes and to the plant's local growing needs (see Chapter 20).

Growers often tell me that they are growing *Cannabis ruderalis*, a wild roadside weed that originated in the Soviet Union. If they are actually growing a *ruderalis*, then they are growing very low-grade marijuana at best. Hundreds of samples of *ruderalises* have been grown and tested in botanical experiments, and the average potency is less than 0.5 percent THC, which is very low grade marijuana. The *ruderalis* collections grown by botanists also put out only a few sets of leaves before flowering and finishing their life cycles. Most collections usually yielded less than half an ounce of marijuana per plant. The potent "*ruderalis*" that I saw grown in the U.S. invariably turned out to be what is actually *indica*.

Recently in the Netherlands and the U.S., *Cannabis* breeders have crossed true strains of *ruderalis* with more potent strains of marijuana.

Figure 60. Leaves show varietal differences of six different seedlings. *Top, left to right:* Durban Poison, Colombian, Afghani (two weeks older). *Bottom, left to right:* Kush, Southern Indian, Thai.

Resulting hybrids mature quickly, yet some have incorporated the genes of potent strains. Most often, these hybrids are available only through mail order. (According to *High Times*, no one has ever been busted for receiving seeds from mail-order seed houses. However, in 1989, legal troubles for Dutch seed companies helped curtail operations. Currently, seed shipments have all but ceased. Some customers reported not receiving seeds although their checks were cashed.

As the art of marijuana growing becomes more sophisticated, true varieties are becoming increasingly common and available from professional seed breeders. For example, Afghani 1 which is sold from Amsterdam was actually developed in California and is very popular among both indoor and outdoor growers. Haze, which is an extremely potent and large-growing sativa hybrid, was also developed in California, but is now distributed from Amsterdam.

Although *Cannabis sativa* is the only botanically recognized species, for the purposes of growing marijuana it's helpful to talk of races or strains of marijuana, and to further divide the general groupings into specific strains or varieties. Four broad and overlapping subdivisions within the species that are of interest to marijuana growers are the *sativas*, *indicas*, *ruderalises*, and hemps. Within these four subdivisions are innumerable variations. A practical outline follows, with the descriptions for plants growing outdoors under natural conditions (time of maturation is given for a midline across the U.S. at about 38 degrees north, roughly a line that runs from Washington, D.C. through Kansas City to San Francisco.

Marijuana Strains and Varieties

Sativas are from eight to 20 feet tall; yields are from 1/3 to five lbs. per plant in sinsemilla buds. *Sativas* may originate from anywhere, but almost all tropical marijuana varieties are *sativas*, and almost invariably all hemps are *sativa*, whether they come from near the Arctic circle or from equatorial regions. Leaf blades are long and narrow and light green in color. Branching is symmetric to uneven, but usually internodes are long and branches are even and well-spaced. Female stigmas (the two "hairs" of a female flower) are most often pure white. Maturation usually is late in the season from mid-October through December for tropical varieties, but as early as the end of July for temperate hemp strains.

Indicas are shorter, usually between four and eight feet tall, and they yield 1/4 to two lbs. of sinsemilla. *Indicas* mostly originate from central Asia, primarily from Afghanistan, Pakistan, Iran, and India. Leaves usually are a very dark blue-green, and may develop a purple tinge. Leaf blades are shorter and much wider than *sativas*. Branching is usually symmetric and thick with short internodes. Flower stigmas are usually white, but may be red or purple; buds tend to be fuller and more compact than most *sativas*. Most often *indicas* mature early, from late August through October.

Ruderalises have narrow, sativa-like leaf blades: plants are short, from one to five feet tall and most of them are very sparse with relatively long internodes. (Botanical collections of *ruderalis* from the U.S.S.R. characterize all *ruderalises* as having narrow blades. Many U.S. marijuana growers describe *ruderalis* as having wide *indica*-like leaf blades, and these might be hybrids.) Often *ruderalis* has only two or three sets of leaves before flowering and typical yields are only 1/4 to two ounces of sinsemilla. Originally from the U.S.S.R., *ruderalis* is very quick to mature and may ripen as early as the middle of July. Generally *ruderalis* begins flowering a few weeks after sprouting but it won't form decent buds, if ever, until the photoperiod drops to about 18 or 19 hours duration.

American hemps are generally six to 12 feet tall with *sativa*-like leaves, coloration, and bud characteristics. These weeds are very hardy (in fact authorities have been unable to eradicate this "troublesome" weed), and mature early, from the end of July to early October.

Any experienced grower has seen considerable overlap among these characteristics. There are *indicas* that might yield five lbs. of buds, and there are *sativas* that have red stigmas. Much of the best stock growing in the U.S. is hybridized anyway, and you're likely to see any combination of the described characteristics.

Choosing Varieties to Grow

Marijuana from around the world responds to the same environmental influences, and the most important influence is the photoperiod, which determines when the plants will mature and if they'll mature before killing frosts arrive. For outdoor gardeners, this is the most important consideration, because if the plants don't mature in time, you're left with only leaf or immature buds to harvest. You're better off growing a less potent but good variety that completes maturation rather than a super-potent variety that won't mature in time. Indoors you need not worry about when the plants would naturally flower since you control the photoperiod and hence maturation.

For straightforward growing or for sophisticated breeding programs, three primary characteristics are most important to all marijuana growers: potency, time of maturation, and yield. Some secondary characteristics to consider are fragrance and taste, hardiness and resistance to disease, bud formation and ease of manicure, and the quality of the high (i.e., an energizing versus a debilitating high, to name two extremes).

Under natural light, time of maturation for the most part depends on the latitude from which the stock originated and the local photoperiod. In general, the farther from the equator a stock originated, the earlier it flowers and ripens. The actual time of maturation varies also with the local conditions to which the variety is accustomed. For instance, if the plants have acclimated at a high altitude, they may mature up to a month before their cousins at sea level, even though they are at the same latitude. This is why varieties from roughly the same area can differ significantly as to when they ripen. The best stocks for breeding for early maturation are South African, Afghani, Pakistani, American weedy hemp, Chinese, and *ruderalis* varieties.

The second consideration, potency, may come from any variety worldwide, since potency does not depend on origin, and any marijuana variety or stock may be exceptionally potent (see Chapter 20).

Besides overall strength or potency, the "quality" of the high also becomes much more apparent when you gain experience with a wide selection of varieties. Different marijuanas have been described as debilitating, stupefying, and numbing versus energizing, uplifting, cerebral, or hallucinogenic.

Yield from individual plants is not usually a major consideration when you are choosing a variety to grow unless you're growing outdoors. Indoors you can fill your garden with healthy plants and space limitations restrict yield more than varietal differences do. Even indoors though, you'll find that certain varieties outgrow and outproduce others. The yield under lights depends mostly on how thickly buds form along branches and how tightly the individual buds grow. This is one important reason why many growers prefer *indicas* to *sativas* (especially Southeast Asian *sativas*), because *indicas* tend to grow more compactly and their buds are thicker and heavier. Native hemp develops well-formed buds compared to the sparse flowers of most *ruderalis*, an important consideration when crossbreeding.

You might also consider when breeding for yield that *ruderalis* varieties yield so little pot that they're nearly worthless for any characteristic other than early flowering. A breeder might decide to use an American weedy hemp for its early maturation characteristic, because these plants also produce good yields with well-formed buds (see Breeding in Chapter 20).

With some experience, eventually you'll want to grow a number of distinctly different varieties. Perhaps most of the crop still will be devoted to a proven *indica*, whereas, for example, several Mexicans and several Thai plants also are grown to give you a selection of different tastes and different highs. After repeatedly smoking one variety, you may get tired of the high, and a selection of markedly different stocks makes smoking much more pleasurable.

Once successful growing becomes routine, you'll want to experiment with breeding and developing your personal hybrid stock. Breeding for exceptional potency, unusual looking plants, or different tastes and highs is what gets experienced growers enthusiastic. Besides great smoke, it's fascinating fun, and *Cannabis* is one of the most responsive plants you can breed.

Table 10.2 Cannabinoid Concentrations in Sinsemilla from California					
Variety	THC	THCV	CBD	CBC	CBN
Mexican 1.5	6.88	0.41	0.03	0.30	0.10
African 3	8.89	0.15	0.04	0.17	0.12
Colombian Chiba 60	9.72	0.05	0.03	0.08	0.12
Thai 3	7.03	0.05	0.02	0.24	0.06
Afghani 1	8.10	0.08	0.03	0.28	0.10
Nigerian 1	10.29	0.16	0.04	0.27	0.07
Cambodian 2	6.71	0.03	0.03	0.19	0.12
Congolese 2	11.11	0.17	0.04	0.23	0.07
Brazzaville Congo 2	7.84	0.11	0.02	0.14	0.10

*Figures are the percentage of cannabinoid to dry weight of sample. Analysis was by gas-liquid chromatography after the procedures developed by the U.S. government marijuana research program at the University of Mississippi at Oxford. Duplicate analysis with average given for all samples. Analysis was done in 1978 from plants harvested in the fall of 1977. In most cases, average buds from typical plants were taken. Varieties were grown in soil in a greenhouse with bright light and about four hours of daily sunlight except Afghani 1, which was grown outdoors in full sunlight. Afghani 1 is ancestral to the commercial seed stock Afghani 1. Notice the near absence of CBD, and the very small amount of CBN in all samples. Varieties were chosen for the perceived differences in the quality of the high, and a discussion of the results appears in *Marijuana Grower's Guide Complete Edition* by Red Eye Press, 1989. For a brief explanation of cannabinoids, see the section on Potency in Chapter 21.

Don't assume that because one variety in Table 10.2 is higher in THC than another that this country has the "most potent" varieties. There are stronger and weaker varieties from all of the countries represented (notice the difference between the two varieties from the Congo). Many individuals of the Afghani 1 variety were obviously more potent than the sample shown here. Subsequent selective breeding by several breeders has led to the development of a number of Afghani 1 seed stocks, including those sold from Amsterdam, and they have varying amounts of THC.

Marijuana Varieties (*Sativas*)

Colombian. Colombian is the tropical *sativa* standard for most pot and pot growers. Everyone is familiar with Colombian, and it is a consistent performer. Colombian grows a little slower, slightly shorter and more compact than standard Mexican. In a perfect environment with room to grow, a Colombian may reach 16 feet tall and yield five pounds of buds after only a six-month growing season. Usually, Colombians are conical or classically Christmas-tree shaped, with the longest branches at the bottom of the plant. Colombians have the typical form of *sativa* leaves and branching profile. Some Colombians grow their longest branches at the middle or upper reaches of the plant and the branches grow more upward than outward. The matured females exhibit a robust oval or diamond shaped profile. When Colombian is good it can be very, very good. Above all, the growth and potency of Colombian plants is consistent, making it a good candidate for both experienced and inexperienced growers.

Colombian is one of those seed sources where the homegrown can turn out to be more potent than the original pot. Commercial Colombian pot growers practice some of the worst of curing and drying procedures, which degrade THC to less active CBN (see Chapter 21 for an explanation of THC and CBN). Homegrowers might be pleasantly surprised to find that their homegrown is about 20 to 50 percent stronger than the original grass.

The lowest grade of commercial Colombian usually is about two percent THC with one percent CBN for an overall potential of three percent THC. More often, the THC + CBN potential is about six percent for Colombian. In carefully dried homegrown, there will be no CBN, and all of the plant's production of THC is retained. The best Colombian can reach 12 percent THC, which is about as potent as any marijuana gets. All in all, it's a good selection for the indoor grower without access to a proven variety.

Figure 61. *Left:* Looking up at a giant Colombian. Notice the "diamond-shaped" profile. *Right:* This grower (hidden in the bottom left) is dwarfed by her Colombian plants.

Mexican. Mexican can turn out to be the best selection that you've planted. Mexicans tend to grow fast and tall, and they thrive under less intense light than Colombian, Thai, and most African varieties; so they do well under artificial lights or in partially shaded greenhouses. If you have good Mexican, particularly a Mexican that you really want to experience again, then plant a sizable proportion of your garden with Mexican seeds.

Mexicans are most often classically *sativa,* with symmetric, conical, Christmas-tree shapes, although because of continual importation, almost any variety is possible from Mexican seeds. Mexicans grow fast: the largest sinsemilla plant I've seen was a California-grown Mexican which was 22 feet tall and yielded more than seven lbs. of sinsemilla (see page 157).

The appearance and growth habits of Mexican and some Nepalese is very similar; many Mexicans look as if they originated from Nepalese stock. Buds tend to be well-formed, but sometimes "feathery", and usually they're deliciously sweet or sometimes spicy. The high is cerebral, spacey, and energizing, but not especially long-lasting. One Mexican variety grown often in California has a distinctive metallic taste, and is called "Ironweed."

Southeast Asian. Thai, Laotian, and Cambodian varieties, although enticing, should be avoided or planted experimentally, especially indoors. Raise only a few Southeast Asians because about half the time these plants become hermaphroditic, causing serious and exasperating problems when they continuously give rise to male flowers that randomly pollinate your sinsemilla. Some varieties tend to grow erratically, by sprouting fast-growing shoots that outgrow everything else in the garden, or by growing with long internodes so that you begin to think you're growing stems rather than pot. Southeast Asian buds often "run", but some varieties do form compact, solid buds.

Thai weed may be the best pot you've experienced, so if you have seeds that you want to grow, plant only a few. Then if hermaphroditic problems ultimately develop, at least they are merely an experiment rather than an investment. The high from Southeast Asian plants is an excellent, uplifting high, and the buds have a sweet or a tangy, very spicy taste.

Jamaican. Jamaican is between Colombian and Mexican in terms of growth habit, high and tastes. Upright, classically *sativa*, most Jamaican is slightly faster-growing than Colombian and a little behind Mexican. Jamaican reaches about 14 feet tall under optimum conditions, and generally is better-branched than Mexican. Jamaican is a good candidate for indoor growers if they like the original pot. Like

Figure 62. *Left:* A typical, hermaphroditic Southeast Asian (Cambodian) bud with "running flowers". *Right:* "Running or foxtail buds" are occasionally seen on other varieties such as this Mexican.

Colombian, Jamaican can turn out stronger in potency than the original grass, because of the poor curing/drying procedures used by Jamaican growers.

Indian. Varieties from India are among the most diverse you are likely to see. India is between Pakistan and the Southeast Asian marijuana growing countries, and you can see the influence of their strains. India is an enormous country that includes Eastern and Western influences, and the country spans tropical to temperate geographical areas.

The "typical Indian" is *sativa*-like, and not as large as typical Mexican and Colombian. Most commercial Indian is considered good, standard, *sativa* pot. Rare varieties are very small (three feet tall) up to the more common varieties of about 12 feet. Varieties may have *sativa*-like leaves, monophyllus leaves (only one to three blades per leaf), or typical Afghani leaves, all of which represent the diversity among Indian varieties. Maturation ranges from as early as the earliest Afghani, to as late as Southeast Asian. Potency is likewise as variable. One of the sweetest, most delicious to smoke varieties comes from a southern Indian that reaches 14 feet tall, and has very graceful *sativa* looks with loose airy buds, and long, arching branches.

Figure 63. *Left:* A Jamaican/Afghani hybrid with a typical Jamaican profile. *Right:* A delicate, "feathery" South Indian bud.

Central African. Nigerian, Congolese, and Kenyan may be the largest plants with the largest leaves you'll ever see. These plants potentially grow to more than 20 feet tall, and one Nigerian grown in full sunlight had leaves 18 inches long. Nigerian plants are among the most potent and debilitating of all marijuana (after two tokes, experienced growers had enough and shortly went to sleep). Although Nigerian buds are not very tight, they don't run like Southeast Asians. Buds are extremely resinous, with an unusual rich, earthy, organic taste and fragrance unlike any other variety. Nigerians mature very late, and often don't ripen until late November or even late December in San Francisco.

Congolese and Kenyan are also very large but appear more like Colombian than Nigerian with similar tastes and fragrances. Congolese and Kenyan mature earlier than Nigerian and ripen in November. The strongest marijuana tested in this plot (see Table 10.2) was Congolese (over 11 percent THC) followed by Nigerian (over ten percent THC) which is about as strong as marijuana gets using this particular system of testing THC (standards set by the U.S. government program at the University of Mississippi).

Figure 64. Field of Afghani in upstate New York.

Marijuana Varieties (*Indicas*)

Afghani. Afghani and Kush plants (*indicas*) grow smaller and thicker than *sativas*. Afghani leaves often are a very dark green, almost blue-green color, with wide blades that sometimes overlap each other. Usual height is between four and eight feet. Generally buds are compact and dense, and stigmas sometimes are pink, purple, or deep red. Full maturation ranges from the end of August through October. Afghani and Kush (from the Hindu Kush mountains in central Afghanistan to the Pakistan border) often are interchangeable, and growers interchange the names enough so that either description may apply. Kush generally are slightly taller than Afghani and the leaves are between Afghani and *sativas* in both broadness of blades and in color. Potency can be mediocre to very strong, and the high of the stronger plants is often debilitating, stupefying, or "knock-out". Both Afghani and Kush have a range of tastes and fragrances, but the term "Skunkweed" came from the common, strong, skunk-like fragrance of many of these varieties. Fragrances may also be spicy or wonderfully sweet.

Pakistani. Pakistani shows the influence of both Afghani and Indian. Varieties most often are like standard Afghani or Kush. One unusual variety had the narrowest *sativa*-like, long and delicate leaf blades that I've ever seen. These plants reached only seven feet tall, but with very long, graceful and profuse branching. Large but lightweight buds formed in such profusion that a continuous line of buds obscured the branches. Branches actually hung down from the weight of the buds, so that the plants looked like dense "fountains" of buds. Flowers were pure white with unusually long stigmas. Potency was considered only good, but taste was exceptionally sweet. This variety matured by the end of September.

Chinese. I've only experienced one variety from the People's Republic of China. Leaves resembled Afghani although they were a lighter green. Plants were very fast to mature and often reached only three or four feet tall when ripened by the end of August. Branching patterns were erratic, with branches of differing lengths appearing from the top to the bottom of the plant. Potency was average but good enough so that, with its early maturing habit, this stock was an excellent candidate for hybridizing. This Chinese variety (Chinese 1) had some unusual characteristics, including enormous seeds, mixed red with white stigmas, rounded and very full buds, and the unusual occurrence of buds developing along leaf stalks.

Figure 65. This Chinese variety had the unusual tendency to grow buds from its leaf stalks (petioles).

Hemp varieties from China are purportedly medium to extremely tall, and *sativa*-like in appearance. Maturation may be very early to late, since China is a vast country that covers many degrees of latitude.

Other Marijuana Varieties

Nepalese often is similar to classical Mexican although there are short varieties, four or five feet tall, with either broad Afghani leaves or *sativa*-like leaves. Nepalese along with South African often has the cannabinoid THCV along with THC. You feel the effects of THCV almost immediately, so that with one hit you might feel high. THCV doesn't last as long as THC, but the effect is cerebral and uplifting. Nepalese may taste very sweet, and it can form good but not the tightest of buds. Most plants ripened in October.

South African (called Durban Poison by some) is the most inconsistent or, more accurately, has the most strikingly different varieties of all marijuana originating from a single country. South Africa is at the crossroads of major trading routes and shipping lanes. Within South Africa are a number of traditional pot-smoking cultures, so it's no surprise that marijuana varieties from this country are so diverse in potency, growth habit, appearance, taste, fragrance, and earliness of flowering. If you come across what is called South African or Durban

Figure 66. *Left:* Young Afghani seedlings. Afghani leaves have wide blades that may overlap. *Right:* Afghani plants of four to five feet tall dwarf a tiny South African "bush" in the foreground.

Poison in the U.S., quite probably it originated from stock developed in the 1970's by breeders in the San Francisco Bay area.

Many growers immediately associate the name Durban or South African with very early maturing, potent stock. In practice, neither of these assumptions is true. There are South Africans that are practically worthless for marijuana, and others that are some of the best the world has to offer. South African varieties may mature very quickly or they may hang on indefinitely before ripening, mimicking the latest-maturing of the equatorial varieties. Most South African that you might come across probably is descended from the "Durban Poison" developed in the 1970's in California.

The unnamed breeder had two primary concerns — high potency and early flowering — and he succeeded wonderfully with both goals. This stock is perfect for the indoor gardener no matter what the growing conditions. This Durban Poison strain has broad leaf blades almost like Afghani but long internodes like *sativas.* Stigmas may be pure white, red, pink, or a delicate purple. Branches grow with differing lengths like Thai, and the profile may be from an eight-foot ovoid down to a four-foot squat bush. This Durban is fast-growing, hardy, very early to mature, very potent, tastily sweet or spicy, and fragrant. What more could a grower ask? A last caution: of the six original

Figure 67. *Left:* This short plant (center) was believed to be from Lebanese seed. Notice that it's ripe while the *sativa* (right) has just begun to flower. *Right:* Durban Poison plants (left) have ripened before Afghani plants (right) have begun flowering.

varieties from South Africa that this breeder grew, only one variety, and only two out of 16 female plants from this variety, were worthwhile for breeding. You might also come across hybrids of Afghani 1 crossed with Durban from this stock under the numbers 214, 417, 418, and 419 on the East Coast and they're some of the best pot and best early-maturing performers grown anywhere.

Of the other five South African seed sources, one was unusual (Swaziland) in that it looked rather like a miniature Thai variety, although it was not hermaphroditic. The leaves had rounded serrations common to Thai varieties, but the leaves were much smaller overall; final stature was short, about six to seven feet tall, and the shape was uniformly like a Christmas tree. Potency was considered only "good." Of the other four varieties grown, none were unusual and none had any characteristic deemed important enough to breed. Three varieties looked and smoked like slightly smaller Mexican or Nepalese. The other variety, from Transkei, had leaf and maturation characteristics in between Mexican and the now famous Durban Poison, although its potency was mediocre. There are two

Figure 68. *Left:* Hybrids of Kush and Mexican parents formed straight stalks with unusually little branching. *Right:* Afghani/South African hybrids grown in New York averaged seven feet tall at harvest.

important lessons here: first, although seeds may come from a certain country with a particular reputation, the actual performance of each seed is unique; second, you can examine a specific seed source closely, and you might find certain individuals that are exceptional for the characteristics that you're looking for. You might find one female that matures several weeks before any other, or one plant that is much more potent than any other. This is what breeding is all about. There are individuals out there that have rare and desirable characteristics; all you need to do is to find them and propagate for those characteristics in an enlightened breeding program (see Chapter 20).

North African and Mideastern. (Morocco, Turkey, Lebanon, Iran and Iraq.) Most of these marijuana varieties have been cultivated for hashish rather than marijuana. The plants tend to be very resinous, but much of the resin consists of nonpsychoactive cannabinoids such as CBD.

Table 10.3 Cannabinoids in Marijuana from North Africa and Central Asia *			
Country of Origin	THC	CBD	CBC
Ethopia	1.29	3.05	0.15
Lebanon	1.07	1.68	0.05
Turkey	1.56	2.79	0.23
Iran	0.18	1.63	0.03
Morocco	0.08	1.61	0

*Percentage of cannabinoid to weight of dried sample (marijuana). Notice that CBD is the predominant cannabinoid. There are also much more potent varieties grown in these countries.

There are innumerable varieties from Central Asia and Northern Africa, and they range from very short (under four feet) to fairly tall (up to 14 feet). Varieties usually have *sativa*-like leaves. Some unusual varieties have broad, *indica* leaf blades and reach up to ten feet tall. If you have original potent stock, it should do well under lights. Northern African or Mideastern stock may also produce an abundance of CBD, a cannabinoid that had been suspected of altering or influencing the quality of the overall high, although this assumption has been refuted by recent research. **Apparently CBD has little if any effect on the overall high.** I've never found any Northern African or Mideastern strains that were exceptional, but other growers have told me of good Lebanese and Moroccan stock.

Other Varieties (*ruderalis* and hemp)

Ruderalis is a very small, roadside weed (probably "escaped" hemp) growing wild in the Soviet Union. They are low potency weeds, and American growers have mistaken some small *indica* varieties for *ruderalis*. The only valuable characteristic of *ruderalis* is its very early flowering. In the last few years, breeders in the U.S. and Netherlands crossed *ruderalis* with potent *sativas* and *indicas* to produce fairly potent, early-flowering hybrids. Hybrid seed stock is appearing now in the U.S., and these plants do well under lights.

Some growers think that they're growing pure *ruderalis*. They're not. Of about 300 varieties that were scientifically tested, potency usually ranged between only 0.05 percent to 0.5 percent THC, a mediocre grass at best. Growers who think that they're growing a potent strain of *ruderalis* are either growing a hybrid, or they're growing something entirely different, most likely an *indica*. *Ruderalis'* only value is for breeding early-maturing stock, because the plants flower almost immediately.

American growers who wish to develop an early-maturing yet potent stock should look to the native weedy hemp strains, such as those that grow wild in the Midwest along river banks, streams, railroad lines, cultivated fields, and roadsides. This native hemp stock matures early; plants grow much larger and more full than *ruderalis* and they form much thicker buds; potency at worst equals *ruderalis'*, but usually hemp's is much better, and the plants have had time to evolve alongside native pests and diseases. These weedy stocks have had time to incorporate some resistance to local fungi, molds, and insects, since weedy hemp patches have been growing in the Midwest for at least forty years and in the East for up to three hundred years.

Figure 69. Distribution of hemp in the U.S.A. in 1965. A dot indicates that a "wild" hemp specimen was collected at least once in the county. The range of "wild" *Cannabis* is still proliferating and expanding in the U.S.A. *Adapted by L.P.Kallan* from *Haney and Bazzaz,* in the Botany and Chemistry of Cannabis, 1970.

**Table 10.4
Percentages of THC and CBD in
Weedy Midwestern Hemp***

Origin	THC		CBD	
	Average	Range	Average	Range
Illinois	0.37	0.05 to 2.37	1.02	0.15 to 7.10
Indiana	0.20	trace to 1.50	2.50	trace to 6.80
Kansas	n/r	0.01 to 0.49	n/r	0.12 to 1.70
Minnesota**	n/r	0.20	n/r	1.65
Iowa**	n/r	0.10	n/r	1.70

*Percentage of THC and CBD to the dry weight of marijuana; n/r is
not reported.
**One sample only.

If you want to develop an early-flowering stock and don't have access to a potent, naturally early marijuana stock, use a native hemp strain to cross with a potent marijuana stock, especially if you plan to grow outdoors.

Hemp patches in North Dakota complete maturation by the middle of August, and weedy hemp in Illinois ripens by early September. In Massachusetts, a weedy hemp patch growing in a vacant field dropped its seeds by Labor Day. In Indiana, Michigan, Kansas, New York, Pennsylvania and other central and eastern states, most of the local hemp matures from mid-August through September. Why not breed these local strains, which grow well, flower early, and are tough and resistant to local disease problems? True *ruderalis* flowers after only three or four sets of leaves and a few weeks of growth. Most *ruderalis* yields about one-quarter to an ounce of scraggly, puny buds which have very little THC. Who needs it? Find a domestic hemp that produces several ounces to a pound of full-budded pot, and you have a much better early-maturing parental stock for a breeding program. The potency of native hemp weeds ranges up to 2.5 percent THC, which is significantly more potent than *ruderalis*. *Ruderalis* has its place in marijuana breeding programs because it's so quick to flower. But the problem with *ruderalis* is that it takes a number of generations to incorporate its early flowering characteristic into a consistent performer that also has a high yield, good buds, and high potency. American hemp is a quicker alternative for developing a fully worthwhile stock since it already has good buds, a decent yield, and a higher base potency (see Chapter 20, Breeding).

Approximate Maturation Times Under Natural Light

Group #1 includes varieties from Colombia, Indonesia, Sumatra, Panama, Kenya, and Nigeria, which originate from latitudes within 0 to 15 degrees of the equator. They mature in November through December under natural light at a mid-latitude of the U.S.

Group #2 includes varieties from Thailand, Cambodia, Jamaica, Southern Mexico, and Central America, which are from latitudes of 6 to 20 degrees. They mature from late October through December.

Group #3 includes Afghanistan, Pakistan, Nepal, Iran, Iraq, northern India, northern Mexico, Morocco, South Africa, and China, which are within about 25 to 38 degrees latitude. These varieties are highly variable, and mature from early August through October.

Group #4 are native hemp weeds (U.S.), which grow primarily in the midwest from 40 to 46 degrees latitude (see map of native hemp distribution, Figure 69). Hemp and *ruderalis* strains from the U.S.S.R. originate from latitudes of 40 to 55 degrees. Maturation is from late July through September.

To give you a relative idea of approximate latitudes: Miami is 25 degrees, Houston and New Orleans are 30, Charleston and Phoenix are 33, Los Angeles is 34, Albuquerque and Little Rock are 35, San Francisco/Oakland is about 38, Kansas City and St. Louis are 39, Denver and Washington D.C. are 40, New York and Salt Lake City are 41, Boston, Chicago, Detroit, and Cleveland are 42, Bangor is 45 and Seattle is 48 degrees.

The times for maturation given for these four groups are for plants grown under natural light at a mid-latitude for the U.S. (actually San Francisco/Oakland area). Your local latitude gives you some idea of when a particular variety will mature under natural light. Tropical varieties may mature late, if at all, in more northern latitudes; early-maturing varieties may mature earlier in more southern latitudes.

Chapter 11

Starting the Seeds

Germination

The potency of marijuana is almost entirely hereditary so always choose seeds from grass that is to your liking. For uniformity of growth, take all the seeds from the same batch of grass. A garden where all the plants grow uniformly and have similar needs is the easiest to care for under lights. On the other hand, for a variety of tastes and potencies, and when you plan to crossbreed, take seeds from different varieties or sources of grass.

Large, plump seeds with good color — brown, grey, or mottled — have the best chance of germinating. Seeds over two years old, or that are immature (green or white), may not be viable. Fresh, mature seeds are quite fertile; usually more than 90 percent will germinate. Seeds from "wild" *Cannabis* such as hemp or *ruderalis*, germinate better if they're first frozen for a couple of weeks. Germination then tends to be more even rather than sporadic. Make sure the seeds are dry, and the container is airtight before freezing.

Seeds gradually lose viability with time, but if kept cool and dry in an airtight container a majority of the seeds should sprout after a year or two in storage. Kept sealed and frozen, more than half of the seeds should still be fertile even after three or more years.

You can estimate the viability of a batch of seeds by soaking several seeds in a glass of water or between wet paper towels. Add two teaspoons of liquid bleach to each cup of water. The bleach solution prevents fungus from attacking any seeds which are slow to germinate. Most of the seeds that will sprout will do so within two or three days of each other. By comparing the number of sprouts to the number of seeds that were soaked, you have a good idea of what to expect when the seeds are planted.

Figure 70. Seeds in a circle are ready to plant. Center seed is too well-developed to survive transplanting.

By determining the viability of the seeds, you'll have a better idea of how many seeds to sow. You want enough sprouts to fill your garden; one for each pot is usual. Also the plants all start within a few days of each other, so they'll be more or less uniformly tall. All the plant tops are then an equal distance from the light.

For fresh seeds, you may need to sow only one seed per pot, plus an extra few for insurance. If only half of the test seeds sprouted after soaking for a week, then plant three or more seeds per pot. You can easily transplant sprouts from a pot with two or three seedlings into any empty pot.

Some growers use the soaking method to sow only the seeds that they know will sprout. Check the seeds daily and plant at the **first sign** of opening. The farther extended the root is before sowing, the less chance the sprout has to survive. Soak the seeds between paper towels wetted with the bleach solution. Most seeds begin to sprout on the third to fifth day. Plant any seed as soon as you see the radical (prospective root) splitting the shell of the seed. If you wait too long, the prospective seedling cannot position itself in the soil. The seedling may never get a foothold and will die, or at best, take some time to recover (see Figure 70).

Figure 71. Some examples of colors, patterns and sizes of marijuana seeds. The smallest seeds are a wild (weedy) strain.

The easiest and surest way to start the seeds is to sow them directly in the soil or in a planting pellet. First moisten the soil and allow the pots to sit for a while so the soil becomes evenly moist. When sowing several seeds per pot, space them apart, so that any transplanting will be easy. Gently press the seeds down to a depth of **1/4 to 1/2 inch,** cover with soil, and moisten the soil surface once more. If you know that the seeds are fresh or if you have purchased commercial seeds, sow only one or two seeds per pot since almost every seed should germinate.

The key to successful germination is to keep the surface of the soil (where the seeds are) constantly moist. The soil surface should be sprayed with a moderate amount of water daily, or stretch a piece of plastic kitchen wrap over the tops of the pots. This acts like a greenhouse or germination box, by containing the moisture and maintaining a high humidity and moist soil without daily watering. Remove the plastic wrap **immediately** when you see the first sprout breaking the soil surface, otherwise the seedlings will overheat or suffocate beneath the wrap.

Some growers prefer to turn the lights on when they sow. The heat generated by the lights warms the soil and hastens germination, but lights also dry the soil, so the surface must be moistened daily. Turn the lights on only if the air or floor temperatures are less than 50 degrees. Seeds can actually germinate at temperatures near

Figure 72. During germination, soil can be kept moist by using plastic covers to create a greenhouse effect.

freezing, although more slowly. It's better to turn the lights on during the third day — that's when fresh seeds usually begin to germinate.

Seeds germinate faster if they're warmed to at least 70 degrees, either by the ambient (surrounding) temperature or by bottom heating. Heating cables are available for germinating seeds: the Park Seed Catalogue, Highway 254 North, Greenwood, S.C. 29647 offers inexpensive cables in several lengths. The shortest is three feet long, and they are also available in longer runs from Park Seed. Heating cables are recommended only if you're planting in a naturally cool space, such as a basement floor or a greenhouse during the winter. Even at temperatures near freezing, fresh seeds germinate by seven or eight days. At 70 degrees, the same seeds would germinate in three to four days.

Most seeds begin to sprout in two to seven days at room temperatures. Older seeds may take up to three weeks to germinate, but this is unlikely. **Once the seeds sprout, discontinue the daily spraying and allow the surface of the soil to dry** to a depth of one or two inches before watering again. When the first seedlings appear, read the section on watering carefully and water according to the instructions for seedlings.

Many growers start their plants in small containers and transplant to large containers later. Starting the plants in small pots conserves space, and many more plants may be started under a small light system to save electrical costs. When you later remove the males, you'll have enough females left to fill the garden space for a sinsemilla crop.

Often growers are advised to start seedlings in peat pots, germination flats, or trays that are only one or two inches deep. This is bad technique. Start your plants directly in large containers or in starting pots that are at least eight-ounce cups or four-inch pots. During germination, marijuana sprouts initially send down a tap root approximately four inches long. Any pot more shallow, such as germination flats, causes the tap root to curl around and not reach the depth the seedling would naturally like. This restriction delays growth and actually contributes to the development of a majority of male plants. According to recent scientific findings in the U.S.S.R. a root system restricted early in growth discourages female development and encourages more males to form in *Cannabis*. This may be why some growers consistently have 60 to 70 percent of their plants turn out to be males whereas other growers always get 60 to 70 percent female plants.

Figure 73. *Left:* The sprout forms an arch to push up through the soil. *Right:* Once free of the soil, the sprout straightens its stem. Remove the seed's "shells" if they don't fall free, otherwise the sprout may die.

Peat pots made of compressed plant fiber (hardened) invite the roots to grow into the sides of the container. This makes transplanting difficult and injures the roots. **Don't confuse peat pots with peat pellets,** which expand on contact with water. Peat pellets are excellent for starting seedlings when the peat pellet is positioned in the soil of a normal size container. Jiffy-7 pellets are a must for starting seeds in hydroponic mediums such as pea gravel or aggregates. The pellet expands on contact with water, and marijuana's roots easily penetrate the sides of the pellet. Plant your seed 1/4 to 1/2 inch deep in the pellet, and position the pellet directly in the gravel, lava rock or sand. For hydroponic, fast-draining mediums, nothing works better than these expandable peat pellets.

Another method that works equally well for hydroponic gardeners is to make a planting pocket of vermiculite or Jiffy-mix. For instance, in gravel, fill a pocket about three inches deep in the center of the pot with pure vermiculite or Jiffy-mix. Position the seed, and water as usual. The pocket retains moisture better than the gravel, sand, lava rock, etc., and holds the seed in the original planting position.

Eight-ounce cups are the minimum size that work well for starting and transplanting. One-quart milk cartons cut to six or seven inches tall are also good makeshift containers for starting seedlings. Half-gallon milk containers will support a seedling almost twice as long (see the section on Transplanting in Chapter 15). Plastic starting bags (four or more inches) are inexpensive, work well, and are available at most garden shops or nurseries. You could use styrofoam or wax paper cups, as long as they are at least five inches tall; six or more inches is better. Punch drainage holes in the bottom of any starting container to ensure that water doesn't accumulate at the bottom, which sours the soil and contributes to suffocation of the roots.

If you have no experience with growing any plant, start the seeds in one of these small containers. Small containers minimize the possibility of overwatering; any errors are restricted to that single container. If you've grown plants before, whether houseplants or marijuana, sow the seeds directly in large containers or in Jiffy-7 pellets or vermiculite pockets. The unrestricted room for the roots to grow encourages more plants to develop as females, and eliminates the chore of transplanting.

If you have several light systems or are planning to rotate the plants to successively larger light gardens, small starting containers are your best option. You can start about 70 four-inch pots under a fluorescent fixture with four four-foot tubes, and raise them for

Figure 74. Space apart four or five seeds per four inch pot. Spacing the seeds makes transplanting easier. Transplant within the first two weeks.

about four weeks; or, you can raise 24 plants in six-inch pots for about six weeks before transplanting and moving them to a larger system. This saves you space and electrical costs, and benefits the overall growth of your garden. (See the section on transplanting in Chapter 15 to get a better idea of what starting in small containers requires of you.)

Setting the Light Cycle and Light Distance from the Plants

Seeds don't need light to germinate. They need only water and temperatures above freezing to sprout. However sprouts do need light to grow well once they break the soil surface, and seeds germinate quicker at higher temperatures.

Once the first sprout appears, turn the lights on and position the light system two to four inches above the plant tops for standard fluorescents, two to six inches for HO and VHO fluorescents, 12 to 18 for 400-watt HID's, and two to three feet above the plant tops for sprouts under 1,000-watt HID lamps. Disregard the manufacturer's recommendations for distances, since marijuana needs much more light than the plants that usually are grown under these lamps. However, follow the distributor's instructions if they gear their sales to marijuana growers. They get feedback from their customers, and should know what the most effective distance is for the particular system you've purchased. The short distance and long light cycle encourages the development of robust, bushy plants, rather than elongated, skinny plants stretching for the light.

After the sensitive seedling stage is past (about two weeks after sprouting), position standard fluorescents one to two inches and VHO fluorescents no more than four inches from the plant tops. For MH or HPS lamps, position the lamp 18 to 24 inches from the tops of the plants for 400-watt bulbs; three feet above for 1,000-watt bulbs. Maintain these distances for the duration of the garden.

If you have your HID's moving on light balancers, position 1,000-watt HID's from 12 to 24 inches above the tops of the plants for the duration of the garden. For 400-watt HID's, position them eight to 18 inches above the plant tops.

Growers using MH or HPS lamps often use fluorescents to start the seedlings. Standard fluorescents use much less electricity and generate a lot less heat, which makes germination cheaper, easier, and safer for the tender seedlings. The abundance of red and far-red light emitted by HPS lamps causes seedlings to elongate by stretching toward the light. Fluorescents have a spectrum much more like that of natural light. Seedlings and clones root and establish themselves better under fluorescents.

Fifty to 70 seedlings in four-inch pots fit easily under a four-tube four-foot fluorescent (160 watts). When you compare the electrical cost of running a 160-watt system that's lit for 18 to 24 hours a day for several weeks with the cost of one or more 1,000-watt HID's over the same time period, you'll begin to appreciate why fluorescents are so popular for starting seedlings and rooting clones. Growers using HPS lamps should start their seedlings under fluorescents for best results.

Marijuana may grow more than two inches a day and growers must adjust the light system several times a week to maintain the proper distance from the plant tops. Under full sunlight and optimum growing conditions, *Cannabis* may grow six inches a day during the middle of growth (vegetative growth). (See the section on Training in Chapter 15 for important information on caring for plants under fluorescent lights.)

You want to keep the plants as close as possible to the light source at all times. This encourages stocky growth, and is especially important during flowering when you want to produce thick, compact buds. But you don't want to burn the plants. For any lamp, place your hand near the tops of the plants. If after about 20 seconds the heat makes your hand uncomfortably warm, the lights

Figure 75. Seedlings develop stocky and full when you keep the lights close to the plant tops.

are too close to the plant tops. Remember that the plants are under these lamps for at least 12 hours a day; so if the light feels too warm to you, raise the lights another few inches.

With HID's, what is important is that the entire garden be illuminated, not whether the light is at one or two or three feet from the plant tops. When the plants are younger, crowd them in a smaller circle and place the HID as close as seems safe while it still illuminates all the plants. After the plants have grown and filled the recommended eight-foot-diameter circle beneath a 1,000-watt HID, take a taut string or wooden slat, and lay it along the angle of your reflector toward the perimeter of the garden. Check that the HID is high enough so that the garden is within the cone of light formed by your reflector. Place the lamp as low as is safe, but so that the circle formed by the reflected light meets the plant tops at the perimeter of the garden.

It's very important for normal development that your plants receive a regular and regulated day/night cycle. **Purchase an automatic timer** (about $10.00 for a small, 10- to 15-ampere timer, and $40.00 for a large, 40-amp timer), so that your plants won't suffer from your irregular hours or weekend vacations. A timer relieves you of a major worry, and goes a long way in providing your plants with a natural upbringing. For any marijuana grower, a timer which regulates a consistent day/night cycle is one of the wisest investments he or she can make.

For natural-light gardens which use electric lights to strengthen or extend the natural light, a timer is more than useful — it's essential. Set the timer so that the plants get an additional few hours of light in either the morning or evening, whenever the natural light is weakest or when the light attracts the least attention. Set the lights to "on" long enough to extend the natural daylength to at least 16 hours of light. You want the lighted hours to be 16 to 18 hours long, including the supplemental hours provided by the artificial lights.

Set the timer so that the plants are not disturbed by light during their usual dark period. Two weeks prior to flowering, and during the flowering period, plants exposed to even a moment of light that interrupts their dark period may not flower, or flowering will be delayed. Set the dark period to coincide with natural darkness or your sleeping time, to ensure that the plants are in darkness and not disturbed by your nighttime activities.

For electric-light gardens, keep the light cycle at a constant 18 to 24 hours of light, and keep the timer on this setting for the duration of the seedling and vegetative growth stages, or until you wish to force the plants to flower. Reduce the light cycle to a duration of from 11 to 14 hours of daily light to force the plants to flower (see Chapters 4 and 18).

Initially, gardens may be illuminated under 24-hour photoperiods for constant light during growth and before flowering, if the cost of electricity doesn't concern you. Plants develop 15 to 25 percent faster under 24 versus 18 hours of light. Some growers prefer the 18-hour regimen to constant light, not that anything is wrong with constant light, but plants naturally have a daily "rest" period, and certain aspects of a plant's metabolism change during these nighttime rests.

HID's require a few minutes of warm-up before the bulb lights. Also, if there is a power outage or you turn the lamps off, usually it takes about 15 minutes for the bulbs to cool before they'll relight properly. This is all perfectly normal.

For flowering, set the light cycle so that the lights only supplement the natural light. At this time you don't want to **extend the length** of daylight; you want to **strengthen** the light during the time of weakest natural daylight. (See Chapters 4 and 5 if you don't understand why). Again, during flowering, the nighttime or dark period must not be interrupted by any artificial or natural light.

Part V
Care and Problem Solving

Chapter 12

Watering

Water is the basis of life. Without water, life cannot exist. More than 80 percent of a plant's weight is made up of water. Water is also one of the fundamental components, along with light, air, and soil minerals, that fuels the growth of all green plants through photosynthesis. Water keeps the plant erect and its cells turgid (rigid), and water conducts the nutrients necessary for health and growth to the plant's cells.

Water, and how you water — how much and how often — can make or break your crop. Too much water suffocates the plant's roots; the plants may develop rot or fungus, or nutrient problems. With insufficient water the root system may never develop fully. Even with a good root system, consistent underwatering slows growth and possibly the maturation of your crop.

Marijuana is an extremely fast grower. This fast growth is not so apparent at first because the plant is small. We tend not to notice that this tiny sprout has probably doubled in size in just a week. Once the plant is a month or more old, daily growth is much more obvious when you find yourself adjusting the height of the light system more and more often.

Such fast growth requires a good deal of water, and since the space around the plant is limited by the pot's size, you'll need to water often. This doesn't mean watering daily, especially when the plants are young, and it doesn't mean keeping the soil saturated. In general, allow the soil to go through a wet and dry cycle. Alternately water with a good amount of water, and then don't water again until the soil a couple of inches deep feels dry to your finger.

Any grower who has gone to considerable expense buying HID's, hydroponic units, automatic watering systems, etc., should have his or her water supply analyzed by a commercial laboratory, or by the water-supply company, which may provide a free analysis.

drops of rain
on a dying plant
awake it
from its dream
of death
more drops
revive its growth
and change its dream
of dying
to a crave for life

Figure 76. From *Poems and Pictures II* by Charles Chase

The cost is minimal considering the problems you can prevent or anticipate and remedy. An excess of iron (Fe) in your water tells you not to use a drip-watering system. Iron precipitates and collects, and constantly clogs drip watering systems.

Rainwater is excellent for growing plants, because it contains carbonic acid, which helps remove salts and alkaloids from the soil, and because it has a trace of dissolved nitrogen, which is an important growth nutrient. Rainwater is also well-aerated, and usually slightly acid to near neutral in pH, which is perfect for growing marijuana.

Treat water high in sodium by adding about one teaspoon of gypsum to each gallon of water. Untreated, a build-up of sodium in the soil eventually may poison the plants. Occasionally water may be too acidic because of an excess of natural sulfur. Counteract the acidity by mixing about one teaspoon of hydrated lime per gallon of water and watering with this treated solution once a month. Even better is to check the pH of the water and add only enough lime to bring the pH into the acceptable range.

Never use water that's been processed through a water softening system. Water softeners use sodium (Na++) to displace the water's minerals (K+, Ca++, and Mg++). Use the water from the source before it reaches the water softener. Even if this untreated water is especially high in minerals, it's better for your plants than treated, sodium rich water.

Some growers worry about chlorine (Cl2) in their water and its effect on growing plants. Chlorinated water should have no adverse consequences, but if this is of a concern to you, simply store your water in a pail or open container overnight. Chlorine is introduced as a gas for bactericidal purposes which dissipates when the water is exposed to air. Stirring or shaking the water vigorously helps to eliminate chlorine and infuses beneficial oxygen into the water.

Water around the stem and not on it. Use tepid water; it soaks into the soil more easily and won't shock the roots. Very dry soil may not absorb the water; it will run off the soil surface and down the sides of the pot. To remedy this, add a couple of drops of liquid detergent to a gallon of water. Detergent is a wetting agent and the soil will absorb the water more readily. Water each pot with about a cup of the solution. Let the pots stand for 15 minutes, then finish watering as usual with pure water. You can also water with a large funnel. Insert the funnel's neck deep into the soil and fill it with water. The slower seepage from the funnel allows the soil to gradually absorb the water. A combination of a funnel and detergent works on the driest of soils.

Watering by Growth Stages

Seedlings. The seedling stage is where most growers who have problems with watering run into trouble (see Chapter 11 for information on watering during germination). The tendency is to saturate the pot with water and to water too often. Overwatering is not a common problem if the plants are started in small pots that dry out quickly. But when plants are started in large containers, saturating the soil gradually turns the soil in the bottom of the pot to muck. This displaces the soil's oxygen, and soon the plant develops what looks like numerous nutrient-deficiency symptoms — yellow, grey, or copper/brown areas on dying leaves. The grower then adds more fertilizer (and consequently more water), the condition worsens, and nothing short of transplanting to new soil will correct the problem.

Keep in mind that the seedling and its root system are small. The root system on seedlings is mostly within the top four to six inches of soil. After you first water, probe your finger deep into the pot before you water again. In large pots, if the deeper levels of soil are still moist, then water moderately with only a cup or two of water.

Sprouts and seedlings are most susceptible to problems caused by water with an extreme pH, or which has high levels of dissolved

Figure 77. *Left:* The lower leaves begin to die when the plant is kept overwatered. Notice how the leaves hang down rather than being outstretched. (See page 231). *Right:* A wilted plant will die soon unless watered.

salts and minerals. **Other than drowning sprouts, this is the most common cause of problems for novice gardeners who don't know why they have so much trouble starting plants.** The same water may cause no problems, or only minor, correctable problems, once the plants are larger. If you have trouble (discolored leaves or signs of nutrient deficiencies on very young plants), try starting them again, using purified or distilled water purchased from a supermarket. The cost is only 40 to 70 cents a gallon, and it takes only a few gallons of water to raise a crop through the first few critical weeks.

Middle Growth. The plant's water needs keep increasing with growth, and this need will become apparent to you. Once the plant has reached middle growth (six weeks and more), water enough so that the pots are saturated, but allow the top few inches of soil to dry before watering again. (Saturated means enough water to wet the lower reaches of the soil without having water running out of the pot's bottom. Test one pot to see how much water it holds, then water your plants with about 1/4 less water per pot.) This wet/dry procedure will work well for the remainder of the growing period.

Underwatering is easily recognized. Plant cells are kept rigid by the water pressure within them and if the soil completely dries out, the cells lose turgor (water pressure) and their rigidity. First the bottom leaves droop, and the condition works upward until the top of the plant flops over. Water immediately, and follow the movement of water up the plant as the leaves recover. You'll actually see the leaves move and the top straighten in a matter of minutes. Marijuana is tough and fairly drought-resistant. Completely wilted plants survive for several days, but they may drop some lower leaves.

Once you see a plant wilt, you know that the soil is completely dry, and the root system probably has reached the bottom of the pot. If you are unsure of watering, wait until one plant wilts. This, in effect, gives you an idea of how often to water. For example, if the plant wilts after a week, you know that you should water by the fifth day. The plants will need more frequent watering as they grow larger. Overwatering is much less likely once the root system has extended throughout the pot.

Flowering. During flowering it's even more important to let the soil surface dry before you thoroughly water again. Flowering is the time when plants are most susceptible to rot. You don't want to keep the soil surface moist, because this raises the garden's humidity and encourages rot and molds to grow. Do water the plants well, though. You want to maximize the growth of the flowers so that you'll harvest full-sized, robust buds.

Water and Moisture Testers

If you feel totally ignorant or helpless when it comes to watering or growing plants, then buy a sampler which indicates soil moisture. The simplest soil-moisture tester is basically a tube with a "window" in it that allows you to take a sample soil core and then see or feel for soil moisture. (Your finger works about as well.) More expensive moisture probes have meters indicating soil moisture. Buy them only if you really are all thumbs with none of them green when it comes to growing plants. One inexpensive sampler available by mail-order for $3.00 is from Bob Galbreath, Drip Irrigation Specialists, 6118 West 77th St., Los Angeles, CA 90045. More professional and elaborate soil-moisture samplers are available from Ben Meadows Co., 2601-B West 5th Ave., Eugene, OR 97402, through *High Times* ads, and in most garden-supply and nursery shops.

Another way to gauge the amount of water a pot will hold is to use a funnel. Stick the neck of the funnel into the soil, and then fill the funnel with water. Repeat until water no longer drains into the soil, or the water begins to seep from the bottom of the pot. Stick your finger in the funnel's neck so that water won't spill when you remove the funnel. By measuring the amount of water you have used to fill the funnel, you'll have an idea of how much water the pots hold when saturated. Once the plants have reached the vegetative stage, nearly saturate the pots each time you water, and then allow enough time between waterings so that the first few inches of soil have time to dry. This wet/dry procedure works well for any medium throughout growth.

Chapter 13

The Air

The air affects the growth of plants in many ways: the temperature could be considered a "fifth limiting factor"; oxygen or CO_2 concentration can limit growth, and humidity or dryness of the air affects both growth and the proliferation of insects and diseases. In practice, the air in most homes isn't a source of trouble. Look at the "air" parameters described here, and you'll find that, most likely, the air and temperature typical of most homes need no special modifications for growing healthy, potent plants.

Ventilation. Marijuana is less susceptible than most plants to problems from a stuffy or stagnant atmosphere. A garden in the corner of a room open to the house will be adequately ventilated. When the weather is mild, an open but screened window provides satisfactory ventilation. Gardens confined in small spaces such as closets must be opened daily, preferably for the duration of the light period. Plants may do well in a closed closet for the first month, but they'll need an open door when the plants get larger. The more the garden fills the room and the larger the plants get, the greater their need for freely circulating air. Don't think that one day you'll open the door to your closet garden and find your crop dead — it's just that it won't grow quite as fast, and stagnant air subjects the plants to conditions that encourage rot and the proliferation of insects.

A small fan that moves air throughout the garden is always helpful, especially if the room is closed. You never want to enclose the garden so tightly that air stagnates. Always leave spaces in the reflectors so that air circulates. The higher the temperature and humidity, the more the plants' need for good ventilation.

The best way to ventilate a garden is with exhaust fans. One fan pulling air out of a garden through a window or hole made for the purpose adequately ventilates all but the largest of gardens. The fan doesn't need to be large, just strong enough to create a good draft.

Install vents and exhaust fans at a high point in the garden walls. If you position the exhaust fan high, it pulls hot, stagnant air out of the garden, which effectively circulates the air. This high placement also lessens the amount of CO_2 withdrawn from the garden since CO_2 sinks rather than rises and therefore is more effectively utilized by the plants.

Fresh air enters rooms beneath all but the tightest fitting of doors so a closed room can still be well-ventilated by an exhaust fan pulling air through the room. By constructing a loose-fitting "light trap" around the fan, you prevent light, and the garden, from being seen from outside through the fan. The light trap need be no more complicated than a cardboard box covering the fan and held in place by having the flaps stapled to the wall. Cut open one side of the box for air passage. (See Figure 31.)

Don't use fans that pull air into the garden from outdoors unless the garden is excessively hot and needs both intake and exhaust fans for cooling. This situation is most common to large greenhouses. Don't use an exhaust fan to direct air to an area with pedestrian traffic, because the distinctive marijuana fragrance is bound to attract attention. Instead, open a window to the outdoors an inch or two, and cover the crack with tightly stretched fine-mesh cloth to keep insects out. Tack a loose-fitting cardboard flap over the crack to prevent the light from being seen from outside. Position an exhaust fan at an interior door or opening to draw fresh air from the outdoors through the window to the interior. Negative-ion generators, which are described next in this chapter, also help remove telltale fragrances.

Ventilation is important not only for the overall growth and health of the garden, but also as an important preventive measure against the two most devastating pest problems you may encounter. Both fungal rots and spider mites flourish in stagnant air. Simply by keeping the air moving, you'll go a long way toward preventing these problems from becoming established.

If there is no practical way to install an exhaust vent, then set up a small table fan. Use an oscillating fan that moves back and forth, and position the fan to cover the entire garden. Mites prefer stagnant, dry air; molds and fungi prefer stagnant, humid air. Both of these problems may never get a foothold in your garden if you simply keep the air moving.

Good air movement is essential for optimal growth. When the air moves freely, it increases the flow of CO_2 and oxygen to the plants. If your garden is secreted in a closet or other small, confined space, and you find that the air is not moving freely, remove some of the large fan leaves from the stems of each plant, and open the door whenever it's safe. By removing some leaves you create more space for gentle air currents to circulate.

Negative-Ion Generators

If you have no safe way to vent your garden of marijuana fragrances, negative-ion generators may be the solution. Negative-ionizers mimic the effects of sitting by a waterfall or breaking waves, which make anyone feel better, more relaxed, and generally "feeling good." Many pollutants and aromas floating in the air are, or are carried by, positively-charged ions. Negative ions effectively diminish marijuana's bouquet by attracting and precipitating pollutants and positive ions that carry its distinctive fragrance. Negative-ion generators sell for roughly $10 up to $180, and they draw only from two to 20 watts. If you think you might have a problem with the telltale fragrance of marijuana, or if you are concerned with environmental pollutants, set up a negative-ion generator, or several if needed. Place the units on sheets of newspaper or foil away from the plants, since a layer of grime will collect on surfaces near the generator. The more expensive ion generators include a "collector"

Figure 78. *Left:* Typical negative ion generators draw under ten watts of power. *Right:* This hanging version reduces grime that collects on nearby surfaces. It also eliminates the possibility of electric shocks or damage that may occur on contact with water.

on which the pollutants settle. Some generators automatically alternate between emitting negative ions and then collecting the pollutants, and some are equipped with reusable filters.

An ionizer may activate a fluorescent tube to flash even when the lights are unplugged. When you turn down the light cycle for flowering, go into the darkened room and make sure the lights don't flash, because the light flashes will prevent flowering. Move the ionizer farther away from the lights, or turn it off at night if the space is limited. (Do not use ion generators near computers or magnetic media, since they will scramble data.)

Temperature

Temperature control should be no problem. Marijuana grows well at room temperatures: 70 to 80 degrees during light hours, and 55 to 70 degrees during darkness is ideal. The plants do well with temperatures typical of most homes, and indoor gardeners rarely need to do anything to change the ambient temperature in their garden. Marijuana survives temperatures from just below freezing to well over 100 degrees, but neither extreme is desirable. If you're comfortable in the garden, your plants will be too.

Plant growth is closely related to temperature. For marijuana, photosynthesis and metabolism increase with higher temperatures, up to about 95 degrees, depending on the particular variety. Generally, the heat from the lights raises the temperature in loosely enclosed light gardens about five to 15 degrees higher than the surroundings. This is a fortunate coincidence, since this raises the temperature typical of most homes (about 68 degrees) into the optimal range for gardening. Daytime temperatures below about 60 degrees slow growth and ripening. For maximizing potency, keep the daytime temperature between 70 and 80 degrees during flowering.

The best way to heat a garden is to add more lights. Watt for watt, lights and their ballasts radiate nearly the heat that electric heaters do. Obviously, your plants will benefit from the additional light besides the heat they generate at this crucial time. Add an HPS (sodium lamp) in large operations or hang 100-watt incandescents or Warm White fluorescents in a fluorescent garden. The strong red light that these bulbs emit enhances flowering considerably.

Propane catalytic heaters do a good job of heating. They're safe and clean, and they increase the CO_2 in the air. Electric and natural-gas heaters also work well. Don't use kerosene or gasoline heaters. The fuel doesn't burn cleanly, and the exhausts are harmful to you and the plants. All things considered, adding lights of any kind is

Figure 79. In a cold room, place pots on a fluorescent fixture to warm germinating seeds. Plastic wrap keeps the soil moist.

your best option for increasing the temperature. Simply circulating the air with a small fan moves the heat from the lights and their ballasts throughout the garden.

If your grow room is either too cold in the winter or too hot in the summer, turn the light cycle to "on" during the night and to "off" during the day. During cold winter nights, the lights warm the room, and daytime temperatures in most homes should be warm enough for the plants during their dark period. In the summer, daytime temperatures may become too hot. Turn the light cycle to "on" during the cooler nighttime, which might maintain temperatures perfectly for growth. Since the lights are off during the heat of the day, the whole cycle is moderated by this off-hours regimen.

Temperature and Potency

Despite what some marijuana myths purport about high temperatures increasing potency, every scientific study that has looked at the relationship between temperature and potency has found that temperatures in the 70's are the best daytime temperatures for optimal potency. Night temperatures could drop from the 70's into the 50's without seriously diminishing potency. Daytime temperatures as low as 81 degrees (90 degrees was much worse) seriously lowered the potency in comparative tests. A hot chamber (90 degrees in the daytime) also dramatically increased the amount of THC lost as CBN (see Table 13.1). Keep temperatures in your garden in the moderate range (where you're comfortable), and this will be in the range (70's) which best maximizes the potency in relation to the temperature.

Table 13.1
Percentage of THC Oxidized to CBN under "Hot" and "Warm" Temperature Regimes*

Temperature Regime			Origin of Variety			
	Day	Night	Panama	Jamaica	Nepal	Illinois
Hot	90°F	73°F	14.3	21.4	27.7	9.8
Warm	73°F	61°F	6.5	2.2	10.8	0

*The higher the percentage, the more THC is lost by oxidation to CBN.

Humidity

Marijuana flourishes through a wide range of relative humidities. It grows well enough whether the atmosphere has the dryness of a desert, or the wetness of a jungle swamp. Ordinarily, the humidity seldom has a substantial effect on the growth or health of the plants. However, extremely dry air such as the direct airflow from a heater or air-conditioner is too dry for for good growth, particularly for germinating sprouts and seedlings. Germinating sprouts may shrivel and die if placed too close to a heat source. Move the sprouts away from the dry air source, or loosely enclose the sprouts in a germination box until they're well established.

A very humid garden is much more susceptible to fungal diseases and rot. The most practical solution is to provide adequate ventilation. If price is no object, **dehumidifiers**, although expensive ($90 to $400), work well, but they also draw a lot of current (five to 15-amperes). **Humidifiers** draw from one to five-amperes, cost as little as $20 to $100, but they're entirely unnecessary in almost all gardening situations.

Marijuana responds best when the relative humidity is between 40 and 80 percent. You'll find that generally, growth is more luxuriant under higher humidity; leaf blades form larger and broader, and plants grow a little taller. In a dry atmosphere, development is more compact overall, and the leaves are smaller with thinner leaf blades.

The few scientific studies that have looked at humidity in relationship to potency reported that plants were slightly more potent in a drier atmosphere (50 to 70 percent relative humidity) than under humid conditions (over 80 percent relative humidity). The atmosphere in most homes is already quite dry, especially when it's heated or air-conditioned.

Spraying Leaves. Spraying the leaves with water cleans the leaves, helps to control and prevent insect attacks (particularly spider mites), and helps increase growth when the atmosphere is very dry such as when the home is heated in winter. Spray the leaves, especially the leaf undersides, several times a week if you've had mites in past gardens, the room is very dusty, or is especially dry. Don't spray a garden that is naturally humid, since this encourages stem rot, molds, and fungi to grow. Most gardeners should spray their garden to wash the leaves no more than about once a month. Stop spraying the plants altogether once the first flowers appear. It is a good idea to spray plants with plain water if you've been foliar feeding. The spray dissolves unabsorbed nutrients, and

Figure 80. Empty household spray bottles can be used if they're cleaned of residue. The short sprayer connects to a garden hose and relieves you of pumping a handle. The solution (fertilizer or insecticide) is automatically diluted while spraying.

washes possibly unhealthy compounds (e.g. nitrate fertilizers) from the marijuana before it's harvested. **Whenever you spray the garden, whether it's with pesticides, fresh water, or nutrient foliar sprays, be extremely careful that you don't get mist on your lights.** Any bulb that burns hot may implode or crack on contact with water. Turn the lights off, raise them as high as possible, and wait until they cool before you start spraying. A cavalier attitude when spraying any water solution near hot lights is dangerous, so take these precautions seriously.

Carbon Dioxide (CO_2)

CO_2 is an invisible, odorless, nonflammable gas that is a natural component of the atmosphere. Carbon dioxide or CO_2 is a byproduct of respiration (breathing or oxidative metabolism) by both plants and animals. CO_2 is an essential raw material for photosynthesis: plants assimilate, incorporate, and biochemically alter CO_2 through energy derived from sunlight to transform CO_2 into sugar compounds necessary for both energy and growth.

When a person at rest exhales, about four percent of the expired air is CO_2. This is over 100 times more concentrated than in the atmosphere, which averages about .030 to .035 percent CO_2 (or about 300 parts per million of atmospheric gases). A byproduct of photosynthesis is oxygen (O_2). During photosynthesis, plants produce more oxygen than they use in respiration. In fact, the oxygen in the Earth's atmosphere was and is produced by plants during photosynthesis. Plants also expire (through respiration) CO_2 constantly, but only at night does their expiration of CO_2 exceed their assimilation of CO_2. The net result of photosynthesis and respiration by plants is that much more oxygen is produced than consumed. CO_2 is harmless unless present in concentrations high enough to asphyxiate you, an unlikely situation even if you add copious amounts of CO_2 to your grow room.

During hours of darkness, plants enrich an enclosed grow room with CO_2. Simply visiting with your plants increases their CO_2 supply, since every breath you exhale releases a concentration of four percent CO_2. During daylight hours, photosynthesis enriches a grow room with oxygen. This richness of oxygen might explain in one small way the exhilaration growers feel when working with their plants. It may also explain why *prana yama* yoga and exercising feels so good in a room filled with fast-growing plants. Visit your plants regularly, it's mutually beneficial.

Supplementing a grow room with CO2 is not necessary to raise a potent, fast-growing crop. However any healthy garden will grow faster if supplied with CO2. In any closed or limited space, plants use up the available CO2, and growth then stalls. Once CO2 concentrations fall below about 200 ppm, growth may stop altogether. This is one reason **all gardens must be open or ventilated.**

Growers who make a substantial investment in setting up a large greenhouse or installing several HID lamps should use CO2-supplementing systems. Gardeners growing a continuous system, where the plants are rotated from one system to another, benefit considerably from using CO2, since there is a premium on fast growth. Some commercial gardeners add CO2 during flowering to enhance growth during the final ten weeks. When no other factors are limiting, **additional CO2 increases growth from 20 percent up to double the usual rate.**

The addition of CO2 does not affect potency, it affects only the rate of growth. Plants grow faster only if all other "limiting factors," such as the amount of light or nutrients, are present in abundance.

Plants can use much more CO2 than is naturally present in the atmosphere. An enrichment of five to six times what is naturally present (1,500 to 2,000 ppm or 0.15 to 0.2 percent of CO2) is the highest concentration necessary to maximize growth when no other "growth factors" limit growth.

For the CO2 enrichment to be most effective, make sure that other factors aren't limiting growth. Generally, the temperature should be about ten degrees higher than recommended (in the 80's or 90's with CO2 enrichment, except during flowering). Keep HID's closer to plant tops for light saturation, about six to 12 inches for 1,000-watt HID's mounted on light movers. Soil must be rich and regularly fertilized. If any nutrient deficiencies appear, hydroponic gardeners should increase concentrations of N, P, and K by 20 percent, and also foliar feed. Don't increase the minor elements or micronutrient concentrations.

Increasing CO2 Concentrations

There are two good ways to increase the concentration of CO2. First is the use of a CO2 generator, which is workable only in large greenhouses or spacious, multiple-HID grow rooms. The second (emitter system) uses a compressed CO2 gas tank with associated hardware to periodically release CO2. The emitter system works well for both large and small grow rooms.

CO2 Generators. CO2 generators produce CO2 by burning a clean-burning fuel such as propane or butane. Notice that these are the same gases recommended for fuel burning heaters for grow rooms. CO2 is an exhaust from heaters that burn these fuels. Anytime you use these fuel burning heaters, close down the vents, and you'll effectively raise the concentration of CO2.

CO2 generators work best when the grow room also needs to be heated. CO2 generators produce a lot of heat, and to be effective the garden must be enclosed to hold the CO2, which also holds in the heat. Especially during the summer, the additional heat tends to be excessive, and ventilation fans must be turned on to cool the growroom. Venting the growroom removes generated CO2, which of course defeats its purpose. Whichever CO2 unit you decide on, place the outlet or dispensing tubing just above the plants; CO2 is heavier than air and gradually settles over the plants.

Greenhouse suppliers sell CO2 generators with instructions for calculating the amount of fuel to generate the appropriate amount of CO2 for the size of your room. For daylight hours (when you want to generate CO2), it's best for growth if the amount of CO2 is .15 to .20 percent. Since atmospheric CO2 is about .03 percent, you'll want to supply between .12 to .17 percent CO2 to raise the garden levels to the desired level of .15 to .20 percent. Meters for detecting CO2 levels are often prohibitively expensive, so the best procedure is an estimation made from the instructions that come with the generator or emitter.

Compressed-gas-tank CO2 (emitter system). For most gardeners who want to add CO2, compressed CO2 gas tanks are the most practical. They don't burn fuel so you need not worry about an unattended flame as with CO2 generators, or about ridding a garden of excessive heat. Compressed CO2 is relatively inexpensive and safe to use, and with any good system, it's easy to control the amount of CO2 released into the garden. The compressed gas units that are sold through *High Times* ads or greenhouse suppliers should come with a regulator and solenoid valve, a flowmeter, and a timer (programmable), and they may include distribution tubing, which is set above the garden. All reputable dealers include detailed but simple instructions for calculating the flow rate to maintain about a .15 percent concentration of CO2. The CO2 tank must be rented from a welding or compressed gas supplier or from a beverage company supplier. Look in the Yellow Pages for local suppliers. For home use, CO2 tanks come in 20-lb. and 50-lb. sizes. The tanks are rented and refilled, and require a refundable deposit on the tank.

Figure 81. A complete emitter system. Emitter systems are easy to set up and cheap to run.

If your room needs ventilation to lower humidity or keep it cool, use a timer for the exhaust fans. Set the timer for the CO_2 emitter to turn on about 30 minutes after the lights turn on, and keep the unit dispensing gas for about two hours (actually, you calculate the amount of time according to the dimensions of the room and the instructions included with the unit). This brings the concentration of CO_2 into the desired range. About 30 minutes to an hour after the CO_2 unit stops dispensing, the exhaust fans turn on long enough to cool the room. For efficient use, set the dispensing of CO_2 to run again after the room has cooled, and the fans are off. The cycle is: release gas; wait 30 minutes to one hour; turn exhaust fans on; after the vents are closed or fans are off, dispense again. Repeat this cycle throughout the light period. In this way, you maximize the use of CO_2 and the benefits of exhaust fans. Follow the instructions that come with the unit if they differ from these recommended intervals.

You now know that CO_2 dispersion works best when the room is enclosed and ventilation fans are off, so that the CO_2 doesn't vent from the garden while being dispensed. The most efficient systems alternate dispersion, a wait, then ventilation, then dispersion, etc., during hours of light. This requires programmable timers to control CO_2 release and to turn exhaust fans on and off. Gardens that don't alternate dispersion with ventilation run the risk of serious rot or insect problems especially during flowering.

Gardens that don't get too hot may work well enough when sealed if you use a fan to keep the air moving within the closed room. At night, run an exhaust fan to help prevent rot and insect problems. Buy your system from a supplier who includes both pro-grammable timers and distribution tubing for best results.

Home Devised Systems. In an enclosed room without active ventilation, additional CO_2 is used up or lost in about one to four hours. When using just a tank or a CO_2 generator without associated distribution tubing and controls, dispense CO_2 one hour after the lights come on from a tank, generator, or any heater that burns propane or butane. Check air flow by blowing smoke above the tops of the plants. Now position the generator or dispenser in a place where most of the CO_2 flows among the plants and not straight out of a vent.

Greenhouse growers can open vents in the greenhouse roof to allow heat to escape. Much of the CO_2 stays in the room because it settles toward the floor, whereas the heat rises. Position distribution tubing directly among the plant tops.

With no automatic dispensing unit, you could release CO_2 and close off ventilation for a few hours, and then turn on ventilation fans two hours after dispensing has stopped. It's also possible to use dehumidifiers and circulating fans in an enclosed, sealed garden employing supplemental CO_2. You're much better off buying a complete dispensing system and a timer for the exhaust fans, since it's cheaper, and relatively problem-free.

Chapter 14

Fertilizing

Nutrients

Marijuana can outgrow practically any plant, and certainly any other plant you might see growing indoors. Marijuana draws heavily on the soil to maintain fast growth by withdrawing the soil's nutrients (minerals or fertilizers). You must replenish these nutrients by fertilizing with soluble fertilizers during growth. This simply means dissolving a soluble fertilizer in water, and watering as usual. This section is mainly for growers using soil, either in pots or in their yard, although a read-through for hydroponic growers can only help.

The Major Nutrients (N, P, K)

The three numbers on fertilizer packages correspond to the percentage of the three major nutrients that the fertilizer contains, and are always in the order nitrogen, phophorus, potassium, or N-P-K. Ra-Pid-Gro is 23-19-17, which means it has 23 percent N, 19 percent P_2O_5, and 17 percent K_2O. You'll need to fertilize with a "complete" fertilizer — one that supplies ample amounts of N, P, and K — in almost any soil several times during the course of the plant's life.

Nitrogen (N) is the most rapidly depleted of all nutrients in soil-grown marijuana, and you should anticipate the need to fertilize the plant with a soluble fertilizer containing nitrogen several times during growth. N is associated with fast, lush growth throughout the plant's life.

Phosphorus (P) is needed immediately after germination and during early growth. Good flower formation in marijuana depends on an adequate supply of P. In outdoor plots, place super-phosphates close to the plant's stem. Super-phosphates won't "burn" the plant, and you want the fertilizer to be as close as possible to the plant for good assimilation.

Potassium (K) is also needed early in growth to establish a healthy, strong plant with sturdy stems. During flowering, K helps in flower formation, and also contributes to good burning properties of the dried marijuana. The best fertilizer to use during flowering is potassium nitrate (KNO3). Studies with tobacco farmers have shown that potassium nitrate, besides providing both elements to the plant, helps the tobacco (marijuana) burn uniformly after drying. Nitrogen fertilizers, such as ammonium nitrates, negatively affect burning properties, whereas potassium nitrate combines good properties of both elements.

The Secondary Nutrients (Ca, S, Mg)

Calcium (Ca) deficiencies should not be a problem, since any good soil contains adequate Ca, and it's part of the nutrient salts of many different fertilizers (e.g. calcium nitrate used for nitrogen also has calcium).

Sulfur (S) is another necessary element that shouldn't cause you any problems. Sulfur is plentiful in any good soil, and it's also part of the salts of many fertilizers (e.g. ammonium sulphate for nitrogen and potassium sulphate for potassium).

Magnesium (Mg) is the only secondary nutrient that you might have to add. Mg is the central element of chlorophyll molecules, and when it's lacking, leaves turn yellow or white, and growth slows. Most commercial and mineral soils have plenty of Mg, but if leaves begin to yellow, see the section on Nutrient Deficiencies later in this chapter.

Trace Elements (Micronutrients)

The trace elements **boron (B), copper (Cu), iron (Fe), manganese (Mn), zinc (Zn), and molybdenum (Mo) are not needed** by the plant in large amounts to spur growth — they're necessary in minuscule amounts to regulate normal, healthy growth. Indoor soils don't usually need additions of trace elements unless the soil or water has a pH outside the recommended range. An extreme pH prevents the uptake and utilization of trace elements. (See Nutrient Deficiencies in this chapter).

Fertilizing

If you have added bulk fertilizers (manures, worm castings, rose food, etc.) when making your soil mixture, you may never need to fertilize again, but most likely you will. Bulk (solid) fertilizers shouldn't be added to potted plants after growth has started since they may "burn" the plants, promote the growth of molds or fungi, or attract gnats and flies.

Figure 82. The importance of fertilizing: a lack of nitrogen has stunted the growth of this 15 week old plant.

While indoor plants are growing, always give nutrients in solution; dissolve the fertilizer in water, and water as usual. If the fertilizer doesn't completely dissolve, first dissolve it in a few cups of hot water, then add cold water to make up the final solution. Never fertilize dry soil: first moisten the pots, and allow them to sit for a while before fertilizing.

Soluble fertilizers may be organic (natural) or inorganic (chemical), and it makes no difference to the plant which fertilizer you use as long as it's properly applied. Ultimately, both organic and manmade fertilizers are utilized by the plant in identical chemical forms. Organic fertilizers, however, promote a healthy soil and soil ecosystem. For backyard growers, organic fertilizers are much better than chemical fertilizers for the long-term health of your soil and garden. Soluble organic fertilizers such as fish emulsion (5-1-1 or 5-2-2), liquid manure (about 1.5-1.0-1.5), or an organic "tea" (see page 142), are very safe to use (there is little chance of overfertilizing or poisoning the soil), and plants respond very well to their application whether they're growing in pots or in a backyard garden. Liquid seaweed is an excellent natural source of all micronutrients.

How much fertilizer to use and how often to fertilize depends on the fertility of the starting soil mixture and the size of the pots relative to the size of the plants. A small plant in a large pot probably won't need fertilization but a large plant in a small pot will need regular fertilization. The rate of growth indoors is limited by the amount of light and space to grow once adequate nutrients are supplied. Increasing nutrient applications doesn't necessarily spur growth unless the plants are low or deficient in a nutrient.

It's impossible to give instructions for the amount and frequency for fertilizing that would cover all growing situations since each garden has different requirements. You want to supply your garden with its nutritive needs without overfertilizing and toxifying the soil. When in doubt, one way to find out what your plants require is to double the frequency of fertilizer applied to one plant and not to fertilize another. If the unfertilized plant grows slower than those fertilized or it shows nutrient deficiencies, then probably all the plants are depending on soluble fertilizers and must be fertilized regularly. If the plant fertilized twice as often grows faster than the rest, increase the amount or frequency of fertilizer to the other plants. On the other hand, if there is little difference between the plants, the soil is providing enough nutrients; so don't fertilize, or else fertilize with a solution diluted to half the concentration recommended on the fertilizer package. This half-dilution procedure probably will work well enough to carry the plants through the growing season.

Another guideline or signal for fertilizing is N deficiency. N deficiency is very common and to be expected. With healthy plants that are growing well with rich, green leaves, fertilize only once every three weeks with a general "complete" formula. If the plants show signs of N deficiency, then fertilize at regular intervals with a complete fertilizer during growth, and a fertilizer rich in P and K during flowering. Table 14.1 lists some common and popular fertilizers that are available in supermarkets and garden stores throughout much of the country. One fertilizer is not necessarily better than another, and there are many locally distributed fertilizers that work just as well.

Table 14.1
Examples of Soluble Fertilizers for Growth

Fertilizer	N	P	K	B	Cu	Fe	Mn	Zn
Miracid	30	10	10		.05	.33	.05	.05
Ra-Pid-Gro	23	19	17	.02	.05	.10	.05	.05
Deep Feed	16	4	2			.10	.10	.10
Pentrex*	16	4	2			.10	.10	.10
Peters**	20	20	20					
Miracle-Gro	20	20	20	.02	.05	.05	.05	.05
Fish Emulsion	5	1	1					
Fish Emulsion	5	2	2					

*Contains a soil penetrant to combat alkaline "lock-up."
**Peters comes in many different formulas and several also have micronutrients.

Table 14.2 — Examples of Soluble Fertilizers for Flowering								
Fertilizer	N	P	K	Mg	Cu	Fe	Mn	Zn
Miracle-Gro	15	30	15		.05	.10	.05	.05
Miracle-Gro	18	24	16	.5	.05	.10	.05	.05
Hi Bloom	2	10	10					
Bloom	0	10	10					
Peters	15	30	15					

There are numerous other fertilizers that have excellent formulas, and include trace elements, but they're not likely to be available in your local gardening store. You must mail order them. Some are Hydrofarm, Eco-Grow, Dyna-Gro, and Dansco. See their advertisements in *High Times* and *Sinsemilla Tips*. These mail order fertilizers often come in several formulas. For example, Hydrofarm has three formulas: All-Purpose at 12-10-22, Grow at 20-6-16, and Bloom at 10-30-18, and all three contain every secondary or trace element necessary for growth. Most of these "marijuana" advertisers have become quite sophisticated, and offer high quality products that are very well suited to your growing needs. (For more information on fertilizing see the sections on Hydroponics in Chapter 9 and on Nutrient Deficiencies later in this chapter.)

Foliar Feeding

Foliar feeding (spraying the leaves with a fertilizer solution) is a good way of fertilizing your plants without building up excessive concentrations of salts in the soil. Foliar feeding with almost any fertilizer is highly recommended as long as the concentrations don't exceed package instructions. Any time you're not sure whether to fertilize or not, foliar feed for safety. Dilute your fertilizer according to package instructions. Use a fine-mist sprayer (e.g. a cleaned Windex bottle) to thoroughly wet the undersides and top surfaces of the leaves. The next day, spray both surfaces of all leaves with plain water to dissolve unabsorbed nutrients. Foliar spraying also helps to correct nutrient deficiencies, since the plant absorbs them directly, which circumvents any problems with soil lock-up or other soil related problems.

Overfertilization (Toxifying the Soil)

In an effort to do their best, some people do the worst for their plants. You can toxify or poison the soil if you apply too much fertilizer. Excessive applications of N, either too often or too concentrated, cause the most problems. If plants are a healthy, uniform green and growing well, don't keep pumping them with N-rich fertilizers. Too much N changes the osmotic properties of the soil so that water is drawn out of the plant, instead of into the plant, and the plant dehydrates. Leaves wilt even though the soil is wet. Leaves very quickly (sometimes in one day) turn gold, brown, or grey and the plant, in fact, will soon die. See Overfertilization at the end of this chapter to remedy. Anytime you're in doubt about general fertilizing, either foliar feed, or water with a safe concentration of an organic fertilizer at half the dilution that the package recommends.

Nutrient Deficiencies

Before you assume the plant has a nutrient deficiency, make sure the problem is not due to plant pests. Search carefully for insects, especially on the undersides of damaged leaves, along the stem, and in the soil.

Under weaker artificial light, lower leaves may not receive enough light to carry on chlorosynthesis. Lower, shaded leaves may gradually pale, turn yellow, or develop brown areas as they die, which is perfectly normal. Not every leaf in a garden forms perfectly and small leaves that formed on young seedlings usually yellow and die within a month or two.

Chlorosis and necrosis are two terms used to describe certain symptoms of disease in plants. Chlorosis means lacking green (chlorophyll). Chlorotic leaves are pale green to yellow or white. Chlorotic leaves may show some recovery after the deficient nutrient is applied. Necrosis means the tissue is dead. Dead tissue can be brown, gold, rust, or grey, and it's dry and crumbles when squeezed. There is no way to resurrect dead tissue.

When diagnosing nutrient deficiencies, first note where on the plant the affected leaves first appear. Almost every nutrient deficiency clearly starts either at the **bottom** or at the very **top** of the plant. In general, symptoms of primary and secondary nutrient deficiencies start at the bottom of the plant. Symptoms of micronutrient deficiencies start at the top of the plant. When symptoms start at the bottom of the plant, the **"fan leaves"** on the **main stem** are affected first. Symptoms that first appear at the top of the plant are most prominent on the **topmost growing shoots,** and the condition progresses to the shoots of all actively growing branches. Always observe first where on the plant the condition is most prominent, and you will have already narrowed the possibilities by about half.

Whether affected leaves remain strongly attached to the plant or whether they easily separate and fall is another clue used in diagnosis, although this is the least telltale of all the general symptoms.

Symptoms of Major Nutrient Deficiencies

Nitrogen (N) deficiency is the most common of all deficiencies in a marijuana garden. Expect nitrogen deficiencies in potted soil even with the richest of soil mixtures. Simply fertilize according to package directions with a **complete (contains N, P, and K)** soluble fertilizer that has a good percentage of N. If your diagnosis is correct, visible recovery should be apparent in three to four days. Pale leaves regain some color but won't increase in size. New growth is much more lush and vigorous, and new stems and leaf stalks (petioles) return to a normal, green color.

N deficiency first shows as a gradual and **uniform** yellowing of the **bottom** leaves on the main stem. Once the leaves yellow, necrotic (dead) tips and areas **might** form as the leaves dry to a gold or rust color. With small plants, the whole plant may appear pale or lime-colored, with red stems and petioles, before many of the bottom leaves yellow and die. **Symptoms include smaller leaves, slow growth, and a smaller, sparse profile. Most often you'll see red/purple-tinged stems and petioles, and a rapid yellowing of the lowermost leaves that progresses to the top of the plant unless remedied.** Affected leaves sometimes drop easily, but at other times hang tenaciously to the plant.

Nitrogen is closely tied to fast, robust growth; hence marijuana quickly depletes the N from soil and soilless solutions. Fish emulsion (5-1-1) is a good source of organic N. Rapid-Gro or Miracid both provide good amounts of N in a chemical fertilizer. If the plants show severe symptoms, spray them with the concentrations of fertilizer recommended on the fertilizer package, along with a good application of fertilizer while watering. The yellowing of older leaves should stop within a few days, lime-colored leaves become greener, and all new growth should have renewed vigor and a rich green color.

Once the deficiency has shown, fertilize at least twice a month to prevent any reoccurrence of the symptoms. In hydroponic gardens, increase N by 50 to 100 ppm. For best results hydroponically, use a nitrate form of nitrogen. (Look at the list of contents on the fertilizer package.)

Figure 83. Nitrogen deficiency: the lower leaves turn a uniform yellow. Also see Figure 82.

Avoid applying too much N fertilizer during flowering. An excess of N causes leafy and therefore less potent colas. During flowering, fertilize abundantly with N only if many of the leaves are yellowing. An excess of nitrogen also may delay maturation and inhibit flowering, so during flowering, go easy with nitrogen fertilizers.

Phosphorus (P) deficiencies are uncommon to plants in any decent soil mixture or hydroponic garden. The most serious problem occurs when the grower continuously adds Fe to the mixture when an Fe deficiency is mistakenly diagnosed. Fe interferes with P uptake.

P deficiencies often start with plants that superficially look healthy, but have an uncharacteristic dull, dark, blue-green color. Stems, petioles and the undersides of leaves often have a red or purple tinge. Unfortunately for anyone diagnosing this problem, some healthy plants develop a purple coloration characteristic of some varieties (Afghani is the most common). Check the leaf edges (margins), particularly on the lower leaves to see if they have a **downward curl.** Affected leaves should also **drop** or **easily separate** from the stem. Tips of the older leaf blades sometimes turn brown or copper. Leaves may develop some grey or purple discoloration, but more often lower leaves form blotchy yellow areas before the whole leaf yellows and dies. In severe cases you'll see stunted plants, more often, just slow growth. An acidic soil or acidic water supply may be the cause.

A number of other, benign conditions also cause dying leaf tips (just the very slender ends): too dry an atmosphere, nickel deficiencies, and slight overwatering or lack of soil oxygen. Don't use the fact that the very tips of your leaves are turning brown to diagnose a P deficiency, and don't use purple stems and petioles as decisive factors, since purple coloration is likely to be perfectly normal.

A diagnosis of P deficiency is reasonable only after the following symptoms have appeared: **small leaves and stunted, abnormally dark green plants which grow very slowly, with leaves that have a downward curl along their margins.** (This is similar to a description of plants with suffocated roots. P deficiency most often will show on developed plants; plants with suffocated roots usually are seedlings.) With P deficiency, lower leaves may have a red or purple coloration in or along the veins.

If you think your plants may be experiencing P deficiency, fertilize with P or a general fertilizer high in P (e.g. Bloom 0-10-10) but don't go overboard. Increase P concentrations in hydroponic gardens by 20 ppm. **Try the addition of detergent as described later.** Continue to foliar feed with phosphorus if you're in doubt. If there is no improvement in the rate of growth after a couple of weeks, reevaluate your problem.

Potassium (K) deficiencies are not as common as growers believe, partly because some problems superficially look like K deficiencies, including simple shading or inadequate light on the lower leaves in electric light-gardens, or an excess of sodium (Na) in the soil or water. K deficiencies show up more often in low-output light gardens than in gardens illuminated by sunlight or 1,000-watt HID's. Without going into a long explanation, this is because during protein synthesis a plant illuminated by strong light can use K more easily. Symptoms also appear more often if the soil or water is acidic since potassium is less readily absorbed in an acidic medium.

Symptoms of K deficiency start at the **bottom** of the plant, where you'll see yellowed areas, or necrotic grey or rust-colored areas and spots that start at the tips and **along the margins of main-stem** leaves. Unless corrected, leaf tissues continue to yellow and die starting at their margins and working inward. Rust-colored, brown, or grey, pinhead-sized spots or mottled areas may appear on the leaves and stems. K-deficient plants may be the tallest in the garden. Stems and petioles often develop red or purple coloring. Diseased leaves most often separate easily from the plant.

If you've fertilized with a complete fertilizer, and you haven't added too much Ca or Fe, then it's unlikely that your growing medium is deficient in K or P. Plants may absorb Na instead of K, and the symptoms of this "K deficiency" will be crinkled "burned" edges on the older leaves. Surprisingly, the addition of a few drops of detergent (not soap) to each gallon of water may help your problem immeasurably. Detergent contains N, P, and K, but more often than that, its **wetting properties** help the plants absorb nutrients, and it is particularly effective when there are excessive salts (e.g. sodium) in the soil. Try a few drops per gallon of water if you suspect P or K deficiencies and have fertilized with them. You should see improvement within a week or two. A good, fast-acting, and natural source of potassium is wood ash (not paper or other burnables). Mix one tablespoon of wood ash to each quart of water and water as usual during the next two waterings.

To summarize the symptoms of major nutrient deficiencies: all three start first on the lower, main-stem leaves (fan leaves); N deficiency should be expected since marijuana draws heavily on this nutrient. Deficiencies of P and K are unlikely in any good soil or hydroponic solution, unless there have been additions of other nutrients (Fe and Ca) in excess or there is an abundance of Na in the soil or water. Make sure that you don't use artificially "softened" water since softening replaces the minerals in hard water with Na. Softened water will surely cause sodium burn and symptoms of K deficiency, among a number of other problems.

Symptoms of Secondary Nutrient (Ca, S, Mg) Deficiencies

Calcium (Ca) deficiency should not occur in any indoor garden, unless you have concocted a home made-mixture that includes only acidic amendments, such as peat moss combined with an organic fertilizer. Almost any general fertilizer has plenty of Ca, and any commercial soil or hydroponic solution will also have plenty of Ca.

Symptoms for Ca deficiency are a dark **green but stunted plant that grows very slowly.** Notice that this is similar to symptoms of P deficiency, but before serious symptoms of Ca deficiency appear, you will probably have all sorts of other soil-related problems, including micronutrient deficiencies. With a severe deficiency of Ca, leaves may be **green but crinkled, and young shoots soon develop with yellow or purple coloration, and they twist or contort before they die.**

Dissolve one teaspoon of fine dolomitic lime, or half a teaspoon of hydrated lime to each gallon of water to remedy. Monitor the pH of your growing medium, and don't exceed the pH recommended earlier. Look for another probable cause: Ca deficiencies should not ~ccur in indoor gardens.

Sulfur (S) deficiency is rare indoors. S is also the other component of many fertilizer salts: ammonium sulphates, potassium sulphates, etc. In any decent soil, or if you have added fertilizers, it's extremely doubtful you'll ever see this problem. Don't confuse S deficiency with N deficiency. Sulfur deficiencies usually start at the **top** of the plant although they may appear more prominently in the middle of the plant. There is a general **yellowing** or paleness of the **new leaves or shoots** and in potted plants, much of the plant may be pale or lime-colored. In severe cases, **veins** of growing **shoots** turn yellow, with dead areas (sometimes purple) developing at the base of the leaf where the blades join.

In the very unlikely instance that you actually have a sulfur deficiency, correct by applying 1 tablespoon of epsom salts to each gallon of water each time you water, until the condition no longer progresses. Foliar feed periodically with a sulfur spray (e.g. copper-sulphate) used to control fungus and rot problems. Once an S deficiency appears outdoors, add gypsum (hydrated calcium sulphate) to outdoor soils before planting, and work it into the soil.

Magnesium (Mg) deficiencies are common outdoors and indoors both in soil and hydroponic gardens despite what you may have heard or read. Symptoms of Mg deficiency **start at the bottom** of the plant but often they also progress to the growing shoots.

Figure 84. *Left:* Magnesium deficiency starts on the lower leaves. Leaf veins are green with yellow or white tissue between the veins. Leaf tips curl and die. *Right:* Iron deficiency starts on the top growing shoots. The leaves are normal except for yellow or white tissue between the veins.

Chlorosis develops on the tissue between the leaf veins. Leaves may be **yellow to white with a network of green veins.** One good indication is that **leaf tips severely curl and die,** accompanied by chlorotic or dying tissue between the veins on many **lower** leaves. To distinguish Mg from other deficiencies, notice that the condition is most prominent on the lower leaves, and that the **whole leaf** is affected. Purple color usually develops on stems and petioles.

It's easy to correct Mg deficiency in any situation with epsom salts ($MgSO_4 \bullet 7H_2O$), which are available from supermarkets and pharmacies. Add half a teaspoon of epsom salts to each quart of water and water as usual. Spray the undersides of leaves on affected plants in the same concentration, and you should see some improvement in about four days, when top shoots regain some green color. All new growth should be normal and healthy. Continue applications until no new symptoms are seen on any plants. Thereafter, one application every two weeks should be enough to carry the plants until harvest. (See "Fe deficiency" below for more information.)

Symptoms of Micronutrient Deficiencies
(Fe, Mn, Zn, B, Cu, Mo)

The most common micro-nutrient deficiencies are Fe, Zn, and Mn, and as with **all micronutrient deficiencies, symptoms first appear on the growing or new shoots.** In hydroponic gardens, make sure that you don't go overboard when raising the concentration of a micronutrient. Micronutrient concentrations that are too high cause root injury or stunted roots, necrotic leaf tissue or leaf veins, or abrupt death of the plant. Hydroponic gardeners should first test applications of increased concentrations on one plant if they have doubts about diagnosis and treatment. Remember that all micronutrients are necessary, in minuscule amounts, only to **regulate** or facilitate normal metabolism and growth. They are **not used in quantities to spur growth** like other nutrients. Micronutrients can be likened to our need of vitamins and minerals for good health.

Despite what you may have read elsewhere, **Fe, Zn, and Mn deficiencies are quite common.** They often give growers serious problems since they're seldom diagnosed correctly, and treatment requires more than simply adding a general fertilizer. Problems with Fe, Mn, or Zn are very common to plants growing in areas with hard (alkaline) water. If you lower the pH of your water or nutrient solution to about 6.5, these three micronutrients become available to the plant. If any of the following symptoms appear in hydroponic gardens, lower the pH of your solution (make it more acidic), and apply all three nutrients in quantities only slightly above average concentrations.

The micronutrient deficiencies Fe, Mn, Zn often occur in conjunction, and usually an alkaline water is responsible. You should apply all three together to alleviate any serious consequences of these deficiencies. However, if distinctive signs of only one deficiency routinely appear, apply only that element.

Iron (Fe) deficiency is easily recognized by the chlorosis of leaf tissue on the growing shoots. **Leaves in the shoots have a network of green veins which stand out among the yellow or white tissue between the veins.** Otherwise, the leaves appear normal, except that they may be slightly undersized. Chlorosis generally starts at the base of the leaf, where the blades originate, but rapidly spreads evenly throughout the entire leaf. (See page 229 after Zn symptoms for treatment with Fe, Mn, and Zn.)

To distinguish Fe from Mg deficiency, notice that Fe deficiencies are prominent only on the growing shoots. Deficiencies of Mg affect lower leaves, and often affect growing shoots also. If lower leaves look unhealthy with spots or dying areas, or **if the leaf margins or tips are curled and dying,** the problem is a deficiency of Mg.

Figure 85. Iron deficiency: leaves are normal except leaf tissue is white or yellow against a network of green veins. The Colombian on the left has more advanced symptoms than the *Indica* on the right where the deficiency has just begun to show.

Manganese (Mn) deficiency is much more common than most growers realize, but, fortunately, the symptoms are very distinctive and easy to recognize. Symptoms appear at the top of the plant and all growing shoots. Older leaves seldom show any signs. Symptoms begin as chlorosis or a bleached blotching of tissue starting at the base of the leaf where the blades join. As the condition progresses, the interveinal tissue turns pale green to yellow or white, but the veins remain dark green. Veins may be pale green. **The telltale sign for Mn, as distinguished from Fe or Zn deficiency, is that the margins of the affected leaves remain dark green, so that each affected leaf is outlined with dark green, but all inner tissue between the veins turns yellow or white.** The leaf is chlorotic, but outlined by a perimeter or ring of green tissue along the leaf margins. In mild or incipient cases, a "halo or yellow shadowline" outlines the leaves **within** a perimeter of **dark green** on the leaf's margins. Shoots or young leaves may sometimes show yellow or dead spots without the distinctive rim of green.

Mn deficiencies seriously affect good flower formation. Maturation is delayed, and flower development is noticeably slowed and inhibited. Buds may be 12 weeks old, and still look immature, since the buds never fill out but remain skimpy like two-week old buds. It is therefore very important to correct this deficiency quickly and to continue applications of Mn throughout flowering. Once you

Figure 86. Manganese deficiency. The leaves begin to lose their green color starting at the base of the leaf blades. Also see Figure 87.

know that your plants have a deficiency of Mn, limit the amount of Fe and P in your fertilizer, since both elements interfere with Mn utilization.

Zinc (Zn) is another fairly common deficiency, especially in neutral to alkaline mediums or water. Chlorosis of tissue **between the veins of top shoots starts at the base of the leaf,** where the leaf blades join. Zn deficiency may look like Mn or Fe deficiency at first, but **a radial or horizontal twisting of the leaf blades in the growing shoots is a dead giveaway.** Under severe conditions, the blades twist 90 degrees in a horizontal plane. Picture the fingers of your hand bending horizontally at right angles at the middle knuckle. Upward growth slows and may cease altogether, and instead a **gnarled, undersized top knot of leaves forms.** During flowering, developed buds may contort and twist, and then turn to a crisp hardness. Stigmas may be very short and undersized. "Hook" buds are caused by a lack of Zn during flowering. Zn deficiency seriously affects all new growth, including buds. Unless corrected, growth may all but cease, and at best, only puny buds develop. Internodes almost

Figure 87. Zinc deficiency. *Left:* Notice the distorted, very small top-knot of leaves. The leaf where the blade bends at the right angle (*mid-left*) is a telltale indication of zinc deficiency. The leaves just below show both manganese and zinc deficiency. The perimeter of green surrounding inner white tissue is from manganese deficiency. The dying and distorted blade tips are caused by zinc deficiency. *Right:* "Hook" bud with very short stigmas is caused by zinc deficiency near the end of maturation.

always are shortened when the plant is deficient in zinc. To treat deficiencies of Fe, Mn, and Zn use a solution that provides all three nutrients. You'll commonly find "transplanting solutions" that contain B-1 vitamins plus "plant tonic", which includes Fe, Mn, and Zn. Read the label to make sure that the needed element is present. For example, Chacon transplanting solution has Fe (.125 percent), B (.02 percent), Mn (.125 percent), Zn (.125 percent), Mo (.0005 percent), with chelating agents. (Chelated elements circumvent problems associated with an extreme pH, i.e. they're absorbed despite a pH outside the desired range.) Other products are Ortho transplanting solution or Nitron, both of which contain chelated Fe, Zn, and Mn. Many other similar solutions contain only one or two micronutrients (e.g., Angel City Liquid Iron has 5.3 percent Fe and .07 percent Zn), and any garden store should carry several brands. Use the most appropriate solution, preferably in chelated forms.

Drench the soil and foliar feed. In a few days, affected leaves should show a little improvement (chlorotic tissue gets a little greener), and new growth gradually returns to normal. Continue to foliar feed twice a week until growth is normal. Spray two or three times during flowering even if all growth appears normal.

Boron (B) deficiencies should never occur indoors, and are very rare except in fields under continuous cultivation with no additions of fertilizers. Symptoms first appear on the growing shoots, which turn brown or grey and die. The shoots may look "burned", and you may think that your lights have touched and burned the shoots. **A good indication of B deficiency is that after the top shoot dies, actively growing side shoots start to grow but also die.** Dead areas develop along leaf margins and between leaf veins of growing shoots before the shoot dies. The top shoot may be bright green and twisted where the leaves are emerging. B deficiency is very unlikely, and it's easily corrected with a solution of half a teaspoon of boric acid (available from any pharmacy) to a gallon of water. Spray the undersides of the leaves and water with this solution as usual. One application should be enough to correct the problem. In hydroponic gardens, do not exceed 20 ppm even in one application, since it's easy to kill the plant with excessive concentrations of B.

Copper (Cu) deficiencies are extremely rare; be careful not to confuse this deficiency with the symptoms of overfertilization. If you have been regularly applying N-rich fertilizers, discontinue and water with plain water for a while. Shoots and young leaves show interveinal chlorosis, and necrotic tips and leaf margins develop that may turn copper or grey in color. **Sometimes the whole plant is**

somewhat limp, although the pot is well watered. Cu deficiencies might at first mimic problems associated with impending overfertilization. In the unlikely occurrence of a Cu deficiency, foliar feed with a Cu-containing fungicide, such as copper-sulphate (CuSO4), or with any general fertilizer that contains Cu, such as Ra-Pid-Gro which has .05 percent Cu. Cu is severely toxic in excess. In hydroponic gardens, concentrations over one ppm can outright kill your plants. Look for another cause, because Cu deficiency is extremely unlikely in any indoor garden.

Molybdenum (Mo) and deficiencies of other elements such as silicon, nickel, and chlorine are extremely rare and unlikely. In fact, it's very difficult to create these deficiencies in any normally grown garden. Contaminants in fertilizers and water will abundantly supply all of these minor nutrients. Don't even consider that Mo deficiency is a possible problem unless you're growing under laboratory conditions and are using distilled water.

Mo deficiency symptoms start at the middle of the plant, where leaves gradually yellow. Symptoms progress under severe deprivation to the growing shoots, which are also twisted and distorted. **Extremely rare, look for another cause.**

General Fertilizers to Treat Deficiencies

Several general fertilizers to use for most micronutrient deficiencies as well as major nutrient deficiencies are: any of Applied Hydroponic or Eco-Grow line of fertilizers for hydroponic gardening, since they contain every necessary nutrient; Miracle-Gro for tomatoes has every nutrient except B and Mo; Miracid is another good foliar treatment for Fe, Mn, and Zn problems. Fish emulsion is a good organic source of nitrogen. Miracle-Gro and Ra-Pid-Gro should solve most deficiencies except Mg. Many general fertilizers now contain all or most of the micronutrients, along with N, P, and K. Read the labels to see which brand contains the most of the nutrient you need. For micronutrient deficiencies, fertilize the soil once, and foliar feed until symptoms disappear.

When foliar feeding for micronutrient deficiencies, make sure to saturate the growing shoots. Micronutrients are relatively immobile in the plant and this is why symptoms appear in new shoots. The major nutrients are translocated easily by the plant, and this is why symptoms appear on the old leaves first. The plant withdraws nutrients from the older leaves to nourish new growth.

Final Thoughts on Deficiencies

In conclusion, expect N deficiencies, and don't be surprised by Mg deficiencies. Fe, Mn, and Zn deficiencies often show up in neutral to alkaline mediums. Any other deficiency isn't likely, or is nearly nonexistent under the conditions for growth recommended here.

If one nutrient is abnormally high, its high concentration may interfere with the absorption of other elements. You then may see a deficiency of a nutrient when actually your problem is an excess of another. For example, a high concentration of Ca interferes with the absorption of K, and vice versa. High concentrations of Fe interfere with Mn absorption. High Ca or Cl concentrations may interfere with Mg absorption. The point here is to keep this in mind, so that if you have added a considerable amount of Ca and see K deficiencies, the culprit is excess Ca, not an absence of K. And general fertilizing should always be done with a complete fertilizer, one that contains some of each of the major nutrients (N, P, K), and usually some of the secondary nutrients, such as Ca and S (which are present in most complete fertilizers). Foliar feed with the deficient nutrient if you suspect that an excess of another nutrient is interfering with uptake of the deficient nutrient.

Excess P causes Fe to precipitate out of the solution, leading to symptoms of iron deficiency. An excess of Na causes K and Fe deficiencies, which is one reason you should never use "softened" water. Adding the deficient nutrient to the soil in the presence of an excess nutrient won't correct the problem. Foliar spray with the deficient nutrient.

For all the micronutrients, the most important consideration is not to apply any single micronutrient in gross excess. An excess of any micronutrient can cause innumerable problems, which makes diagnosis difficult or may kill the plants.

Other Soil Related Problems

Poor soil aeration. Lower leaves turn grey-green, wilt, and fall from the plants. Yellow, grey or brown areas spread from the leaf tips, which die. **Leaf margins droop and curl down and inward.** The plants are actually dying because their roots don't get enough oxygen. Compacted soil or muck suffocates the roots. Empty one pot with the "sickest" plant to check the soil. If the soil smells sour (ammonia), or feels like muck or ooze, remedy by transplanting all plants to a new, looser medium, and **water less often.** This problem is quite common with small plants in large pots of soil, (Fig. 77) and something to watch for if you're inexperienced in growing plants.

Overfertilization is common and quite sad to see, since usually the plants are very healthy and growing rapidly before the condition becomes apparent. By fertilizing excessively, you toxify the soil. **Leaves may wilt even though the soil is moist — this usually occurs after a single overdose of nitrogen fertilizer.** One more dose of nitrogen may be all that's necessary to kill the plants if they aren't already dying. Leaves rapidly turn gold, rust, brown or grey, and the plant dies shortly, sometimes overnight and just after you've fertilized. If the plant hasn't died, proceed as directed below.

Figure 88. A single overdose of nitrogen is killing this plant. Starting at the top of the plant and its growing shoots, the leaves die and in this case have turned rust- colored.

Overfertilizing gradually. Leaves are a very dark, dull green. Leaf margins fold in toward each other. The plant folds its leaves, trying to conserve water. **Leaf blades severely curl down and in, forming flat circles.** Circular leaf blades usually signify a gradual and continuous buildup of too much fertilizer salts in the soil. Stop fertilizing altogether. Excess nitrogen is the most likely cause. If your medium drains well, bring the plants outside or to a bathtub. You must flush out the excess build-up of salts from the soil. Discard the top two or three inches of soil; it has the highest concentration of poisonous salts, and probably is devoid of roots due to the toxic salts. Run a couple of gallons of lukewarm, fresh water slowly and continuously through each pot. New leaves gradually resume their normal turgor in a day or two if the treatment is successful. Hereafter, water with plain water unless serious symptoms of nutrient deficiencies appear. For cautious fertilizing, foliar feed only.

The foremost culprit is excess nitrogen. Too much soluble nitrogen (nitrates) changes the osmotic properties of the soil or hydroponic medium. Instead of water being drawn into the plant, the medium actually draws water out of the plant by reverse osmosis. Leaf margins fold trying to conserve water. Death is, in part, caused by dehydration.

Chapter Fifteen

General Care

Supports for Plants

Healthy plants ordinarily don't need supports to remain upright. Under natural conditions stems undergo stress from wind and rain. These stresses, that indoor plants don't ordinarily face, strengthen the stems. Vibrations stimulate a plant to strengthen its stem. Greenhouse-raised tree seedlings are shaken daily before they're moved outdoors.

Under moderate light such as under fluorescents and some window gardens, you might find that some of the plants need support. Hanging any artificial light higher than the recommended distances causes plants to stretch for the light and elongate on a spindly, delicate stem that may not support the weight of the leaves. Too much red light (HPS, LPS, incandescents, and floodlights) will cause elongation too.

When the usual accidents occur during the care of your garden, or if your plants suffer the catastrophe of a fallen light fixture, support your plants so that they may recover their original sturdiness. For sprouts and seedlings, the simplest method is to take a rigid piece of wire, form a "C" at one end, and bend the "C" to a right angle to the wire. Set the straight end in the soil and rest the stem in the "C". Pipe cleaners are ideal for seedlings. Straighten a coat hanger, and use the same procedure for larger plants. You could use dowels, cane sticks, or wood lathing, and affix the stem to the support with string or wire twists. Don't tie the string too tightly, because a tightly tied string can injure the stem when the stem's girth increases. Remove the support as soon as the plant can stand on its own.

Hydroponic gardeners probably have the most trouble with plants that need support. Hydroponic growing mediums may be very loose or lightweight, and it's easy to knock plants over. Because hydroponic media may not support plant stakes, run taut strings from wall to wall or from upright studs. Stand the fallen plants upright and attach them to the string runners with wire twists. Once they can stand by themselves, remove the twists, since the plants strengthen their roots and stems when not supported.

Thinning

Depending on the viability of the seeds, you should have several sprouts in most pots if you planted several seeds per pot. When the garden becomes filled with foliage, remove the excess plants, so that each pot has one plant. In vegetative gardens, don't thin the plants until they begin to crowd each other and compete for space and light. The longer you let the plants grow, the more potent the new leaves and shoots will be.

To thin your garden, remove any plants with yellow, white, or disfigured leaves. Remove the less vigorous and those that lag behind in development. Try to leave seedlings that are healthy and vigorous and that are about equal in development. Cut the unwanted plants at their base; the old root system can remain in the pot. These harvested seedlings will be your first taste of your crop. Young plants may produce only a mild buzz, but the top shoots will be stronger no matter what the age of the plants. Usually by two months of age the upper shoots have become potent enough to whet your appetite for the finished product.

Most growers start one plant per pot, but they plant many more pots than they expect to bring to maturity. Thin (cull) the garden of males as soon as you discover each plant's gender, and the plants have filled the garden. (See Chapters 17 and 18 on how to decide which plants might be males, and Chapter 22 for harvesting leaves at their peak potency.)

Transplanting

If you planted several seeds in each pot, some pots probably will have several sprouts and other pots may be empty. If there are any empty pots, transplant a seedling from a multiple-sprout pot during the first two weeks of growth.

First, (**and always when transplanting**), moisten the soil in both pots, and wait a minute or two. Prepare a hole for the transplant in the new soil. Take a spade or a large spoon, and insert it between the transplant and any plant that will be left to grow. Try to leave at least an inch of space from spoon to stem. Lever the spoon so that you take up a sizable wedge of soil. Place the transplant in the prepared hole at the same depth it was growing before. Replace the soil in both pots. Tamp the soil down firmly, and water moderately to bond the new soil with the original. If carefully done, a wedge of soil with all the roots can be removed intact. The plant is undisturbed when moved, and it survives with little or no transplant shock.

To prevent drop-off and wilting from shock, you may want to use Rootone or Transplantone. These powders contain root-growth hormones and fungicides that assure a safe and trouble-free transplanting. However, if transplanting is done carefully, neither is actually necessary.

Another way to remove transplants from among a group of seedlings is to use a tin can with both of its ends removed. Place the can over the transplant and push the can into the soil. Wiggle the can until the soil loosens. Carefully maneuver the can upward, and you should be able to remove the transplant with its roots held intact within the can. Place the can in a prepared hole, and slide the can away.

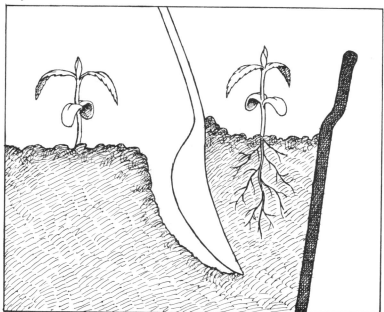

Figure 89. To transplant sprouts, take a spade or large spoon and lever the spoon so as to take up a sizeable wedge of soil. *Drawing by O. Williams.*

Transplanting from Small to Large Containers

Transplanting is simple and easy to do if the plant is rootbound. Rootbound plants benefit by being transplanted to a larger pot, and you'll need to water and fertilize less frequently. A few days before you plan to transplant, fertilize with a solution about half the strength recommended on your fertilizer package. When you transplant, the original soil is more concentrated in salts (fertilizer) than the new soil, which encourages the roots to grow outward, seeking water, so your transplants will establish themselves in the new soil more quickly. As usual, anytime you transplant, **first moisten the soil in both pots;** doing so protects the roots, and makes the whole process cleaner and easier. Also, never allow a naked root system to contact or sit in dry soil, to remain in sunlight, or to be exposed to air for an extended period of time; any of these damages the roots.

Cover the soil surface of the plant to be transplanted with a sheet of newspaper or foil. While holding the base of the stem and pot, rap the pot sharply against the floor. The root system, held intact by the protective foil, is loosened from the sides of the pot, and with all the soil adhering to the root system, should pop out cleanly. If it doesn't come out, squeeze the pot or run a knife around the sides of the pot to loosen any roots sticking to the pot's sides. Make sure that the drainage holes are not plugged; if they are, air cannot enter to displace the soil, and the soil won't slide out easily. Once the transplant is moved, fill all empty spaces with fresh soil and patiently water until the soil is evenly moist.

Position transplants at the same depth that they were growing before. This helps prevent stem rot. If you're experienced, you might bury the stem up to the first set of leaves. This saves a few inches of vertical space. The stem gradually forms roots, but burying the stem is helpful only if you're using large pots, and the overhead space is limited. Plants with buried stems actually may be a little more robust by season's end, but try only a few plants at first, because success depends on the particular growing conditions in each garden, and you don't want to lose plants to stem rot.

At the times shown in Table 15.1, give or take a week or two, the plants should be rootbound. If the soil at these times comes out in a small ball or if the root system is obviously undeveloped, then the soil mixture is unhealthy, or you have consistently overwatered. You should replace the old soil mixture with a different mixture, or correct your watering habits; otherwise you'll have future problems with slow or very poor growth. If the root system looks healthy, but hasn't yet filled the pot, wait another week or two. Prepare the new pot by placing some moistened soil in the bottom of the pot, so that the transplant will be raised to near the top of the new pot.

Table 15.1 Guide to Times for Transplanting	
Transplant	**During**
Eight-ounce cups	about the third week
Four-inch pots	third to fourth week
Six-inch pots (half gallon)	fourth to fifth week
Eight-inch pots (one gallon)	sixth to eighth week
Two-gallon pots	eighth to twelfth week

The times in Table 15.1 are for average light gardens. None of these times is perfectly fixed. Always check one plant to make sure that it's rootbound before you transplant all of your seedlings. You don't want to transplant when the soil is still loose and the pot isn't yet filled with roots, because much of the soil will fall from the roots. The plants suffer and require time for their roots to recover before resuming normal growth.

Figure 90. Transplant when the plant is rootbound.

If you have used small plastic starter bags for seedlings, they should transplant as easily as those in rigid pots. Simply stretch the sides of the bag so that the roots or soil aren't sticking. The intact cylinder of soil should easily slide from the bag.

Plastic bags larger than eight inches may be a little tricky to transplant from and to cleanly. First, put some soil in the container into which you are going to transplant, enough to raise the transplant so the base of the stem will be at the same height as the new soil surface. Place the transplant into the new bag, and adjust the bottom soil to the correct height. Cut the old plastic bag away, and fill the side spaces with new soil mixture. Two people, one to hold and the other to cut and fill, make the job much easier.

Repair

If heavy branches break from the main stem or a plant has fallen over, all is not lost. Marijuana plants recover and heal themselves when given the proper care. If a branch splits from the main stem, use electrician's black tape and a splint to hold it in its original position. After a few weeks when the break has healed, remove the tape.

Cover severe breaks with tree-pruning compound to prevent any invasion of disease organisms. Even if the plant has been knocked down or branches have been broken, don't give up. Repair the

Figure 91. A creased stem is easy to repair with splints and tape.

Figure 92. *Left:* Use tape and splints to hold branches and stems in their original positions. *Right:* This plant needed only tape to repair branches that split during a windstorm.

Figure 93. *Left:* Cover any breaks or wounds with pruning compound. *Right:* Cloth protects the stem from being cut into by cord used to support the plant.

damage or position the plant in its original upright position, and after a few weeks you'll discover that surprisingly, your plant has miraculously healed.

Other than a complete break and separation, marijuana heals from what at first seems a devastating injury. As long as some of the roots are still in the ground or still hold a ball of soil, or some of the cambium layer (outer stem covering) is still connected, the plant or branch can recover. Pruning compound, slats for splints, and electrician's tape are your best aids for repair. Whatever the injury, try to return the branch/plant to its original position, and hold it there. Tie string to a cloth loop around the stem of heavy plants that need support. Cloth protects the stem from being cut into by the string. You'll find that marijuana is a tough, resilient plant, that doesn't easily give up. Look at the accompanying photographs, which should give you the incentive to repair broken plants. The plants shown here recovered enough to yield about what was anticipated.

Promoting Even Growth

The light intensity from any electric light source drops dramatically as the distance from the light source increases. Mathematically the amount of light is divided by the square of the distance from the light source. (Intensity = Output at source divided by Distance squared). In other words, if a plant one foot from the light gets one unit of light, then a plant two feet from the light gets 1/4 unit of light, and a plant three feet from the light gets 1/9 unit of light, and so on.

Of course in sunlight, shorter plants receive as much sun as taller plants, unless they're shaded. Under electric light, the top of a plant two feet from the light receives only 1/4 as much light as a plant top that's one foot from the light.

When the plants' heights are uneven, shorter plants receive less light and consequently grow more slowly than taller plants, which compounds the problem. All plant tops should be kept at the same distance from the lights so that they grow equally fast under the light system, no matter what electric-light source is used. The weaker the light, the more important it is to keep the tops' height equal. You can help the growth of your crop considerably if you rotate the pots by moving the shortest plants under the center of the bulb. Try to minimize shading. Every day, check your plants and spread them out to optimize their space and the light illuminating each plant.

Figure 94. Hang the fixture at an angle corresponding to that of the plant tops. *Drawing by O.Williams.*

One way a grower with fluorescent lights can deal with uneven growth is to line the plants up by height, and hang the light system at an angle corresponding to the plant tops. This equally illuminates even the shortest of plants.

Or put the smaller plants on boxes, empty pots, or anything else that raises their tops up to the height of the tallest plants. This is particularly useful if you are growing plants of different ages and different growth stages under the same light system, or if you are growing with HID's.

The light emitted from a fluorescent tube is not uniform along its length. The light at the center is stronger than the light emitted at the ends. Likewise, the light at the periphery of a HID-light garden is weaker than the light directly below the center of the bulb.

Female plants need more light than males. Once sex shows, move the males to the ends of a fluorescent light system, or to the periphery of a HID or natural light system, or remove them from the garden altogether. Males do quite well under low-light conditions. Always place the females in the brighter, stronger, central light. (See Male Flowering in Chapter 16.)

Marijuana, like many other plants, produces a hormone in the growing tip or topmost shoot (apical meristem) which inhibits new branches (lateral shoots) from developing. The hormone establishes a gradient from the top of the plant down. The farther branches are from the growing tip, the less is the effect of the branch-growing inhibitor. This is why many plants that grow in sunlight form a Christmas tree or conical shape, with progressively longer branches growing toward the bottom of the plant away from the hormonal inhibitor.

Under artificial light, the situation is balanced somewhat, because lower branches receive weaker light, and consequently they grow more slowly than the upper branches. Upper leaves also shade the bottom of the plant more than when in sunlight. In most electric-light gardens the plants are cylindrical rather than conical. This works out just fine under electric lights, since the cubic area of the garden is filled more evenly. Cylindrical plants fill the space completely in most electric-light gardens.

Training

Often, you'll find a plant or two that rapidly outgrows the rest of the plants. If you don't want to cut its top, train the top to grow horizontally. Bend the topmost growing shoots of the tallest plants and hold them in position with wire twists, string, weights, or any other means that you devise. Bending neutralizes the effects of the growth-inhibiting hormone: the top grows more thickly and lower branches grow more quickly.

Figure 95. Use wire twists to train plant tops. You can buy wire twists in quantities at garden shops.

Keep the main shoot slightly below the upper part of the plant. Side shoots now grow faster and the rest of the plant and shorter plants gradually catch up in height. Use this method to keep tall plants even with the tops of average plants. Bending down the tallest shoots keeps the tops of young plants or buds on maturing plants strongly illuminated, no matter what light system you have. Remove the string or wire twist after a few days so that the growing tip doesn't break while twisting up toward the light. After a couple of days, again bend and secure the top in place. During flowering, repeat the process several times until you have a snake-like plant top covered with vigorous buds.

By training the tops, you can keep the lights lower, and more strongly illuminate all of the plants as well as their lower branches. The effective growth area under electric lights is a cubic area limited by the strength of the light. Under fluorescents, this effective cubic growth area may be only one foot deep for a small system, but can be up to about five feet deep under the strongest HID-light systems.

The idea, especially under weaker fluorescent systems, is to have a cubic area filled with vigorously growing buds. Train the tops to grow horizontally, and you'll force more buds to develop within this effective growth area, then you'll get more and larger buds whatever light system you use. **This is critical for fluorescent gardeners. By training, you'll get a decent return of buds, because training the**

Figure 96. A trained plant top early in flowering. Notice that side branches have grown as high as the top of the plant. By training the top, you'll harvest much more in worthwhile buds.

Figure 97. *Left:* Plant top trained in an "S" shape. *Right:* A young plant clipped at the fourth internode now has eight strong branches.

top branches keeps their developing buds within the effective cubic growth area. A single trained top may return 1/8 to almost 1/3 ounce of pure bud under even small fluorescent light systems. The larger the light system, the more weight you can expect to harvest.

Without any bending or close attention to the plants' growth, you'll end up with much more leaf than decent buds. **If you're using HID's, this isn't critical,** but for any fluorescent gardener, it's ridiculous to spend time and energy necessary for raising plants then not to take more time to assure yourself of a good return of buds by training tops. These last weeks of flowering are most important. Train those tops and watch the plants each day. You've come all this way; now is the time to be paid in potent dividends.

Pruning (Clipping)

Under any light source, to quickly fill a garden's space and to control height, prune or clip the fastest growing plants early in their growth. You may find that cutting a plant's top is emotionally difficult, but it doesn't harm the plant; it may actually help the overall growth and return of your crop. Use scissors, knife, or a razor blade to cut the shoot in the middle of an internode (midway between the growing shoot and the next pair of leaves below).

Don't clip any plants before they have at least three leaf pairs; otherwise you'll delay that plant's development. Cutting the top shoot encourages lateral shoots (side branches) to develop. After clipping the top on a plant with four internodes, you'll soon see from six to eight strong branches grow and quickly cover all spaces open to the light. The crop develops with a cubic layer of buds for harvest rather than a number of single tops. Clipping a plant anywhere from one to two months old yields a rounded, very bushy plant with many strong colas (highly recommended for greenhouses). In sunlight, it's also popular to clip all tops when the plants are from ten to 14 weeks old, because by this time these top shoots are usually very worthwhile to smoke.

Indoor-light gardeners usually prefer not to clip their plants' tops because they want to fill the area with as many plants as possible. Clip the top of a plant only if it's markedly outgrowing every other plant. Or clip the tops if you have just a few plants and want to fill the horizontal space. **Don't repeatedly clip the top shoots.** If you do, you'll end up with plants with numerous slender flowering shoots that are a pain to manicure and have little substance or weight.

Where many growers go wrong is in pruning too often or too early in growth. If you prune too often, repeatedly cutting the strongest shoots, you'll harvest few, if any, large colas. Pruning too early in growth, during the first two weeks, and before any lateral shoots have developed, delays the plant's progress until new leaves form and fast growth resumes. Wait until the plant is about one month old before clipping its top.

Pruning During Flowering

Under sunlight, you can expect to harvest a plant with strong colas on every branch, rather than one large top cola and much smaller branch colas, if you clip the top growing shoot about two weeks before flowering. Under weaker electric light, removing the top shoot may result in smaller buds and possibly a smaller harvest. Don't use late pruning as a general procedure under artificial lights, except as a last resort when one or two plants are outgrowing the rest of the crop. These fast-growing plants prevent the light from being positioned closer to all the plant tops. Bending and training these tallest plants is the best procedure.

When the plants first start to flower, clip off the lowest, under-developed branches. These branches won't bear worthwhile buds anyway, and by removing them, the stem and root system feed only

Figure 98. You can tie plants in a horizontal position during flowering to keep them below the top of a fence. The colas will grow upward and in a line along the stem.

the stronger branches, which consequently yield larger buds. Removing lower branches also allows reflected light to better illuminate the whole plant and promotes better air circulation.

Once the buds begin to form, remove some of the large fan leaves along the main stem. This allows the light to reach the lower buds and they'll develop more fully. Don't overdo it; once a leaf forms it produces more "growth energy" for the rest of the plant. If you strip a plant of its leaves, you're lessening its capacity for growth. Removing most of the healthy leaves also can delay flowering. In an outdoor plot, plants stripped of leaves flowered two weeks later than their sisters that were left intact. Under lights, remove only some upper mainstem fan leaves that shade the lower branches.

Chapter 16

Control of Insects and Pests

An indoor or greenhouse garden is an artificial habitat. For this reason, your plants may never experience the insect infestations that outdoor plants naturally undergo. For this same reason, once contaminated, indoor plants are particularly susceptible to the ravages of almost any infestation since they do not have wind, rain, cold, and natural predators to help them withstand the onslaught.

The insects that infect marijuana indoors do best in a warm, stagnant atmosphere. A constant stream of moving air that draws fresh air from inside and vents air to the outside helps immeasurably in preventing initial infestations. Adequate and continuous ventilation also helps prevent the establishment of fungus and rot diseases.

Never cultivate houseplants in your marijuana garden, and never go from caring for houseplants or garden vegetables to your marijuana garden, because you or your pet may transport the problem insect or disease. Whiteflies and spider mites — the two most devastating insects — are extremely contagious. Mites may gain entry to the garden on your hands or clothing, or on your pet's fur. Pests may float through open windows, or they may crawl through cracks in walls or floors.

Young marijuana plants are most vulnerable to pest attacks before the plant has begun strong production of the cannabinoids, which are natural deterrents to disease and insects. The younger the plants, the more devastating an infestation might be, not only because the plants are small, but also because an infestation may stay with the plants for the rest of their lives. Even though mites and whiteflies won't kill the plants outright, they do weaken them, and the plants become more susceptible to fungus and rot diseases. If you discover mites or whiteflies, you may choose to induce flowering immediately so that the plants ripen before the infestation does serious damage.

Once a grow room has had pests, before starting any new crop, employ foggers or bug bombs intended for fleas and roaches (available from any supermarket or veterinarian). Foggers kill just about everything that crawls, and since no plants are yet in the room, they're safe to use according to package directions. Siphotrol, from a veterinarian, works very well and has residual killing power that lasts for up to 17 weeks.

Prevention is the best policy, since after infestation you might only contain the attack rather than completely eradicate the pests. Most insecticides that promise to rid your garden of pests rarely destroy all of the pests and eggs. You'll probably notice that after a few weeks pests are still present. Special problems occur near major farm areas. After years of ever-increasing applications of pesticides, insects develop resistance to sprays that would be effective in other locales. For example, whiteflies and mites are very difficult to treat effectively in cotton-growing areas, such as California's Imperial Valley and in Louisiana because years of constant spraying have left only the resistant strains. Prevention or containment measures will prove more effective than insecticidal sprays.

There are several insecticides recommended to control the pests described here. All of them require that you spray **regularly and repeatedly** to have any chance of actually ridding your garden of the targeted pest. Repeat the sprayings at the recommended intervals several times, even if you don't see any more pests, because egg and certain pupae stages are resistant to any insecticide; otherwise the pests soon reappear in abundance.

It's also a good idea to add a drop or two of liquid dishwashing DETERGENT to each quart of insecticide spray. Detergent is a wetting agent which helps the insecticide penetrate marijuana's "hairy" leaves, and the insecticide better contacts the underlying leaf surfaces and the pests. There are other sprays not listed here that might be effective against a particular pest. When you are searching for an appropriate spray, notice that the insecticide package lists the pests controlled. Make sure that the spray is intended for **vegetables (human consumption), and note the number of days after spraying to wait before you can safely use your product.** Don't use a spray that is intended solely for ornamentals since the ingredients may never break down into harmless substances. Whenever you spray, plan a major attack. Wear old clothes, goggles, a painter's mask, hat and gloves. Turn off the lights and fans and give yourself room to move. Raise the light system as high as possible out of the way of the spray. Allow time for the bulbs to cool before spraying and make sure the bulbs are dry before turning them back on.

First, discard heavily infested leaves and remove them from the garden. Close all doors and windows and start at the back of the garden so you work your way out to the exit. Spray thoroughly, and spray enough to drench all parts of the plants. Pay special attention to the undersides of leaves, where insects and larvae usually congregate. Remove clothing for washing, and shower. Repeat the spraying at least two more times at the intervals recommended on the pesticide's directions. Thoroughly spraying at the recommended intervals is the only chance of eliminating pests or at least curtailing a major infestation. Any pests that survive may reproduce a new population that's worse than the first. A haphazard spraying leads only to frustration and claims that the spray doesn't work. Follow the manufacturer's directions.

The insecticides recommended in the rest of this chapter are given in order of preference for the targeted pest.

Aphids, Mites, Whiteflies and Other Pests

Aphids, mites, and whiteflies are the most common and potentially devastating of pests indoors. You should be able to eradicate or at least reduce the population of aphids to the point that they no longer pose a serious threat.

Aphids are the most common, especially outdoors or in green-houses. Fortunately, they're also easy to kill and eliminate. Aphids are soft-bodied, ovoid insects with antennae, and they may be from pinhead to match head in size. They may or may not have wings. Aphids may be pink to black, but on marijuana aphids are usually green or black. Infested leaves or shoots might be distorted, curled, or crinkled. Aphids are parthenogenic (they can produce offspring without fertilization from a male), and proliferate in enormous numbers if left unchecked.

Aphids initially congregate on growing shoots and on undersides of younger leaves where they're easily visible and accessible. Start your eradication program by simply running your fingers over the shoots to crush the aphids. Or, take each plant outside or to a bathtub, and wash the aphids away with a forceful stream of water before spraying with an insecticide.

If a column of ants is running up the stem, then the aphid population is well-established and is being managed by an ant colony. You must rid the grow room of both the aphids and the ants, because ants use aphids like we use milking cows. Ants carry aphids to other plants and harvest their honeydew excretions. Set out standard ant traps or other ant-control concoctions from any supermarket. These contain a poison sugar solution that the ants transport back to their nest. It will take a few days to a week, but soon they'll disappear since the whole colony dies from eating the poison (commercial ant poisons are usually arsenic or very slow-degrading organic toxins). Don't put ant traps in your pots. **Don't ever let the poison wash into your soil.** Place the traps near the ants' entrance to room, or as far from your garden as practical. Eliminating the ants stops them from further spreading the aphids, and from bringing new aphids into the garden and reinfecting the plants. Follow the column of ants, and seal their entry into the room. Or place cardboard collars around the stem of each plant and spread Tanglefoot (a sticky substance sold in garden shops) on the collars to stop the ants from spreading the aphids. You might also circle each pot with masking tape and cover the tape with Tanglefoot. This prevents almost any crawler from reaching other plants.

Aphids are one of the few insect problems that soapy water treatments reasonably control. A thorough washing with a soapy solution of Ivory soap reduces the population to acceptable proportions on seedlings. A better, non-chemical control is a spray made from three hot peppers (or cayenne powder), an onion or two, and a couple of cloves of garlic. Grind, pulverize, or mash the ingredients. Let them sit in two quarts of water for a few days and occasionally shake the mixture. Filter the solution through a very fine mesh screen, or several layers of cheesecloth. Use a coffee filter if the solution clogs your sprayer. Add a few drops of detergent and spray as you would an insecticide. This spray works very well outdoors, and the aphids seem to gladly seek greener, or perhaps cooler, pastures. This spray also helps with almost any other pest. Try it if you want to avoid using chemical pesticides, but don't use it close to harvest.

Supermarkets, nurseries, and plant shops carry a number of sprays that eliminate aphids. **Pyrethrum** is a natural insecticide produced by plants in the *Chrysanthemum* family. It's not toxic to mammals (you), and it quickly degrades to harmless natural compounds. Pyrethrum compounds are the insecticides of choice for many growers, because of their safety, natural origin, and effectiveness. Ortho, Chacon, Attack, and many other brands of pyrethrum sprays or general insecticides for vegetable gardens should be very effective for a wide range of problem insects.

Malathion, orthene, diazinon, nicotine-sulphates, and other safe-to-use insecticides are also effective against aphids. **Safer Insecticidal Soap**, sprayed every ten days, controls aphids well.

Make sure you repeat the sprayings and thoroughly saturate all of the plant at the recommended intervals.

Mites and whiteflies proliferate quickly, and both have a lifecycle that makes complete eradication difficult. If you keep their populations under control, you have succeeded in your main objective.

Mites are tiny (about 1/100th to 1/16th of an inch) crab or spider-like creatures that may be black, red, green, or yellow (usually they're part black and part transparent). Probably you'll first notice that the **top surfaces of lower leaves have speckles** — tiny white or yellow specks caused by the mites sucking plant juices. Look up to the light through a damaged leaf, and you might see transparent specks from mite damage, or black specks, which are the mites. Poke them with your finger, and they'll run away (you now know that, sadly, you have a problem). One mite, the *eriaphyid* mite (*Acrilops cannabicola*) is specific to *Cannabis*. If the infestation is well-established, you'll see spider **webbing** at the crooks of branches and leaf stalks. By this time you're in real trouble, and if the plants are nearing maturity, just try to keep the damage to a minimum before harvesting.

Orthene is the most effective; it and diazinon, malathion, and pyrethrum sprays are the only reasonably effective and safe sprays

Figure 99. The head of a match dwarfs tiny spider mites.

Figure 100. Mites appear as black specks when you look up to the lights through the undersides of the leaves.

to use. Kelthane, which works well against mites, is harmful to the environment, and to you, and is not recommended. Diazinon, pyrethrum, and malathion sprays might work if you are not in a major agricultural area. In such areas, where the mites have become resistant, they're useless.

Spray at seven day intervals at least three times. Don't spray if you're within three weeks of harvest. Washing the plants with soap is not worth the hassle. Soapy sprays work well for some plants, but with mites on marijuana, they don't help much at all. Mites are protected by marijuana's "hairy" or cystolith-covered leaves. No soap or water remedy for mites on marijuana seems to work effectively, even when used with detergent penetrants.

To prevent mites, periodically spray your plants with fresh water. Mites like a dry, stagnant environment. In several grow rooms, a twice-weekly spray of fresh water to the undersides of all leaves helps significantly in preventing mite infestations to all plants, including marijuana. A vent-fan or directed fan also helps prevent initial contamination. Spraying the undersides of leaves periodically with water, and keeping the air in your room moving are the best non-insecticidal procedures to use if you anticipate a possible mite attack.

For infested gardens, lowering the temperature slows down the mites more than it affects the growth of the plants. Lower the temperature at night (open windows) to slow the mites' life cycle. Lowering the temperature and spraying with water are both helpful if you're nearing harvest and don't want to use insecticides.

If you discover that only one or two plants have mites, remove them from the garden, or move them to the garden's periphery so that their leaves don't contact another plant's leaves. Encircle all pots with a band of masking tape or surround the lower stem with a cardboard collar. Cover the tape or collar with a layer of Tanglefoot or heavyweight motor oil. The sticky barrier captures mites and stops their spread to other plants.

One worthwhile treatment for mites, and almost any other insect is a fogger generally used for fleas and roaches. These "bug bombs" are very effective, but possibly poisonous on plants you intend to ingest. In fact, use them only in the seedling or vegetative stages of growing if other insecticides haven't worked.

Holiday Fogger seems to work the best, probably because its concentration of active ingredients is relatively mild compared to other foggers, such as Hartz, Ortho, or Germain's and other concentrated foggers which can damage the plants. Close all ventilation to

Figure 101. *Left:* A spider mite through a microscope (x16). *Right:* This mealybug (center) is 1/20th of an inch long.

the room and place the fogger so that it doesn't directly contact the plants. Raise a bedsheet or newspapers above the plants to protect them from direct contact with the spray (these foggers actually spray the insecticide rather than creating a fog). Don't enclose the plants; just position the protective sheet so that droplets don't land directly on the plants; then follow package directions. One or two deployments of **foggers can completely eliminate mites** and anything else that crawls in your garden. After seven to ten days repeat the fogger treatment for best results. Foggers and **systemic** treatments may be your best options for dealing with mites. They're useful for seedlings, but don't use them if your plants are flowering.

Whiteflies are white (you probably guessed that), but they're not flies; they're small moths about a tenth of an inch long. You'll see the adults fluttering erratically about the garden anytime you disturb the plants. Eggs, pupae, nymphs, and tiny honey-like balls of adult excretions dot the undersides of leaves. You can eliminate many of the larvae by running your fingers along the undersides of the leaves, and by disposing of heavily infested leaves altogether. Whiteflies also attract ants, but ants don't "cultivate" whiteflies the way they do aphids. As with all insects, if you want to "search and destroy" them, lower the temperature in your grow room, which makes any insect sluggish.

Control whiteflies by spraying with **diazinon**, malathion, orthene, or pyrethrum sprays. Spray at six to eight-day intervals, particularly on the undersides of the leaves. Wash the plants with soap (Ivory flakes), to help lower the general population, but this is a pain if the plants are beyond the seedling stage. Try one of the other treatments suggested here. If you don't want to use a chemical insecticide, maintain population control by spraying weekly with Safer soap, and by hanging sticky attractor cards that are available at nurseries, and by vacuuming the adults.

Whitefly Attack is one commercial brand of attractor card that captures the adults. These sticky cards act like flypaper, and the color of the cards attracts whiteflies, gnats, leaf hoppers, and flying aphids. Bright yellow-green or yellow-orange color attracts white-flies. The yellow-orange color is similar to the color of Kodak film envelopes and boxes. Cover any facsimile (Kodak slide boxes, card-board painted yellow, etc.), with either a very heavy motor oil, or Tanglefoot. Hang the colored cards or fly paper near the plant tops and periodically shake the plants. Adult whiteflies land on the cards and stick to the tacky surface. These cards won't eliminate the problem but they do help to curtail a population explosion.

Figure 102. *Left:* Close-up of an adult whitefly next to unopened male flowers. *Right:* Close-up of a whitefly infestation on the underside of a leaf blade. The shiny "balls" are the whitefly excretions that attract ants.

Also very helpful for whiteflies and any other flying insects is a vacuum cleaner. Yes, vacuuming does help. Simply shake each plant vigorously, which should force the adults to take to the air, and you can suck them up like an undersea monster out of *Yellow Submarine*. Then vacuum the undersides of leaves. You won't completely rid the garden of pests, but especially if you're nearing harvest, this is a worthwhile control.

Mealybugs are white, about 1/8" long, and look like small, fuzzy, white sowbugs. Once mealybugs are well-established, you might see cotton-like or wooly materials or "tents" at the crooks of branches, or where a leaf stalk meets a branch. Marijuana is not a mealybug's favorite plant, and it's easy to eliminate them, or at least reduce their population to nondetrimental proportions.

Kill mealybugs with a cotton swab dipped in standard rubbing alcohol — seek and saturate each bug or cottony mass. **Diazinon,** nicotine-sulphate, orthene, and malathion are all effective and safe insecticidal controls for mealybugs if the "search and destroy" procedure with alcohol doesn't control the pest.

Scale insects encase themselves in a waxy or hardened protective covering in the adult stages. They're about 1/12" to 1/6" long. The adult females are brown and stationary, and they establish themselves along stems and large branches, but the larval stages move about the plant. Check along the stems, where you may see a hardened, brown protrusion, or what looks like a blemish or raised node clinging tightly to the stem, which contains an adult.

Scale infestations are seldom serious, but if they appear when the plant is young, you'll want to eliminate them. **Diazinon,** malathion, orthene, or a number of oil-based general plant sprays should eliminate the pests. Scale proliferates slowly, making control or elimination with alcohol on a cotton swab touched to each pest a leisurely task. You can also scrape them off with a sharp knife. The hand/scrape or alcohol method works well enough for minor infestations if you watch carefully and keep after them.

Leaf Hoppers. If you've ever had an outdoor garden, you've probably seen leaf hoppers. Usually they're green with red stripes and about one-half inch long, although they also come in other colors or color combinations. Leaf hoppers shouldn't be an indoor problem, but if you see many of them, take the time to spray with **pyrethrum,** malathion, or diazinon before any serious problem occurs. Two thorough sprayings with any of these insecticides should eliminate leaf hoppers. Yellow hanging cards with a sticky coating, or vacuuming, also helps in small gardens.

Flea beetles are tiny, black, beetle-like creatures that jump like fleas. They generally attack only flowers, and rarely appear on marijuana. One treatment with a **diazinon** or malathion spray should rid the garden of flea beetles.

Figure 103. Leaf hoppers are very common in outdoor gardens. Don't worry about them unless there are many.

Thrips are speck-sized insects which shouldn't be a problem. Thrips are more insect-like than flea beetles, and with a close look you'll see their wings. To check for thrips, spread white paper below the plant and jar the plant repeatedly. You should see tiny, shiny, black specks if thrips are present. **Orthene** or malathion sprayed twice, one week apart, should eliminate all of the thrips. Flea beetles and thrips only occasionally invade a marijuana garden and neither pest should be a serious problem.

Caterpillar is a general term for many larvae of moths and butterflies. They have enormous appetites and the first sign of their presence is that portions of leaves will be eaten. Some caterpillars take on the color of the host plant, and therefore are hard to spot. The "hunt and destroy" method is effective if you take the time to search them out. Some caterpillars naturally gravitate to the more succulent shoots; so first look along the stem of the top growing shoots. Orthene and diazinon are effective killers of most caterpillars. For long-term control, repeated spraying with *Bacillus thuringiensis* (a beneficial bacteria) prevents and eliminates caterpillars, and many other larval or grub problems. If you find leaves with portions eaten but can't find the caterpillars, wait a few hours after the lights have gone off. Turn the lights back on, and you'll probably find these nighttime feeders near the tops of the plants.

Ants and termites are major problems only when the plants are rooted in the ground. Any decaying matter such as composts or manures attracts both pests. If they are a problem, avoid the use of composts, humus, and manures in future crops. Pull out any old stumps in the planting bed. The best preventative is to mix some **cedar chips** into your planting mixture, or for outdoor growers, to mix the chips throughout the planting bed. This procedure works very well in repelling termites, which may eat into the main stem. Simply flooding the bed repeatedly may drive termites away. Or buy Arab termite control to rid any garden of termites. It's safe to use, and doesn't harm the plants.

Ants also present problems by damaging roots or woody parts of the stem. Ants also may encourage aphid problems. Standard ant traps, ant stakes, or ant poisons are completely effective in eliminating all ant problems indoors. Or surround the base of the stem with a cardboard collar. Cover the collar with Tanglefoot or a heavy-weight motor oil.

Earwigs, sowbugs, gnats, and any other insect living in the soil can be controlled by a **rotenone soil drench**. Two applications should eradicate all pests. All of these soil-borne insects prefer and thrive in soils rich in composts, humus, and other organic materials.

Usually they're fairly harmless, and only a moderate nuisance. However, earwigs and sowbugs may eat and kill germinating sprouts, and many soil pests eat roots. Get rid of them unless you're nearing harvest.

Mice and rats may eat seeds and shoots and hence, devastate a newly planted garden. Most problems with mice and rats occur in autumn or winter, because rodents come indoors to escape the cold.

If you've had a problem, the surest protection is to surround the plants with window screening or another barrier. Once plants are past the seedling stage, mice are not a problem, but rats may eat shoots or strip away layers of the stem (cambium layer), which can kill the plant. Repellents sold for rodent control and numerous poisons available from supermarkets and hardware stores should work well enough. **Be careful with rat poisons. Some can kill pets and people too. Keep poisons away from the plants; never let water wash over the poisons and run into your soil.** Mothballs laid in the perimeter of the garden are purported to repel rodents. Set up a barrier or enclosure for the surest way to protect precious seeds.

Figure 104. Rats may strip the outer part of the stem (cambium layer) which will kill the plant. *Photo by A. Karger.*

Figure 105. *Left:* This grower encircled the stems with chicken wire to protect against rats and woodchucks. *Right:* Open both ends of tin cans and place them over seedlings to protect against cutworms. The can is painted so as not to reflect light to overflying aircraft.

Cats and dogs. Don't rely on training your pets to stay out of the garden. Dogs may dig or eliminate into the soil. Soil is more natural to a cat's instincts than a kitty-litter tray, and the jungle ambience of marijuana gardens is irresistible to most cats. Cats and some dogs also love to chew on leaves, and they can easily destroy young plants. Devise a cat-and-dog-proof barrier before you plant. Once the plants are larger, your cats will spend hours in the garden, and an occasional munching of a leaf causes no harm.

In General

Aphids, mealybugs, mites, scale, whiteflies, thrips, flea beetles, leaf hoppers, cutworms, cabbage worms, leaf miners, and many other insects and grub or larval pests are susceptible to diazinon, pyrethrums, orthene, or malathion. Alternating one insecticide (diazinon or orthene) with another (pyrethrums or malathion) works better than repeated sprayings with only one insecticide. Pests often build up resistance in agricultural areas, and you should try several sprays if the first isn't working.

Liquid Sevin also kills almost any insect or bug, but it's extremely toxic to beneficial insects, bees, and fish. Use Liquid Sevin only if other sprays are ineffective.

Rotenone is a general, natural insecticide derived from the roots of the flame tree and other legumes. Although quite effective against a wide range of insects, rotenone is particularly useful against caterpillars in a spray or dust form, and as a soil **drench against sowbugs, gnats, and other soil-borne insects.**

Safer Insecticidal Soap kills and controls aphids, mealy bugs and root mealy bugs, scale, spider mites, thrips, whiteflies, leaf hoppers, and many other problem insects. Safer soap is very popular with growers. Use up to one week before harvest. Be sure to protect eyes when spraying!

Systemic insecticides are applied while watering. The insecticide is absorbed and distributed throughout the plant. Systemics are especially lethal to all pests that suck plant juices or chew leaves, and they're **an excellent preventative** for all the insects described in this chapter. Systemics might be your best choice for controlling mites and whiteflies. If you have had previous problems with mites or whiteflies, try applying a systemic when the plants are young, before you see any pests. Repeat the application one month later.

Many systemics are intended solely for ornamentals, since they do not break down into harmless by-products quickly. Make sure that the systemic you choose is intended for use on edible crops, and note the number of days before harvest when you should stop using the systemic. The average time between the last application and harvest is about 30 days. Dexol Houseplant Insecticide is one safe brand, among many, that you can use.

Biological Controls

Biological controls are most effective in growing rooms that are ongoing, that is, continuously growing. Biological controls introduce either a predator that hunts and eats your problem insect, or a pathogenic disease that infects the pests. Predators don't eliminate the pest but they keep the population under control, so that the crop is not seriously damaged.

Pathogenic controls (bacteria that kill the pest) can completely eliminate a pest, and they're most useful in greenhouses and outdoor plots, but you can use them indoors. If you have an ongoing, large growing room, outdoor plot, or greenhouse, you should look into biological controls. In a typical home garden, biological controls are often no more than an added expense with marginal results, but in a greenhouse, they can be very helpful.

Cutworms, cucumber beetle larvae, tomato hornworms, cabbage worms, and almost all borers, grubs, caterpillars, and other harmful larvae can be quite devastating. Usually they're a serious problem only in outdoor plots and greenhouses where cultivation is repeated year after year, and especially if the plants are rooted in the ground. Often the pest's life cycle includes a soil-borne larval or grub stage that emerges from the ground where the pest over-winters. The pest may then eat roots, or bore into stems or branches, thus killing the infected plant, or plant part. Once you see that some of your plants have been infected with borers, make sure you use a preventative spray of *Bacillus thuringiensis* for succeeding crops; otherwise the problem progressively worsens each season, and might devastate your next crop.

If you see a branch dying on an otherwise healthy plant, a borer probably has invaded the branch. Look for a swollen, discolored area on the branch surrounding a small hole. Cut off any dying branches, since they won't recover. If the branch is still growing well but you've found a hole, inject mineral oil with a large-bore syringe. This smothers the borer or forces it out, where direct revenge is swift and sweet.

Two products, Seek and the bacteria *Bacillus thuringiensis*, are completely safe to use, don't harm animals, earthworms, beneficial insects, or you, and both will rid a garden of borers and caterpillars, or at least knock their population down to acceptable levels.

B. thuringiensis is best used as a preventative spray if any borers or grubs were present in the former crop. These bacteria parasitize and kill a wide variety of garden larvae or caterpillars in the grub, borer, or wormlike stage. Many companies offer this product, which is diluted and sprayed like an insecticide at approximately two-week intervals. Dipel, Thuricide, and Attack are three brands, but any product that lists *Bacillus thuringiensis* as the active agent will work just fine.

A new product, Seek (The Nematode Farm, 3335 Birch St., Palo Alto, CA, 94305) can be used as a preventative or applied during an infestation, and early results have been promising. Cutworms, Japanese beetle grubs, wireworms, white grubs, and corn borers are among the 250 or more insect pests (larval or wormlike stage) that are susceptible. Apply Seek in a preventative mulch or inject it directly into channels, tunnels, or other borer holes to kill established pests.

Lacewings, when they can be encouraged to stay and reproduce in a greenhouse, work fairly well for a biological control. Lacewing larvae eat a number of pests, including aphids, mites, mealybugs, and a number of problem "worms", including budworms and corn earworms.

Aphids. One effective predator for home or greenhouse situations is the larvae of the green lacewing. Ladybugs (*Hippodamia*) are often recommended but rarely stay around long enough to be of any real help. Ladybugs are said to stay around when released in the cool of the evening and if prey are present. Introducing ladybugs may be a wasted effort and expense for the home gardener. Because of their lifecycle, ladybugs must be fed a special diet that awakens their reproductive instincts so that they feed and reproduce when released. You also need an ongoing garden with an appealing habitat. Look for insectary distributors that advertise this *preconditioned feeding,* otherwise ladybugs are useless.

Whiteflies. *Encarsia* wasps are tiny wasps (that don't sting or bite) that parasitize whiteflies. They're best used when released consistently in an ongoing grow room where whiteflies are a constant problem. The garden must be at least 64 degrees for *Encarsia* to be effective. Release at least twelve per plant at two-week intervals.

Biological controls also include repellents. Interplanting marigolds and garlic among plants in outdoor or greenhouse plots discourages many insects from invading the garden. The Peruvian Ground Cherry (*Nicandra physalodes*) is very effective for greenhouses in which you anticipate a whitefly problem. Scatter a few *Nicandra* plants inside the greenhouse to repel any initial whitefly invasion. (A complete review of companion planting for outdoor growers is detailed in the *Marijuana Grower's Guide Complete Edition,* Red Eye Press, 1989.)

Mites. Control spider mites naturally by releasing predatory spider mites during the peak infestation periods of the summer months, or any time an indoor grow room has a mite problem. It helps mite predators if the temperature in the grow room is moderate rather than hot. Don't expect the release of predators to clean up a thoroughly infested garden. Predators reduce, but don't eliminate the prey.

Three predatory mites for control of prey mites are *Metaseiulus oxidentalis, Phytoseiulus persimilis,* and *Amblyseius californius.* (Order the first two from Rincon-Vitova, Oakview, CA 805/643-5407. Several other species of predatory mites are also available through mail order.) Try two species at a time, to find which is most effective.

Lacewings are also an effective biological control for mites. Try both lacewings and mites to determine which can live and be helpful in your particular garden.

Before releasing predatory mites, always wash the leaves or at least give a heavy misting to remove some of the dust. Dust gets in the way of predatory mites in their search for prey. Bring small plants to the shower for a thorough washing after covering the top of the pot with a layer of aluminum foil.

Fungal Diseases

Because *Cannabis* is not native to the Americas, few diseases that specifically attack marijuana are present in this country. *Cannabis* is remarkably free of microbial diseases, with the exception of certain fungal diseases. Fungal stem and root rots are fairly common. Shot-hole leaf rusts and *Botrytis* grey fungus rot are the most common microbial diseases of consequence.

Fungal stem and root rots occur mainly because of improper care. Watering too often coupled with a warm, stagnant, and humid atmosphere, is the main problem. Stem rot appears as a

Figure 106. A cola covered with *Botrytis* fungus, commonly referred to as bud rot. On the surface is a grey, wispy cover and the inside of the bud is a mushy black.

brown or black discoloration at the base of the stem, and it's soft or mushy to the touch. Allow **the soil to dry** between waterings, and be sure to water around the stem rather than directly on the stem. Wipe away as much diseased tissue as possible. Dust the stem with a sulfur dust. Treat the stem with a fungicide if the rot reappears.

Bud rot is the most devastating microbial problem that you might confront. The worst problem is from *Botrytis*, a grey fungus that rapidly destroys buds. You might first discover *Botrytis* when you notice a grey or yellow leaf blade sticking out of an otherwise healthy bud. Tug on the blade and if it comes out easily, and is soft and mushy at its base, you know that you have some form of rot. Open the bud to see if it's slimy and black inside. Once the disease advances, whole colas can be covered in a day or two with a grey, wispy cover before they turn a mushy black.

Simply reducing humidity and increasing air flow throughout the garden helps immeasurably. Ortho Multi-purpose Fungicide Daconil 2787 controls many molds and rusts, including *Botrytis*. **A combination of Ortho Funginex with True-Ban (Mallinckrodt Co., St. Louis, Mo.), will control all rot,** including any rot that may attack flowering buds. True-Ban is a liquid systemic fungicide that must be applied very early in growth, preferably during transplanting; otherwise it's ineffective.

If rot has been a problem in the past, spray any fungicide several times during growth, up to just before flowering, and even if you don't yet see rot. Prespraying allows the fungicide a chance to work and prevents the initial growth of fungi. Most fungicides can't penetrate thick buds, they won't kill the sea of fungal spores, and their application during flowering may not help at all.

Once you detect rot you must act quickly. Cut out all diseased tissue immediately (it's still smokeable if dried quickly). Mix two teaspoons of liquid bleach to each cup of water (about a six percent solution), and spray all diseased areas. The bleach solution only marginally forestalls the spread of the fungus, but it's helpful. Keep the atmosphere as dry as possible, and set up fans to keep the air moving. Set the fans to direct strong airflow directly on all of the plants. Use oscillating fans to cover large gardens. **Fans help more than most fungicides during flowering,** and they might eliminate the fungus altogether, especially when coupled with a bleach spray or a fungicide.

Some growers stop fertilizing with nitrogen during flowering since they want the buds to be less green at harvest; but any dead or dying (yellowed) leaf is an invitation for fungi to initiate infection. *Botrytis* may attack healthy tissue, but not as readily as yellow

Figure 107. A heavy dew each morning during flowering helped rot destroy this plant in less than a week. The leaves look fine but every cola is completely rotted. Growers should harvest all good-sized colas at the first sign of rot in order to save a large crop. Just harvest colas, not whole plants.

or dying tissue. For all rot problems, it's imperative that you keep the garden clear of dead and fallen leaves.

If you've had rot problems before, make sure you remove all yellowing leaves and keep the plants a healthy green by fertilizing with nitrogen — better to have green buds than rotted buds. Drench the plants completely several times with a general fungicide (such as Ortho Daconil 2787) well before flowering to have any chance of preventing rot; it's safe and effective to use, particularly when sprayed several times prior to flowering.

The fungicide captan has been recommended for controlling rot on marijuana. Captan has been found to cause cancer in laboratory animals, and if it hasn't been banned by the time you read this book, it should be. **The use of captan is strongly discouraged.**

Leaf-spot fungi may cause red, brown, or yellow spots on leaves and occasionally on the stems. The diseased spots may fall away or disintegrate leaving a hole ("shot hole") in the leaf. This condition appears only in a warm and humid grow room on plants that are deficient in nitrogen. Arrest the disease by fertilizing with nitrogen, decreasing humidity, and increasing air flow or ventilation. After taking these measures, watch for the development of new spots. If the disease is still progressing, use a general fungicide, which should end the problem. Check the label to see that the fungicide is effective against "leaf spot" or "shot hole" disease.

Green slime on pots or soil surfaces indicates too frequent watering, poor soil drainage, too frequent fertilizing, or an acidic water supply. The slime (algae) is not a problem, but the presence of green slime can foretell eventual problems. **Stop watering so frequently.** Wait until at least three inches of topsoil are dry. Add hydrated or dolomitic lime at the rate of of one teaspoon per quart of water, each time you water, for a couple of weeks. Wipe the algae away, and it shouldn't reappear.

Part VI
Flowering

Chapter 17

Preflowering: Is it Male or Female?

Female marijuana plants are more desirable than males. Females form the familiar flower clusters (buds) that ordinarily make up the marijuana most of us buy. The female buds are the desired crop; not only are buds the most potent part of either male or female plants, they make up most of the weight of any good crop.

It is to the grower's advantage to separate the females from the males as soon as possible. Although the male's leaves and shoots are as potent as the female's before flowering, they can't compare to the matured female's buds in potency or in weight. The male's main function in nature, and in marijuana growing, is to provide pollen (genetic material) for the fertilization of the females and the continuance and hopeful "improvement" of the next generation when breeding.

The most common scenario in a marijuana garden is for the grower to identify the males as soon as possible and to harvest most of them when they begin to crowd the females. A few select males are kept to produce pollen to fertilize females in a breeding program. If you want your garden to be sinsemilla, you must remove all males before any of their flowers open. Well-seeded buds are less potent and smaller than sinsemilla buds. You can place males in a moderately lit spare room or window, and they will mature and grow enough to produce an abundance of pollen, more than enough for any breeding program.

During the first six to eight weeks of growth (seedling stage), it's practically impossible to discover the gender of any plant when it's raised under a long daylight photoperiod. Later in growth, female plants generally form more complex branching than the males, and males may be taller. These differences in height and branching are less apparent in weaker light; so your best indications come under sunlight. The most insignificant differences are under low light, such as under a modest, fluorescent light garden.

After at least eight, and usually by 12 weeks of growth, plants commonly indicate their gender to observant growers, who can identify their preflowers. The preflowers become more distinctive and easy to identify the closer the plant comes to actually flowering.

Preflowers on young plants and plants grown under low-light may be difficult to distinguish. Under HID's or sunlight, preflowers are larger and more distinctive, and the predetermination of sex is often completely accurate. Even under low light, you can identify the sex of any plant after you've gained experience. Once you've identified or guessed a plant's sex, mark the plant with a wire twist, soil marker, or whatever means you devise that's easy to see and remember. With some experience, you'll learn from your mistakes, and you'll be able to identify the sex of each plant with confidence.

Sexing the Plants

After the plants are at least eight weeks old, look closely (a magnifying glass or photographer's loupe helps) at the junction (node) where the main stem meets with leaf stalks and branches. About two or three nodes below the plant's top, near the base of the main stem's leaf stalks, and just behind the leaf spurs (stipules), you might see a rudimentary flower (preflower). In the best of cases you'll see a single, well-formed female flower with the familiar two white stigmas raised in a "V" sign. If you see a female flower at each internode at two or three successive internodes, this plant is certainly a female. Commonly, you'll see the base of a female flower, a well-formed bract, with no stigmas. If you're experienced, you'll be able to identify this preflower and the fact that the plant is a female, at least 90 percent of the time.

The male preflower is much harder to positively identify. A male preflower rarely opens but remains a tightly closed knob or a flat, spade-shaped protrusion raised on a **stalk** that characteristically identifies the male flower. **Often the vegetative overlap of the male preflower superficially looks like a female flower.**

Once you've learned the difference between male and female preflowers, you'll find enough prospective preflowers to remove most males weeks before they actually flower. The accompanying photographs should start you on your way to an accurate indentification almost every time. Novices shouldn't harvest every plant that looks like it might be a male. You'll probably find that you've mistaken the gender of several plants. Marking each plant or pot with its presumptive sex is the only way to learn from your mistakes. After a while, by rechecking the preflowers of your mistakes, you'll gain accuracy and confidence, and soon master the procedure.

Figure 108. Look closely at the juncture of the stem, growing shoots, and leaf stalks on the main stem. On these close-up pictures, what looks like branches are actually the leaf stalks on the main stem. There are two stipules that look like the blade of a knife at each junction. Nestled at the base of the stipule is where you'll find the preflowers. *Top left:* Classic male preflower is flat and spade-shaped with a tiny stalk. *Top right:* The vegetative overlap of this form of male preflowers often fool even experienced growers. With a quick look, their tips may appear like a female stigma. *Center:* The third form of a male preflower is a tiny knob raised on a stalk. *Bottom left:* The usual form of a female preflower is a single female flower with a bract from which protrudes two white stigmas (which look like fuzzy white hairs, often in a "V" sign). *Bottom right:* Don't mistake a female flower bract like this one that has no stigmas for a male preflower.

Other Procedures for Sexing the Plants

Outdoor gardeners can take advantage of the results of a 40 year old experiment to discover with certainty, the sex of each plant. This experiment found that the flowering hormone that induces marijuana to flower is locally produced, that is, each part of the plant produces the hormone (phytochrome), and the hormone is not translocated (transferred or moved) throughout the plant.

Once decent-sized branches develop, cover a lower branch on each plant with an opaque (light-tight) paper bag or sleeve (not plastic because the branch must breathe). A double layer of black construction paper or a cardboard mailing tube are two possibilities. Close the end at the branch tip, but **leave a small opening** of the paper sleeve or tube at the other end. After about ten to 14 days you should see flowers developing on the covered branch. The rest of the plant continues to grow normally, with no slowing of overall growth. This procedure works best for outdoor growers, because the plants have a longer life, and branching is better outdoors than indoors. You might start your seeds in March, cover a branch in May, and know before June the sex of every plant. Indoors, branches don't form well enough, and the crop doesn't usually have enough time for this procedure to have any real value.

Indoor gardeners sometimes turn the light cycle down to 12 hours to induce flowering on two-week-old seedlings. After about two more weeks, all of the seedlings will have shown their sex, and the light cycle is lengthened to resume vegetative growth. The only problem with this procedure is that it slightly delays overall development, as the plant must switch from growth to flowering and back to growth again. It's better to practice identifying preflowers, and after a couple of crops you'll do just fine. This procedure however, is very useful especially to outdoor growers who start their plants indoors under lights. They can start seedlings and grow them for only a month; yet they'll be able to transplant only month-old females to their outdoor plot.

Use this text and the photographs on preflowering to get started on identifying both male and female preflowers. With some experience, most growers become adept at identifying gender well before the plants actually flower. Identifying preflowers is the best procedure for predetermining sex, and it's a valuable skill that's useful in all indoor and outdoor growing situations.

Chapter 18

Marijuana Flowers

Marijuana is dioecious: which means each plant normally bears either male or female flowers and is considered either a male or a female plant. Normally about one-half the plants are female and one-half are male. Marijuana gender is determined somewhat the same as gender is in humans. Males have an X and a Y sex chromosome; females have two X sex chromosomes.

There are many variations on this basic theme of exclusively male or female plants. Occasionally an hermaphrodite that has both male and female flowers on the same plant appears, and many varieties are naturally hermaphroditic. Occasionally, flowers may contain extraneous flower parts of the opposite sex.

Male Flowers

Male plants are the bane of marijuana growers. They're necessary for breeding and hybridizing, but otherwise they're in the way. They take up precious room, and their pollen spoils many a good sinsemilla crop. However, they're a necessary evil for the development and breeding of good marijuana seed stock, and to hybridize and incorporate desirable characteristics from different strains within a single variety.

In nature, males usually start to flower about two to four weeks before the females; there is, of course, sufficient overlap to ensure pollination. Males are not as strongly obligated by the photoperiod for flowering as the females are. Under electric lights, males sometimes flower after three or four months, even when the photoperiod is 16 or more hours long. They do, though, respond to a shortened photoperiod by flowering in about eight to 12 days. Males, especially those from temperate climes, sometimes are induced to flower even under long-light regimens. For example, some hemp and *indica*

Figure 109. *Left:* The male flower clusters sometimes look like bunches of little grapes. *Right:* The anthers which hold the pollen look like a bunch of tiny bananas (in center).

varieties flower when the photoperiod is shortened from constant light (24 hours) to 18 hours of light. The same plants started under 18 hours of light may not flower until the light cycle is reduced to 15 hours.

Just prior to flowering, male and female plants diverge in their growth patterns. You may notice that the tops of the male plants (upper internodes) elongate about a week before the first male flower pods appear. By elongating, and ultimately growing taller than their sisters, males ensure that their pollen is released from a high position so that gravity and the wind carry pollen to the females awaiting below. The male top shoots are thin and sparse, unlike the female tops, which thicken and branch at the onset of flowering.

Male flowers are small, ovoid-shaped pods about 1/4 inch long before opening, and they may be green, yellow, or red to purple in color. Individually, the flowers are pale and not striking, but they develop in copious clusters (cymes) concentrated mostly at the top of the plant and on the ends of branches. Male flowers look more like familiar flowers than the female flowers do. They have five tiny tepals (somewhat like petals) and five pendulous stamens.

Pollen develops within the sacs (anthers, which look somewhat like tiny bananas) of the stamens. A line of resin glands forms along the sides of the anther slit, from which the pollen drops. This association lends support to the idea that the resin glands may help dissuade insects, animals, or microbes from attacking the plant's reproductive parts.

A single male is capable of releasing clouds — millions if not billions — of pollen grains. One good male can fertilize all the females in an indoor crop. Outdoors, wind may carry pollen 20 to 30 miles from its source. In November of 1987, the Asthma and Allergy Foundation found that an astonishing 40 percent of the pollen in the air of Los Angeles was from *Cannabis*. This is one reason why outdoor sinsemilla growers routinely find a few seeds, even after they've carefully culled all of their males.

Once the male releases the majority of its pollen, his vigor wanes. He has cast his genetic material to the fate of the wind. The task and cycle for which nature designed him is complete, and soon he'll die.

Figure 110. *Left:* The top of a female plant after two weeks of flowering (Kush variety). *Right:* The top of the same plant after four weeks of flowering. See Figure 111 on next page to see how the buds have developed into a thick cola after eight weeks of flowering. Be patient! The last few weeks of growth are when you gain the most in potency and in weight.

Female Flowers

Females begin to flower eight days to two weeks after you've shortened the photoperiod. Female flowers are small and insignificant at first, but the flowers continually form for six to 14 weeks, until they develop into tightly packed, dense clusters (racemes) popularly known as "buds" or "colas" (colas more often refers to a dense collection of buds).

Figure 111. This mature female cola (Kush) will be harvested within a week.

A single female flower consists of two small (1/4 to 1/2 inch long) fuzzy white stigmas (sometimes pink, red, or purple) raised in a "V" sign and growing out of an ovule enclosed in a tiny green bract (pod). Pollen that lands on a stigma grows a germinating tube down to fertilize the ovule. Most of the resin glands, which contain the active ingredient THC, develop on the bracts (modified leaves), which encase or cover the ovule. The resin glands on the bracts are visible with good eyes or a magnifying glass a few weeks after the flower first appears. Some growers call the bracts "calyxes" or "false calyxes", but *bracts* is the botanically correct term.

Hermaphrodites

Some plants are hermaphroditic (also called mixed gender or intersexes). Hermaphrodites produce both male and female flowers on the same plant. Thai and other Southeast Asian varieties commonly consist of hermaphroditic plants that form some male flowers among the female buds.

Figure 112. Hermaphroditic plant with male (left) and female flowers (right) on separate shoots.

Some hermaphrodites, particularly Southeast Asian varieties, are genetically predetermined, which means that no matter what the environmental influences are, these plants will form both male and female flowers. More common are plants that are basically either female or male plants, but because of an abnormal or unorthodox environment, the plants respond by producing male flowers on a fundamentally female plant, or female flowers on what should be an exclusively male plant. Often the cause of these abnormalities is an erratic, prolonged, or abbreviated photoperiod or life cycle. One very common case of this abnormal flowering is when a grower plants a temperate variety, such as an Afghani; these temperate varieties normally flower when the daily light is from 13 to 14 hours duration. Growers often turn the light cycle down to only nine or ten hours of light. Under this abbreviated photoperiod, female plants quite commonly develop male flowers or, more often, male flower parts on the female buds late in the maturation process: after eight to 12 weeks of flowering, you may notice male anthers (pollen sacs) protruding from female buds — it's time to harvest.

A few male flower parts won't ruin your crop, (although infertile seeds may develop), but the point is significant: any deviation from the norm often has an abnormal effect on the development of the plant. Deviation means too long a dark period, or an erratic day/ night cycle. An excess or absence of fertilizer, or suffocating soil

Figure 113. Close-up view of a hermaphrodite. Male flowers on the left and a female flower bud with its fuzzy white stigmas is in the center.

Figure 114. *Left:* A male plant reversing to female flowering. *Right:* Abnormal flowers. At the middle left, a single female stigma protrudes from a male flower pod. Above and to the right, two male anthers protrude from a female flower bract.

conditions may also lead to abnormal or premature flowering. The point here is to make the environment as natural and healthy as possible. Then the plants respond normally, and you need to confront few, if any, abnormal developments or problems.

Sinsemilla

Sinsemilla has been called everything from overpowering and overwhelming to overpriced and overrated. There is no contradiction here, since sinsemilla, like any other pot, spans the entire range in both quality and price. Saying that some buds are sinsemilla says nothing about its potency.

Sinsemilla (from the Spanish words *sin* and *semilla*) means "without seeds." Sinsemilla is not a particular variety of marijuana: it is the mature, seedless buds of any mature female marijuana.

Many experienced growers believe as I do, that sinsemilla plants are more potent than their seeded counterparts. Some growers may argue that they're equal; but I've smoked hundreds of buds, both seeded and sinsemilla that were taken from the **same plant.** Some loss in potency occurs simply because you must squeeze the seeds out of a seeded bud and the resin is lost on your fingers. Seeded

Figure 115. Sinsemilla colas can grow to impressive sizes.

buds on an otherwise sinsemilla plant were invariably less potent than the sinsemilla buds on the same plant. Try this test yourself.

Sinsemilla buds do take longer to mature, and do form larger buds than when seeded. Once a bud is thoroughly pollinated, energy goes to the production of seeds, and few new flowers form to add to the size of the buds. Seedless buds continue to form new flowers for an extended period of time, often for up to three months. To grow sinsemilla, all you need do is to remove the male plants before they release pollen and fertilize the female flowers.

Part VII
Breeding and Propagation

Chapter 19

Clones

Clones have been much in the news lately. Science notes, newspapers, and popular movies talk about clones as if they were a new miracle of our modern times. For enlightened plant growers, they're old news. Any experienced houseplant grower has raised clones, only they referred to them by their more common name: **cuttings.** Clones are, by definition, genetically identical to their parent. A cutting or clone has the identical potential for growth, flowering characteristics, potency, etc., that the parent plant had.

Clones offer every marijuana grower a simple alternative to starting plants from seeds. The clones can be taken from a single, favorite mother plant; by repeating the cloning procedure, you could grow the favorite continually and indefinitely. Theoretically, you could grow a garden filled with the same, genetically identical plants for the rest of your life.

More than allowing you to continually cultivate your favorite plant, cloning offers every grower several important advantages: cloning gives you a means to grow a crop of completely homogeneous plants; all of your garden space may be devoted solely to females; you know beforehand what the taste and potency of your crop will be; your entire garden can be identical in growth habit, nutritional needs, maturation, and potency; homogeneous plants make cultivation easier, since there is little need for individual attention.

The planning of future clone crops is decided **exactly,** since experience with the first clone crop is applicable to the second and all future crops. You can then, through experience, tune growing practices to the specific needs of your clone, and precisely time when to transplant cuttings, how long to grow them vegetatively, and when to harvest.

There are some drawbacks to growing clones. First, you must be completely satisfied with the marijuana that you're growing, since all of the plants will be identical in taste, aroma, potency, and yield. Second, you must know what you're dealing with. Some growers simply take cuttings from a female plant from a stock that they like. When the clones grow to maturity, the grower may find his plants below average in potency, or find that they are susceptible to rot, mites, or any number of other problems.

Don't trust chance. If you plan to grow with cuttings, be sure you know what the matured, mother plant is like before you devote your **entire** garden to her cuttings. Also, since all the plants should mature within one week of each other, you must have enough drying space, and be ready to handle the entire crop when it comes time to manicure and dry.

Scientific researchers who have grown clones continuously for seven years reported that clones do not "run out"; that is, they maintain their original potency, which does not decline over years as some growers have thought. **These researchers also found (and I have observed) that clones may flower two to three weeks later than the original stock did when planted from seeds, which is an important consideration for greenhouse and outdoor growers.**

Marijuana doesn't root as readily as many other softer-stemmed plants. It may take up to a month before a cutting has enough roots

Figure 116. This garden of clones in Massachusetts grew very well, but flowered two weeks later than the mother plants that were started from seed.

to be planted successfully, although ten to 16 days is more usual. To make a clone, take a cutting two to six-inches long from an **actively** growing shoot of either a branch or the plant's growing tip (three-node cuttings root best). Cuttings taken from lower, rigid or slightly woody shoots root the fastest. If you plan on taking cuttings, refrain from adding any nitrogen fertilizer for one or two weeks prior to taking cuttings, since they'll root more readily. Make a clean cut diagonally rather than horizontally across. The angular cut increases the surface area at the end of the stem, which must absorb water to support the cutting. Remove the lowermost set of leaves. This relieves the stem of some of the burden of supporting its leaf mass. Position the cutting so that all of the stem, almost to the lowermost set of leaves, is submersed in a glass of water or a rooting medium such as Jiffy-mix, perlite, sand, vermiculite, rockwool, or a mixture of these mediums — 1/2 perlite to 1/2 vermiculite, or 1/2 aggregate or gravel to 1/2 peat moss — work very well. Any medium that is loose or airy (perlite, gravel, lava rock, or aggregates) mixed with a water-holding medium (vermiculite, peat moss, or Jiffy-mix) will give you the fewest problems. Small containers such as plastic or paper drinking glasses, peat pellets, or 2" rockwool cubes, work well and save space. Always place the cutting immediately in the rooting medium. If the end of the stem dries or forms callous tissue, cut off the very end and it will root faster.

The most important point for rooting, no matter what the rooting medium or method, is that the potential roots have access to oxygen. Simply changing the water in a glass of water every day replenishes the oxygen. Don't overly saturate your rooting medium. Water moderately to maintain even moisture, and repeat watering with a little water every few days. You may dip the stem in a rooting or transplanting compound such as Rootone or Transplantone which contain fungicides and B-vitamins that purportedly promote root growth, although I've seen no difference in the results when using either. **The oxygen in the rooting medium is the most important criterion.** If you have an aquarium aerator, bubble air into the water between changes of fresh water. Shake a container of water vigorously to infuse it with oxygen. Any loose medium, such as those recommended above, holds plenty of oxygen.

Place the cutting in any moderately lit area: under a small fluorescent system, in a window with indirect light, or in the periphery of an HID system. A 24-hour or constant light cycle encourages the fastest rooting. You don't want the cuttings to be in strong light or sunlight, which overtaxes the ability of the stems to provide water to the leaves. If any leaves dry or begin to die, pinch them off and increase the humidity by loosely enclosing the cuttings in a germination box. If leaves yellow or any mold appears, decrease humidity (open your germination box). As long as there is a living top shoot, the clone has a good chance of eventually rooting.

Clones root best when their stems have access to oxygen and a mild fertilizer. Use a nutrient solution that is half the strength of your usual solution starting one week after taking the cutting. After a few more days, foliar feed with a mild (half-strength) fertilizer. Lastly, gradually introduce your plants to stronger light. Place the planted cuttings under sunlight for two hours the first day, then four, then six, until you've reached eight hours. Under HID's, keep the bulb about three feet from the plant tops at first, and lower the bulb several inches each day up to the recommended distances. Now the plant should suffer little or no transplant shock when placed solely under strong light. Transplant rooted clones directly to large containers, after making sure that all the planting medium is moist. Roots quickly grow to fill the pots in a good medium and strong light; you don't want them in a small pot which constrains root growth.

Creating a Garden of Clones

How do you make your favorite plant into the mother of a garden of clones? How can you take fresh vegetative cuttings from a plant that you've allowed to mature? Here is where you need some preparatory and creative thinking. This is also where small fluorescent light setups help in even the largest of indoor gardens, and where germination boxes, which were just an added hassle for sprouting seeds, become useful.

It's possible to take a cutting from a female plant during flowering and get the cutting to root. But now is the time for flowers and harvests, and you don't want to take prized, budding branches for rooting. Foresight helps immeasurably. If you expect to grow with clones, then take at least one cutting, if not several cuttings, from each prospective candidate when you first decide that the plant is a female.

For example: suppose you are growing three different varieties: a Mexican, an Afghani, and an African. You know from smoking the original that all of the pot is very good, but you don't know what the plants will look like or how well they'll grow because this is the first time you're growing them. After the plants have been growing for about two or three months, you've determined which plants are

Figure 117. *Left:* A sharp blade makes a clean cut. Scissors can pinch the stem. Make a diagonal cut across the middle of the internode. *Right:* Cuttings rooted in rockwool cubes can be placed directly in a larger block.

female by checking preflowers, or by turning down the light cycle to force the plants to flower. As soon as you identify the females, select some healthy shoots from each variety. Shoots from lower branches, which would return little weight to the harvest, are good candidates since they root quickly.

Take a few cuttings from each chosen plant. Label the cuttings so that you can identify not only the variety but also the plant from which the cuttings were taken. For example, African variety #1, plant #4 (Afr 1.4); Mexican variety #3, plant #2 (Mex 3.2), etc. You must keep exact tabs on what is what, not only the variety but also the specific plant. This is the same as when breeding or hybridizing for seed stock. Careful records will serve you well for years to come, and make all crossing or cloning an exacting rather than a hit-or-miss exercise.

Root the cuttings in a bright window, under a modest fluorescent fixture, or on the periphery of your HID system. Cuttings survive much better under high humidity. High humidity is created in a semi-enclosed germination box, which traps the moisture. A germination box is any enclosure that contains moisture (if the box is air-tight, humidity may be so high that rot develops). A germination box may be a box covered with plastic kitchen wrap. A discarded glass aquarium with kitchen wrap partially covering the top is another possibility. Any enclosure that allows light in, contains some but not excessive moisture, and doesn't overheat will serve you well for rooting cuttings.

Cuttings root best under warm (70 to 85 degrees) temperatures, moderate light intensity, and a long photoperiod. Small fluorescent light gardens kept on 18 to 24 hours a day are perfect for rooting cuttings. A bright window, but not with sunlight directed on the cuttings, and perhaps with a floodlight to extend the photoperiod, is another possibility.

After the cuttings have rooted, transplant them to the growing medium you usually use. Poke your finger in the moist medium, making space for the roots. Gently cover the roots with the moistened mixture. Water with a dilute (half-strength) soluble fertilizer.

In the interim, harvest and dry the mother plants. Over a period of time, smoke and evaluate the pot from each mother plant. In a month or two you should have a good idea of which individual plants were the most potent and because you kept records, you know which plants grew well. Now decide which potent, good-growth plants you want to continue as clones. For example, you've decided that Mex #3, plant #5, grew large and was very potent. Go to your clones and find all Mex 3.5 cuttings. You could grow just these few cuttings, but to fill your garden it's better to grow another crop from seed (if you don't have enough clones to fill the garden) alongside the Mex 3.5 cuttings. As soon as these cuttings are growing well, prune their tops to create shoots for more cuttings. In a few weeks you'll have many strong branch shoots, from which you again take cuttings. Root these cuttings. By the time this second crop is harvested, you'll have enough Mex 3.5 rooted cuttings to fill a large garden for the next crop. Keep in mind that given only one cutting, you can prune and clone it repeatedly to produce enough shoots to fill any garden.

The preceding is only an example. The point is to give you an idea of how to go about finding and selecting a superior clone, and how you eventually can fill a garden with your chosen clone. If you've come this far, you'll be experienced enough to have found a favorite, and to have devised several ways in which to fill your garden continuously and exclusively with her cuttings.

You could have one or two mother plants that are kept growing in a window or under a small light system. Continuously take shoots for rooting and replenishing the garden. Replace the mother plant with a new clone when her branches are so numerous and small that the shoots are too small to provide fast-rooting, strong cuttings.

Once you've chosen your cloned stock, propagate the cuttings until there are enough to fill even the largest of plantations. Outdoor growers simply take their clones and grow the sprouts under lights. They pinch the tops a few times in order to force the growth of multiple shoots. Once the shoots are strong, they're cut and rooted. The process is repeated during the winter, until an outdoor grower might have hundreds of rooted cuttings ready for spring planting.

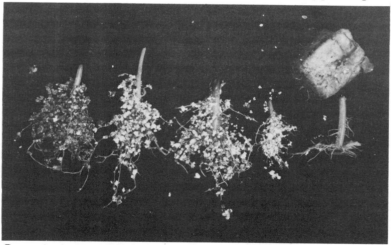

Comparing rooting mediums. *Left to right:* One, vermiculite; two and three; perlite-vermiculite mixture; four, perlite; five, roots in and removed from rookwool cube; Not shown: cuttings died in peat pellets. Best rooting was in a mixture of perlite and vermiculite. Pure vermiculite also worked very well.

Chapter 20

Breeding

After you've grown a crop or two, you'll probably begin to think about breeding. **Breeding for superior marijuana is the high road to success.** Breeding allows you to develop, quite easily, the best pot in terms of potency, disease resistance, early maturation, yield, and other desirable characteristics. After you've bred superior plants to your satisfaction, you then can cultivate a garden of exclusively superior clones.

You do need good stock to begin with, but careful monitoring enables you to develop truly wonderful marijuana from many varieties considered only average by any connoisseur's criteria. You can, by breeding, emphasize characteristics such as dynamite potency. Quite often growers find that their variety "runs out" (diminishes or loses potency) or becomes "spotty" (some plants are still potent and others are mediocre). This happens when the grower hasn't carefully monitored the seed mothers each crop. In fact, most growers have a certain female that they devote to seeds because she's "pretty," the largest, or the earliest. As in love, it's what's inside an individual that counts, and in marijuana, it's that as-yet-unseen potency that you're looking for.

The actual act of producing seeds is very simple. Basically all you have to do is transfer pollen from male flowers to female flowers. The mother plant does the rest. Also, it's easy to fertilize only a few buds, and leave the rest of the plant and garden as sinsemilla; so here, you can have your seeds and your sinsemilla too.

Breeding allows you to cross (hybridize) two different varieties, and eventually incorporate the best of both into a new hybrid stock. One variety may have great potency, another much better growth and yield. Once you find offspring that combine the best qualities from both varieties, take cuttings to clone new plants that you know will be outstanding. This may, at first reading, sound like you have to wait years for the results. But you'll be smoking some good dope from each crop, and you can grow at least two, if not four or more crops each year indoors. After only a few crops with very careful monitoring and breeding, the results are quickly realized. Once you've found a superior individual, clone the plant and grow it for the rest of your life. Most of the great Durban Poison and its hybrids that U.S. growers now use came from seed stock grown in the 1970's in California. Of 16 females only two were very potent. The rest of the mothers ranged from nearly worthless to only good. Yet after only three more crops, a consistently outstanding variety was created through careful breeding. Before embarking on any breeding program, read Chapter 10 for preliminary information.

Hybrid Vigor

Marijuana hybrids also exhibit a phenomenon common in plant breeding called "hybrid vigor." When you take distinctly different varieties and cross them, the offspring (which are now hybrids) are often healthier, and generally more vigorous and desirable than either of the parents. This is commonly seen when crossing a temperate, short-season variety with a tropical, long season variety. Afghani crossed with Colombian or Central African is an example.

Outdoor growers usually want early-maturing plants, and this cross is a typical way to start the search for those few individuals that incorporate an Afghani's early maturation with an African's outstanding potency. Once the individuals are found, they're crossed, always using the best mothers for the next crop's seeds. After several generations, this new hybrid variety begins to "breed true"; that is, all the plants will be similar.

Here is one way to find out indoors which ones will be the earliest flowering individuals in a group of plants. (This is very useful for outdoor growers in the northern parts of the country.) Turn the lights down to 14.5 hours, and wait two weeks for the first sign of female flowering. Those that start to flower will be the earliest. If no plants flower, turn the light cycle to 14 hours. Repeat this process by turning the lights down half an hour each time, and waiting 10 to 14 days for the results. This is a very effective way for outdoor growers to determine earliness of flowering by growing a winter seed crop under lights. The earliest mothers are then used for breeding and producing the seeds for the summer, outdoor crop.

Keep in mind that excessive inbreeding may lead to inconsistent potency if one of the original parents was markedly less potent than the other. If this happens, cross hybrids back to the original African or potent parental stock to reinvigorate the stock.

Figure 118. These hybrids were three-quarters Afghani and one-quarter South African. They were very hardy and yielded more than either of the parents.

Producing Female Seeds

To develop seed that will yield exclusively female plants requires some luck and careful observation, but it is simple. Remember that some female plants occasionally bear an isolated male flower (see Hermaphrodites in Chapter 18). Marijuana plants are normally either female (XX sex chromosomes) or male (XY chromosomes). Marijuana plants, although predisposed genetically to be either male or female, have a degree of latitude that very often is affected by the environment. A plant that should be exclusively female may bear an occasional male flower and vice versa. The pollen from this isolated male flower on a female plant has only X chromosomes, the genes for female plants. By carefully collecting the pollen from this male flower and pollinating female flowers (which also carry only X chromosomes), all the resulting seed will yield prospectively female plants (XX chromosomes).

The only difficulty to producing female seed is in finding an actual source of female pollen. As stated before, many Southeast Asian plants characteristically bear some male flowers among mostly female flowering buds. These plants give rise to seeds that will reflect their parents; that is, female buds mixed with male flowers. Don't breed these natural hermaphrodites. What you want to find is that rare female plant that develops perhaps one or two male

Figure 119. Find that rare female plant that has only one or two male flowers and collect the pollen to produce "female" seeds.

flowers. This plant is genetically female. Carefully collect her pollen, and fertilize an exclusively female plant; all the resulting seeds develop into pure females. The only other certain candidate for female pollen is a female that has flowered well with pure female flowers, but late in life the plant reverses to male flowering. This is not that unusual when the plants are left to grow for an extended time, or if there is an erratic photoperiod.

Usually you have to wait for a fortuitous happenstance to find a solitary male flower on a female plant, but there are presently known at least six different chemical treatments that induce fertile male flowers to grow on female plants. **Gibberellic acid (GA) is the chemical most commonly available.** GA is applied to the growing shoots of female plants either in a dilute spray or by wrapping cotton around the shoots and soaking the cotton with a solution. Concentrations of GA used are 0.02 percent dissolved in dilute sodium hydroxide (NaOH) and then in distilled water for a daily spray, or 5 mg per plant for ten successive days using the cotton-soak method. Shoots elongate within a few days and the first male flowers appear among the female flowers from two to three weeks after initial treatment (the treatment works without being particularly precise with the concentration of GA).

Supplying and Storing Pollen

The act of pollinating females is simple enough, but storing fresh pollen for longer than a month is difficult. Males stop growing and die soon after dropping their pollen, and because pollen loses viability quickly, it is desirable to maintain a continuous supply of fresh pollen. Different varieties mature sooner under natural light than others: an Afghani male may flower in a greenhouse in July; a Nigerian female may not be ready for pollination until late October, after the Afghani male and its pollen are dead. It's better to make the cross the other way; i.e. use a Nigerian male to pollinate an Afghani female, since both will be flowering at about the same time, in September. To keep a male alive longer and to delay flowering, cut the plant back, especially all flowering shoots, when they first appear. The male renews growth, and you'll have fresh pollen weeks later when it's needed.

This cross, however, is not always ideal even for indoor gardeners. Very often you'll have one variety that you know is consistently very potent, and another that is inconsistent or else new and unknown. You should always use pollen from the variety you know, since you're sure it has good genes for high potency. The unknown or new variety should be your female breeders, since you can smoke each female at your leisure and eventually decide which individual is the most potent. Use the seeds from this mother for your next crop.

A Continuous Supply of Fresh Pollen

Male plants don't need the intense light that's necessary to grow healthy females. Before the flowers open, move males to the periphery of your light garden, or to another room. Males survive on low light levels, and males flower normally even if placed in a partially shaded window. For example, hide males in a window from outside view by using a venetian blind. Adjust the slats of the blind to angle downward, which allows light in but hides the plant from the line of sight of outsiders. Or simply place the plants several feet away from a window shaded with a mesh curtain. If you have a large grow room, bring the males through flowering under a small four-foot fluorescent in the corner of the room. Enclose the pollen garden in bedsheets to prevent contaminating the females with stray pollen.

Take male cuttings for an easily hidden pollen source that's separate from the females. Wait until male flower clusters develop, but haven't yet opened. Cut these flowering branches, put them in a glass of water, and position them away from the females, anywhere that gets moderate light. Every two days change the water. Make a fresh cut at the end of the stem if callous tissue forms, or the stalk won't be able to take up water. The shoots slowly mature and open to give you a continuous supply of fresh pollen.

You can even cut the male flowering branches **once they've formed clusters of unopened flowers,** and hang them to dry upside down, in an hidden area. Some flowers slowly open from residual moisture, and release pollen during the next week. Place sheets of paper below the shoots, or suspend them within a paper bag to collect the gradually falling pollen.

Collect pollen by **gently** shaking a flowering branch over a clean plate, a cone formed from paper, a paper bag or cardboard box. If the pollen is to be kept for any length of time, pick out all extraneous plant debris. Place the open container in a cool, dry, light, airy space. Cover the container loosely with newspaper or paper towel. This is all necessary to keep the pollen from germinating and to help prevent fungi and molds from destroying the pollen. Pollen maintains enough viability to produce seeds up to a month later if not attacked by these microbes. **Keep the pollen dry.**

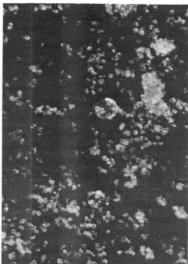

Figure 120. *Left:* Male flowering shoots kept in a glass of water will supply fresh pollen for several weeks. *Right:* Pollen grains. The two spheres are resin glands that have fallen along with the pollen (x40).

Freezing Pollen

You can freeze pollen for at least three months, and it will maintain enough viability for decent fertilization. Pollen may maintain its viability for years if properly frozen, but oxygen, moisture, temperature fluctuations, and microbes eventually take their toll. Put dry pollen in small, glassine (plastic) bags, seal them in small, airtight vials, and freeze immediately. Use many vials since you can't refreeze thawed pollen. Allow the pollen to sit in an open dish at room temperature for an hour or two before pollinating. Now that you have your pollen supply, it's time to pollinate.

General Breeding and Hybridizing

Seeding Whole Plants. Outdoor growers produce seed for their summer crop in small light gardens during the winter. Since they want to pollinate the whole crop, a few males are left to grow among the females. Occasionally they shake the males, which dispense clouds of pollen that thoroughly pollinate any garden.

If you want only certain females to be pollinated, raise the males separately in an area free of wind and drafts. When many flowers start to open, move some of the females close to the males, and shake the males a few times over a period of days. Wait two days to allow the pollen time to fertilize. Now spray the females thoroughly with water. Shake them dry, and bring them back to the female garden. This procedure keeps other females free of contamination from stray pollen carried in by the fertilized females.

Seeding Selected Buds

Most growers don't want to completely seed their crop. Also, you may want to use several varieties to pollinate different branches on one female. No problem. Just carefully hand-pollinate selected buds. A single bud will give you anywhere from 30 to 100 or more seeds (one good branch can give you 500) so you don't need to pollinate much of any plant. You must, though, be methodical. Before you pollinate any bud, label each branch that you intend to seed. Avoid top branches, since there is more chance of pollen falling onto other branches. The buds should be well-formed, and stigmas must be white and fresh. Withered stigmas mean that the flower is no longer receptive to pollen. Use string-tied labels or masking tape to label the bud with your cross. Write in dark pencil (most inks will fade or wash away). Outdoors, check the labels and rewrite them if they're fading. Write the date, the variety, and the number of both the female and the male, and affix the label to the branch. Six months from now, when you're floating in a wonderful high, you'll very likely lose track of exactly which was which and by what, and you'll kick yourself for not knowing.

The simplest procedure is to take a clean finger or an artist's brush, dip it into the pollen, and gently brush the female flowers (stigmas). A little contamination of some other buds occurs from stray pollen, but there will be very few random seeds if you're careful and gentle. You can, of course, remove the plant during pollination into another room with males, or simply perform the pollinating away from the other females, and there will be no contamination. Each time you use a different male's pollen, rinse your hands first then thoroughly wipe dry before applying the new pollen.

To do the job with practically no contamination is a bit trickier if the plant is rooted in the ground or you're outside in wind. Here is another method that works fairly well. First get a clean, medium-sized paper (not plastic) bag. Cinch the bag near its top with a wire twist or string. You are going to place the bag over the end of a

Figure 121. *Left*: An unfertilized female flower with the bracts removed has two stigmas attached to an ovule. *Right*: An ovule three days after pollination. Stigmas have begun to die (top) and the ovule has begun to swell as it forms into a seed. The calyx in *Cannabis* is paper-thin and transparent. It tightly clasps the ovule and is barely visible in this photomicrograph (x16).

branch and close it to fit tightly around the branch. Reopen and put some pollen in the bag; you don't need much. Remove any large leaves from the branch that might be in the way. Very slowly slide the end of the branch into the bag and, again, very slowly tie the bag closed around the branch. (If you don't pre-cinch the bag, or if you close it quickly, you'll force a puff of pollen into the garden.) Give the bag a shake or two, and repeat the next day. In two days saturate the bag with water and then remove it. Much of the leftover pollen will adhere to the wet bag and not contaminate other buds when it's removed. Spray the fertilized branch for the same reason. To further help contain stray pollen, get a friend to hold a large, wet towel over the branch during the operation.

A healthy female forms viable seeds in from ten days to six weeks. Four or five weeks is usual. Wait until you see dark, plump seeds splitting their bracts before harvesting. In most cases, you can't wait too long, but you can harvest too early. If the seeds are still green or white, they're immature, and few, if any, will germinate. The only time you need to worry about harvesting too late is if there is much rain or high humidity. Mature seeds may rot or actually germinate in the buds by absorbing moisture.

Evaluating Potency for the Next Crop

Careful evaluation of the potency of the females by **smoking them over a period of months is the key** to deciding which female's seeds to use for the next crop. You must pollinate a few buds on every decent female, and after harvesting evaluate each mother's potency by repeatedly smoking samples over a period of time. Only by **repeated smoking** can you be certain which was the best, and the best is what you want to grow. It helps if you give friends numbered samples, so they can smoke several joints of each sample at their leisure. Testing by repeatedly smoking the samples is necessary, because mood, attitude, psychology, physical state, time of day, and many other factors strongly influence subjective ratings of potency. It's often best to take only a few tokes, and then wait for a time. If you smoke too much of a joint, it's difficult to evaluate just how stoned you are. Also, if you record how long the high lasts, this is a good, objective determination of potency. For example, at the same time each day, take the same number of tokes from a test joint, and record how long you felt high. Repeat the test from sample joints from each plant, over a period of time. After a month or two, you'll form definite opinions rather than some hazy, emotional feeling about which plant was the most potent. Involve some friends in this blind testing. Ask them to be consistent, and to write down their opinions. Set up a "suggestion list" with specific criteria. They'll help you formulate a consensus. Without access to a chemistry lab, this method of selection is the most effective procedure available to home gardeners and when conscientiously done, it works very well.

You can also evaluate the males by smoking shoots before you pollinate. By the time you're involved in sophisticated breeding though, you'll probably not want to bother smoking male leaves and shoots. Find a "marijuana lightweight." Give him numbered joints so there will be no preconceived notions about which plant or variety might be the most potent.

A good breeder also keeps records of other important factors such as date harvested, disease resistance, and yield. By comparing potency evaluations with the records for other characteristics, you'll be able to make an informed decision on which mother's seeds to use for the next crop. You may be lucky and find a certain mother that has all the characteristics that you want. More often, if a plant has two very desirable characteristics (e.g. potency and rot resistance), this is what to go for. Later, after the variety breeds true (the offspring are consistent), you bring in the third factor, such as early maturation. The whole process is a lot easier than it sounds at first. It's also incredibly enjoyable and satisfying to carefully proceed through the process and develop your own super variety.

Figure 122. *Indica/sativa* hybrids of uncertain ancestry have stabilized into hardy stock after four years in this Vermont garden.

Part VIII
The Reward

Chapter 21

Potency

The potency or strength of marijuana is steeped in myth, misunderstanding and mystery. *Cannabis* is the only plant known to produce cannabinoids, which are the psychotomimetic (mindbending) compounds in grass that get you high. There are more than 60 known cannabinoids, and more than 400 chemical compounds found in marijuana, but only a few of the cannabinoids are psychoactive or known to contribute to the overall high. Almost all of the high depends on the amount of THC (delta-9-tetrahydrocannabinol) contained in the grass. Generally the more THC the marijuana contains, the more potent it is, and the longer the high lasts; the less the concentration of THC the milder the high, and the sooner it dissipates.

Several other cannabinoids contribute to the high, particularly the quality of the high: whether the high is immediate or gradually increases; whether the high feels light or heavy, cerebral or physical, energizing or debilitating, and in certain cases, whether it lasts long or dissipates quickly. The psychoactive cannabinoids are **THC, THCV, CBN**, probably **CBC**, and other unknowns, but not **CBD**, which is apparently inactive.*

---

*THC is the abbreviation for (-)-delta-9-trans-tetrahydrocannabinol. For our purposes, THC also includes (-)-delta-8-trans-tetrahydrocannabinol, an artifact of delta-9-THC, and THCV. (CBN is included when considering potential THC since it's a degradation product of THC.) THCV stands for tetrahydrocannabivarin; CBN is for cannabinol; CBC is for cannabichromene; CBD is the acronym for cannabidiol. CBD previously was believed to be psychoactive, or to contribute to the high by interacting with other cannabinoids. The most recent research indicates that CBD contributes little, if at all, to the marijuana high. Different cannabinoids affect the high in complex ways (see the *Marijuana Grower's Guide Complete Edition*, Red Eye Press, 1989, for much more). To simplify, the quantity of THC is a useful standard when talking about potency.

Resin

The much coveted resin (that contains the cannabinoids) is concentrated almost entirely within the resin glands that cover all plant parts except the roots and seeds: the leaves, stems, and both the male and female flowers develop surface (sessile) resin glands, and on the flowers and small leaves that intersperse the buds, stalked resin glands develop as the buds mature. You can't see the resin glands with the naked eye until the flowers develop. Flowers, and their associated small leaves develop larger resin glands on stalks (up to 500 microns tall), which look (with a magnifying glass or a good eye) like small, glassine mushrooms.

Resin does not flow in the plant, but is manufactured and held within the resin glands and associated cells. About 85 to 95 percent of the active ingredients in marijuana are concentrated in the resin glands; this is why fine hashish-making procedures actually are refined methods for collecting the resin glands. To evaluate the state of "ripeness," the stalked glands visible to the naked eye are the best indicators of freshness, and will indicate telltale signs of degradation. Stalked resin glands are most concentrated and visible on the bracts which encase the seeds (sometimes called *pods, false calyxes*, or incorrectly, *calyxes*).

Figure 123. The small leaves that intersperse the buds are also covered with resin glands. *Left:* The lower (adaxial) surface of a small, fresh Mexican leaf blade (integrals are one millimeter, x16). *Right:* The upper (axial) surface of a Thai leaf blade (x16).

Resin itself, or an abundance of resin glands, is not a good indicator of potency. A marijuana variety may have copious amounts of resin and still be nearly worthless for smoking; another variety may have little apparent resin, but it may be super-potent. This is because much of the resin is made-up of inactive ingredients, and the resin might contain mostly inactive cannabinoids. Also the active cannabinoids (THC, THCV, etc.) are only necessary in amounts small enough that they may not be major components of the resin. Surprisingly, the few scientific studies that have compared the concentration of resin glands or resin to potency, have found that the concentration of resin glands was *negatively correlated* with the potency (in other words, the fact that a variety of marijuana is resinous or has a lot of resin glands has little to do with its potency). Experienced connoisseurs actually may look for a non-resinous but very potent variety — who needs cough-inducing resin if it doesn't add to the high?

Maximizing Potency

The potential potency of any crop is mostly determined by the potency of the parents that produced the seed; the potency depends on the genes for potency (THC production) that the mother and father contributed to their offspring (seed).

To assure high potency, the vital points are: **select a potent seed stock; grow a healthy, vigorous crop; harvest at peak ripeness.** After these three main points, there are several other factors that every grower should attend to.

Once you've cultivated a fully matured plant, the contribution of specific environmental factors diminishes. Considering every environmental influence, only about 20 to 30 percent difference in potency is all that a conscientious grower could expect to achieve by precisely controlling every aspect of the environment: humidity, temperature, soil, fertility, and quality of light, to name only a few of a myriad complex of interrelating factors.

To illustrate, consider that you have a variety that might produce ten percent THC under perfect environmental conditions for maximizing potency. As long as you harvest a fully mature, healthy plant, the potency varies only between seven and ten percent THC. If the plant is immature or unhealthy, the potency might be as little as one to five percent THC. This is why cultivating a healthy, fully matured plant from potent seed stock is so important. If every growth factor was not optimal in terms of potency, you can still harvest a potent plant that in this example would be at least seven percent THC.

Controlling every environmental factor in relationship to every other is impractical and nearly impossible, but by cultivating a healthy, potentially potent, and fully matured crop, you've already assured yourself of a potent return.

Growth factors such as light quality, humidity, and air temperature; soil factors such as fertility, aeration, water, and soil temperature: all these make a small contribution to the overall potency of any crop. Contrary to what you may have read, the production of THC does not depend on the intensity of light. The light spectrum does influence potency. The recommendations given in this book cover the most influential aspects of light in general terms. Excessive heat diminishes the potency of a good crop more than any other environmental factor. **Keep daytime temperatures in the 70's, and below 85 degrees** during flowering for best results.

The foremost consideration for maximizing potency after you've selected good seed is the timing of the harvest, particularly the maturation or **ripeness** of the crop. Pay attention to choosing good seed stock, growing a healthy plant, and harvesting ripe colas, and you'll become a successful grower. (Breeding is the most significant contribution a grower can make to potency, but breeding has to do with future crops, not the present crop.)

The choice of the parents lies with you and your evaluation of the pot from which you chose the seeds. Throughout this book, almost everything said about growing is geared toward the growth of a healthy, vigorous crop, because the health and vigor of any crop is most important to the overall **yield** of potent material. An unhealthy runt of a plant can still be potent, but what fun is a potent plant if it yields only a couple of joints?

To maximize potency, maintain moderate temperatures during flowering. Keep daytime temperatures in the 70's, and nighttime temperatures in the 50-to-70-degree range. Keep the humidity low; don't spray flowering plants, and use ventilation fans to lower the humidity. Fertilize with less nitrogen during flowering, unless the plants obviously need nitrogen (many leaves are yellowing). Fertilize with a solution rich in phosphorus (P) and potassium (K) during flowering. Water often enough to maintain good growth, but don't keep the pots saturated; allow the upper reaches of the pots to dry before watering. Use supplemental lights, rich in the red bands (HPS, LPS, incandescents, and Warm White fluorescents) during flowering. Follow these recommendations to become a master grower, and you'll have done all that you can reasonably do to encourage the development of a superior crop.

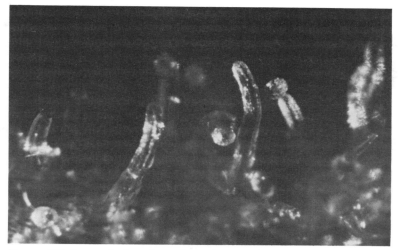

Figure 124. Lower leaf surface along the vein (x40). Harvesting too late decreases potency. Missing gland heads represent a loss of potency. Brown heads indicate degradation and diminished potency.

Seeds from native sources, such as Colombian, Thai, and African, frequently develop into plants that may be from 40 percent to several times more potent than the original grass was. This is simply because the growing and drying techniques described here optimize the production and retention of the variety's potential THC, whereas traditional marijuana growing techniques often retain less than half the potential THC in the finished product (see Chapter 24).

You've chosen good parental seeds, and given the proper care to your crop, so you've covered the two foremost considerations for high potency; this leaves the third critical criterion — the timing of your harvest. (See Chapter 22 for more on when to harvest.)

When to Harvest Sinsemilla

Most important for all growers is the change in potency of the buds through time. Graph 21.1 is based on actual measurements of the changes that occurred to the potency of buds (from a single plant) through time. It's important that you get some understanding of the processes that are happening. Buds increase in potency as they mature; however, once they reach their peak in potency, degradative processes outpace the production of cannabinoids and potency declines. For any grower, the trick is to be able to recognize when the buds have reached their maximum potency, and then to harvest them at this time.

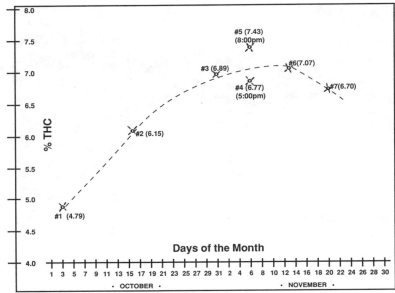

Graph 21.1 Study of the change in potency of sinsemilla buds from a single plant during the course of maturation. *Drawing by L.P. Kallan.*

All samples were taken from a **single** plant (Mex 1.5) grown in a greenhouse (about four hours of daily sunlight) near San Francisco, California. Just prior to flowering, the plant was pruned to produce about a dozen colas of approximately equal size and development. Samples consisted of single colas harvested at 5:00 p.m. on the days shown. Colas were dried under identical circumstances at ambient temperatures. Two evaluations were made of each sample, and their average appears on the graph. The percentage of THC shown is the sum of delta-9, delta-8 THC, THCV, plus CBN (the actual THC potential). The system of testing used was based on that developed by the U.S. Marijuana Research Center at the University of Mississippi, using gas-liquid chromatography. On August 1, the first flower appeared and by August 20, collections of flowers were developing in the axils; this condition was called "beginning bud formation." The first cola (Sample #1) was harvested six weeks later on October 3, and the last (Sample #7) was harvested on November 20. Sample #5 was harvested at 8:00 p.m. on the same day as Sample #4. (Also see Harvesting Sinsemilla in Chapter 22.)

The good news is that in any protected environment, indoors or in greenhouses, the factors that contribute to a decline in potency are nowhere near as influential as when the plants are grown outdoors. Wind, rain, and severe swings in temperature can significantly degrade the potency of a mature, outdoor plant in a couple of weeks. Indoors, growers have much more leeway, and the difference between harvesting mature buds this week or the next won't amount to more than a ten percent change in potency, which is barely detectable when you evaluate by smoking. But look carefully at the parameters for harvesting here and in Chapter 22, and you'll have a good chance of harvesting your buds when they are at their peak.

Time of Day to Harvest

Timing of the harvest also refers to the time of day that the buds are harvested. Research at the University of Mississippi, some of which has yet to be published, suggests that there is a considerable rise and fall of potency during the course of a day. I don't think the swings, if there are any, are as pronounced as the data suggest. In a personal communication, researchers mentioned that the most prominent swings occurred in the leaves well before flowering. However, to get some indication of the possibility of these swings during flowering, one cola (Sample #5) from the plant in Graph 21.1 was harvested at 8:00 P.M. on the same day as sample #4 (harvested at 5:00 P.M.). Sample (#5) was ten percent higher in THC than a comparable bud (#4).

In traditional marijuana growing cultures, growers often harvest at about midday, when the sun is high, following the reasoning that the plant "oozes resin" to protect it from heat and the sun. It is now known that resin doesn't flow in the plant, and that higher temperatures actually decrease potency; so this grass-roots logic isn't justified. The preliminary experiments suggest that the best time to harvest is at night, and the testing of this single bud lends its very slim support to this possibility. To follow this logically (that the THC accumulates during the night), the bud could well be its most potent just prior to sunrise. Harvesting according to the time of day probably doesn't make any, or as big a difference as has been suggested, but there is enough preliminary research to be worth mentioning and investigating. For now, harvest your plants during their nighttime.

Chapter 22

Harvesting

Harvesting Leaves and Shoots

Harvesting leaves and shoots is an exercise many experienced growers could not care less about. When you have plenty of potent buds, who needs leaves or shoots? When you first grow marijuana, you may savor each precious leaf and shoot. If you don't smoke that much, or if you're a "THC lightweight," leaves are satisfying, and shoots may be devastating.

Male leaves and shoots equal the potency of those from females, and shoots approach the potency of mature buds, although few growers realize these facts. A novice smoker/grower could be more than satisfied with smoking leaves; shoots from a primo variety can be very potent. To give you an idea of possible potency, typical commercial Mexican **buds** tested about 0.5 to 1.5 percent THC in 1970. A top **shoot** from a Californian or Hawaiian sinsemilla variety in 1988 may be from three to six percent THC. That is, shoots from today's varieties are from two to 12 times as potent as commercial Mexican buds from pot 18 years ago, because development of superior varieties and selection through breeding have dramatically increased the potency of homegrown marijuana in the U.S.A.

The potency of leaves and shoots depends first on the variety, then on the development of the plant from which they are harvested, and on the position of the leaves on the plant (see Graph 25.1 in Chapter 25). If the variety is hemp versus primo marijuana, it matters not when you harvest, since the leaves will have little THC. With a potent variety, **when you harvest** makes a major difference.

Look at Graph 22.1, which shows how **new** leaves increase in potency through time. This graph shows the probable changes in potency as related to the **development** of the plants, not necessarily the **age** of the plants. This graph is hypothetical, and was formulated in 1977 from dozens of scientific papers on leaf potency, coupled with personal observations of smoking. Even in light of more recent studies, it is still a reasonably accurate and useful portrayal of the changes in potency of the **new leaves** and **shoots** as they appear.

A top shoot from an eight week old plant may have only one-quarter of the potency of a top shoot harvested a few weeks later. Smoke-test one set of leaves to see if they're satisfactorily potent before harvesting others. It may take another few weeks of patient anticipation before you harvest some very worthwhile smoke. Once the potency is to your liking, harvest comparable leaves and shoots from the rest of the plants. Some varieties develop more quickly than others do, and because growing conditions vary so much from garden to garden, the number of weeks shown on the graph does not indicate absolutely when your leaves will be most potent. Some leaf gardens reach their peak potency after nine weeks while others may not peak until the 15th week.

Potency does not steadily increase or accrue throughout the plant; rather, **each leaf reaches a point of maximum potency as it individually appears.** Once a leaf forms it no longer increases in potency, a fact that few growers realize. The leaf still produces cannabinoids, but the rate of decomposition exceeds the rate of production, so leaves actually decrease in potency the longer they stay on the plant. To say that the potency is increasing means that the new leaves that are now forming are more potent than those previously formed. The biosynthesis, or rate of production of cannabinoids **decreases** during the development of each individual leaf. **Each leaf is most potent as it's developing and it declines in potency with time.** This is why shoots are much more potent than leaves that lie just below the shoot. Look at Table 25.1 which shows potency in relation to where (top, middle, bottom) on a plant the leaf came from. Concern yourself with the timing of leaf harvests only if you're growing strictly vegetative gardens. Bottom leaves rarely get anyone high. Top shoots from a potent variety should get all but the most THC saturated of smokers high. Shoots make up a significant amount of weight only in large, outdoor gardens. Indoors, most growers harvest no more than a shoot or two, which is enough to whet their appetites for the finished bud harvest.

Don't strip a plant of its leaves or shoots if you plan to bring the garden to maturity. Anytime you remove leaves, there is less overall

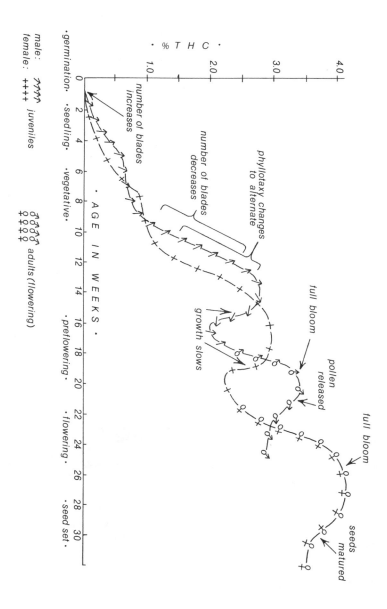

Graph 22.1. THC Graph (hypothetical). *Drawing by E.N. Laincz.*

"growth energy" left to the whole plant, and a denuded plant takes longer to mature. Each developed leaf contributes its surplus biological energy to nourish new growth. When growing for buds, remove only yellowed or diseased leaves or a few leaves or shoots if you need some smoke.

Harvesting Males

Male plants don't have the dramatic increase in weight during flowering that the females do. It's not worth waiting for males to mature, because they take up valuable room that could be devoted to females, they'll pollinate your sinsemilla crop, and male flowers add hardly any weight to the harvest. Males also need relatively little light to complete maturation; so move them to the periphery of your garden, or near a window to complete maturation to maintain them for a constant supply of fresh pollen.

Male flowers continually form and open over a period of three to six weeks. For maximum potency, harvest a male when it has large clusters of well-formed flowers, and a few flowers have just begun to open.

Before flowering, male and female leaves and shoots are about equal in potency. Male flowers **usually** are nowhere near the

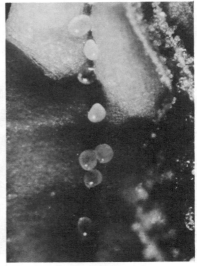

Figure 125. *Left:* A cutaway view of an unopened male flower shows that the resin glands are already well-developed (x16). *Right:* Anther of a male flower (x40). A line of resin glands is in the center. On the right is the pollen slit which opens zipper-like to release the pollen.

potency of female buds, and certainly male plants don't yield anywhere near the weight of potent grass that mature female plants do. For sinsemilla, harvest or remove any male before its flowers open. Allowing the males to continue flowering gives very little increase in potency and literally only a joint or two more in the total yield.

Males serve two purposes: in vegetative gardens for moderate smokers, males provide decent smoke and a good part of the leaf harvest; for any good breeding program, males are indispensable, even when the grower ultimately intends to grow with clones, and even if most of the harvest is destined to be sinsemilla. Selective breeding of a few lower buds is easy to do, while the rest of the crop is devoted to sinsemilla. (See Chapter 20 on Breeding if pollen is desired for breeding in a sinsemilla crop. For maximum potency when harvesting leaves and shoots, see Graph 22.1).

Harvesting Seeded Buds

During sexual maturation, female flowers continually appear, and they accumulate in tight clusters from about 30, to more than 100 individual flowers. The flowers collect into progressively larger clusters (or racemes) for five to 14 weeks. These seed-filled clusters are the "buds" that make up most imported, commercial marijuana. If pollinated, each fertilized flower develops a seed that is encased and protected by resin-covered bracts.

It's not unusual for a single bud to have a hundred seeds, or for one small indoor plant to produce several thousand seeds. A full size, thoroughly seeded outdoor plant can easily bear more than 100,000 seeds.

It may surprise you to know that more than half the weight of that Colombian pot you just bought was wasted on seeds. Typically, seeds make up 40 to 70 percent in weight of seeded, commercial pot. Sinsemilla that is comparable to seeded pot in potency is worth the price at twice the cost. This is why home-grown sinsemilla that is markedly more potent than imported pot is worth the price at two to four times the cost. An ounce of Colombian seeded pot has at least 1,000 and often more than 2,000 seeds.

After pollination, a healthy female takes from ten days to six weeks to form fully mature, viable seeds. Four to five weeks is usual. Seeded plants generally finish maturation two to six weeks sooner than sinsemilla. Some outdoor growers in the North routinely seed their plants to hasten maturation before frosts kill their plants. They reason that it's better to have seeded, mature buds than immature sinsemilla.

Figure 126. *Left:* Top of a seeded bud ready to pick. *Right:* Harvest for seeds when the seeds start "shelling out" (splitting their bracts).

When growing for seeds, harvest the plant once the seeds begin to "shell out" (that is, you see dark-colored seeds splitting their bracts). For a plant devoted to seed production, this often takes place when the plant has ceased growing and begins to die. This is completely normal. The plant's reproduction takes priority, and there is little energy left for sustaining new growth. You'll see colors fade, leaves yellow, and growth generally decline or stop. No need to worry. As long as the seeds have developed fully, the plant has done what the plant needs to have done — to produce healthy, mature seeds for the next generation. Now that the prospects for a new generation have been secured, the plant gracefully succumbs to the ravages of old age and honorably dies. Harvest seeded buds once the seeds have developed good color. Don't wait until the plant is dead. Open an average bud and make sure the seeds are plump and have mature coloration. **In a humid environment, mature seeds may germinate or rot if they're left too long on the living plant.** When harvesting for both seeds and potency, harvest the whole plant as soon as many of the seeds have developed a mature color

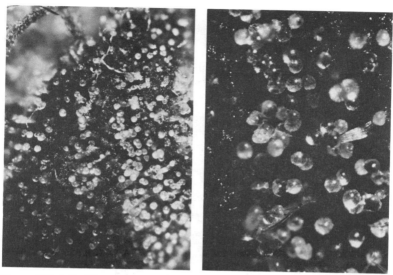

Figure 127. *Left:* Photomicrograph (x25) of a single female flower that holds a mature seed. In a protected indoor environment, even resin glands on seeded buds show little degradation. *Right:* Photomicrograph (x40) of the resin glands of the same flower.

Harvesting Sinsemilla

Sinsemilla plants form new flowers for an extended period of time, from five to 14 weeks after the flowers begin to appear in clusters or, as some growers say, "after the plant has begun to bud." With no seeds to deplete the plant's resources, buds grow larger and take longer to fully form, and to reach optimal potency.

It's only natural to want to harvest as soon as possible. Not only do you want to enjoy the fruits of your labor, you probably can't wait to start again. But you've waited this long, and now is the time for patience. Harvesting too early reduces your return and the buds will be less than their potential potency. After months of care, paranoia, and anticipation, another two or three weeks is well worth the wait.

Not all gardens develop uniformly. Even when they came from the same seed stock, some plants may be ready to harvest up to four weeks sooner than their sisters. This is especially true when the seeds are hybrids between a tropical, long-season variety, and a temperate, short-season variety, because some of the plants have inherited more of one parent's short-season influence, and others have inherited more long-season characteristics.

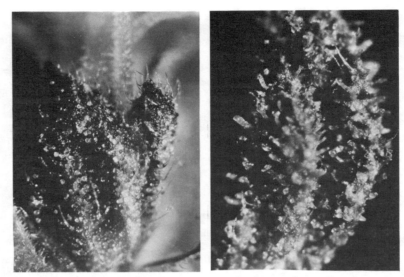

Figure 128. *Left:* A single immature sinsemilla flower shows that the resin glands are not yet fully developed (x16). *Right:* An overripe sinsemilla flower shows many resin gland heads are missing or brown (x16).

Treat the plants gently now: don't rough them up, or run your hands over the buds to "check for resin." That resin on your hands is resin no longer on the buds. Rough treatment knocks the delicate resin glands from the plant. To make *nup*, one of the finest forms of hashish from the Middle East, dried plants are thrashed against a fine mesh cloth enclosed within a tent. The residue of resin that sifts through the cloth is compressed to form *nup* hashish. Leave plant abuse to the hash-makers. Use a tender touch and a gentle hand for sinsemilla.

To determine when to harvest, closely watch the development of the buds and their coating of resin glands. Wait until the appearance of new flowers in the tips of the buds begins to slow. The bracts (flower pods) starting at the base of the buds, should be swollen, and the **stigmas will have withered and browned.** At the top of the bud you'll see fresh, white stigmas. When you see swollen bracts and withered stigmas at the base of the bud, and fresh flowers only near the top, it's time to harvest. About 70 percent of the stigmas should be withered and 30 percent still fresh on a peak potency bud. More important is that about 70 percent of the bracts are swollen and covered with stalked resin glands. A finished cola has a solid, swollen feel. Wait another few days if the bud feels lightweight and "soft", and wait until at least 80 percent of the stigmas have died if you have doubts. Indoors, it's better to wait a little longer. Outdoors, be careful not to wait too long, especially if the weather is anything but mild.

Look closely at the coating of resin glands on the buds; they are visible with good eyes and easily seen with a magnifying glass or photographer's loupe. The majority of glands will be clear and sparkling, and raised on stalks so that they look like miniature glass mushrooms. Almost all of the THC is contained within these glands. You'll see an occasional brown, amber, or missing head, which is no problem. But if many of the gland heads are **brown, colored, or missing, it's definitely past the best time to harvest.** Watch for missing gland heads in outoor plants to indicate an immediate harvest.

The decline in potency from harvesting too late in a protected indoor garden is not as dramatic as with outdoor plants. Indoor plants aren't subjected to inclement weather, which damages the resin glands and diminishes the potency. However, if rot begins to take a toll, any infected bud should be harvested and dried quickly.

Figure 129. *Left:* The base of Afghani/African hybrid sinsemilla buds at peak harvest. *Right*: Close view of the base of Mexican sinsemilla buds ready for harvest. Also see cover.

Some varieties — Thai, Cambodian, and Laotian are the most common — have buds that may mature at different times on the same plant. You don't have to harvest the whole plant. Take the mature buds, and leave the immature buds for further development.

Occasionally after a good part of the plant is harvested, the remaining buds get an added boost in growth, because the root and stem system has only these leftover buds to sustain. The light remains strong and uniform indoors, not diminishing with time like natural light does at season's end. This stable, growth-encouraging environment may stimulate not only the additional growth of existing buds, but also formation of new buds, and you might harvest another small crop in about two months. These second harvests are not common.

Most plants mature uniformly, with all of the buds ripening within a week or two. Often you'll see that the last buds to stop growing and ripen are in the top, main cola, or in the smallest buds toward the bottom of the plant, where there's not much light. Generally, buds mature within a few days of each other starting near the bottom of the plant especially if the plant is in natural light. Under electric lights, you might find that the top cola is the first to mature.

The quickest-maturing varieties (a South African and an especially fast Afghani) were ready to harvest in five and six weeks respectively, after buds first started to form. Usually it takes from seven to nine weeks after buds first start to form for quick-to-mature varieties, such as South African and Afghani, to be ready to harvest. Equatorial varieties take a few weeks longer, from eight to 14 weeks to completely ripen. Look at Graph 21.2 which is an actual examination of potency changes in maturing buds on a typical Mexican sinsemilla grown in a greenhouse. The Mexican was chosen because it's midway between the shortest- and longest-maturing of all marijuana varieties.

Part IX
After the Harvest

Chapter 23

Rejuvenation

Indoor or greenhouse growers can get two and even three harvests from a single plant by returning the plant to a vegetative state for several weeks, then flowering again for a second harvest. Here it's important to harvest most of the plant before its health seriously declines. When you harvest, leave some living shoots and large leaves on the stem and remaining branches.

To rejuvenate a plant for another crop, turn the light cycle up to 18 to 24 hours. For spring-harvested plants in sunlight, just keep the plants in a sunny area. The lengthening days of spring rejuvenate the plant and stimulate new growth. Fertilize with a nitrogen-rich fertilizer.

You could rejuvenate plants in warm, frost-free areas, in heated greenhouses, or in any indoor garden. Outdoors or in greenhouses, you may have started a crop in December, and harvested the buds in May. This is perfect timing for rejuvenating naturally lit plants, and is applicable to Hawaii, California, the deep South and Southwest, and heated greenhouses. The natural lengthening of spring daylight quickly resets the plants growth. By summer's end growth equals or is better than if you planted from seed.

The first new growth you see may look a little strange: the new leaves are simple and entire, i.e. they have one blade, like the first true leaves on germinating sprouts, and the leaf margins (edges) may not be serrated (toothed). This is because the plant reverts to juvenile growth and recapitulates its growth cycle. The size and number of blades increase, just as they did on the seedling.

In natural light, after rejuvenation, simply grow the plant as you would any other, and wait for it to naturally flower in the fall. Under electric lights, wait for at least three and up to ten weeks of renewed vegetative growth before you shorten the light cycle to the appropriate number of hours for flowering. Now repeat the procedures for flowering and ripening.

Figure 130. A plant harvested in the spring and ready for rejuvenation grows beside the spring-started seedlings. Some leaves and buds are left to keep the plant alive.

Figure 131. Rejuvenated plants start with leaves that look like the first leaves on a new seedling. You might thin the plant of some of its shoots to open the plant up for better bud formation.

If you grow winter crops in greenhouses that are harvested in the spring, always regenerate the best females. Over the summer, branches may develop in such profusion that you are better off thinning them out. Remove unwanted branches at their base, and leave a symmetric multi-branched plant.

Over the summer, leisurely smoke and evaluate the potency of buds from each regenerated female. Meanwhile, monitor other characteristics such as size, resistance to rot, taste and fragrance. Rejuvenated plants offer every grower the opportunity to see before them, and then breed for, certain desirable characteristics. Rather than a hit-or-miss breeding program, you know what to expect from rejuvenated plants. Many successful breeding programs use rejuvenated plants. You have the unique opportunity to select with both hindsight and foresight, plants that might have just the characteristics that you're looking for.

If you have artificial lights, or if frost is no problem, encourage the growth of a third harvest. Repeat the harvesting technique by leaving some healthy leaves and shoots. Under sunlight, supplement the natural light with electric lights to extend the photoperiod to at least 16 hours of daily light; 18 or more hours is better.

Chapter 24

Preparing Your Pot (Drying and Manicuring)

Many curing and drying procedures have been practiced and praised by marijuana growers. None of them works better than simple manicure and hang procedures developed by American sinsemilla growers.

Once harvested, no magic process or secret method will increase the potency of the plants. On the contrary, much that is often done actually decreases potency, and may ruin a good crop. Boiling the roots, exposing the marijuana to UV light, or using water-soak, sugar-spray, and then dry procedures, may diminish rather than increase the potency. Don't look for magic formulas. If you started with good stock, and nurtured your plants to maturity, then a careful manicure-and-dry procedure will process your plants into a potent stash.

In Colombia, Africa, and Mexico (although in Mexico they're getting better all the time), the growers ruin or at best diminish the quality of their harvest by their poor drying methods. For example, in Colombia and Africa, the plants are cut, dumped in piles, and left to dry in the sun. The piles are turned occasionally to assure an even drying. Much of the chlorophyll (green color) in the plants is destroyed (bleached) by sunlight, by microbial action, and by heat generated in what is basically a compost heap. This is why imported marijuana is often brown or gold.

Colombian marijuana typically tests 30 to 60 percent cannabinol (CBN). CBN is a degradation product of THC, the active ingredient of marijuana. At best, CBN has about 10 percent of the activity or strength of THC. CBN is not synthesized by the plant; it is the oxidative byproduct of THC. In other words, when THC is exposed to air (oxygen), it quickly degrades (the hotter the faster) to the much-less-active CBN.

Table 24.1
Percentage of THC
Oxidized to CBN

Country of Origin	THC	CBN
Colombia*	2.59%	1.27%
U.S.A. Sinsemilla**	6 to 11%	.06 to .12%

*Average THC and CBN from five samples of Colombian "Golds". The THC + CBN is 3.86 percent which is the potential total of THC when the grass was fresh. Since CBN is 1.27, this is a total loss of about 33 percent of the original THC.

**Average THC and CBN from eight samples of California sinsemilla collected in California and prepared by the simple hang and dry procedure recommended here. Average loss of original THC to CBN is only about 1 percent (see Table 10.2).

Carefully prepared American sinsemilla usually has about 0.1 percent CBN. Hence the figures in Table 24.1 show that the manicure/drying procedure recommended here results in only about a hundredth of the THC being lost to oxidative degradation. Follow the procedures described here, and if the plants are handled carefully and dried in a **dark** and airy space, there will be practically no loss of THC. This is why homegrowers can take seeds from medium-grade imported pot, and find that what they grow turns out markedly better than the original pot. A Colombian might test four percent THC and two percent CBN, but the seeds grown in the U.S.A. would yield plants with six percent THC and virtually no CBN. This is a 50 percent increase in potency.

Light is perhaps even more devastating than oxidation in degrading THC. Light very quickly degrades THC to a number of nonpsychoactive cannabinoids and other inactive substances. Undamaged buds effectively protect THC from the effects of light and exposure to air. The worst thing any grower or user of marijuana can do to his finished pot is to run it through a screen, or break it up, and expose the sifted marijuana to light and air. This could render potent pot almost completely inactive in a year's time (see the Tables in Chapter 25).

Manicuring

Manicuring removes the less-potent leaves that dilute the potency, and showcases the buds. With fresh pot, hold the colas upside down so that the leaves hang down to expose the leaf stalks. Cut away the larger fan leaves at the base of their stalk (petiole), and then progressively remove the smaller leaves, or shear away their ends, until all that's left are well-formed buds. You need not remove the very small leaves that intersperse the buds, since they are about as potent as the buds are. Use fingernails, scissors, or a ring blade. Any scissor with a spring action works well, since your hands won't tire as easily. Some fingernail and toenail scissors open with a spring or lever action, and their small size and precise points do a delicate and efficient job. Head shops sell a number of spring-action cutting tools for manicuring. You'll need a bottle of rubbing alcohol to clean resin from the scissors and your hands. Scrape resin from the scissors, and rub your fingers together to collect the resin — presto, hashish! (For manicuring, see photo on page 325.)

Manicuring goes much faster after the colas have been dried. With a dry manicure, the finished cola is right in front of the worker, and precise and finished touch-up is easy. Dried leaf is much easier to cut than wet leaf, and contrary to what you may have heard or read, limp marijuana is much more difficult and time-consuming to

Figure 132. Tools of the trade. You need alcohol to keep the tools free of gummy resin. You need joints to maintain interest in an otherwise boring task.

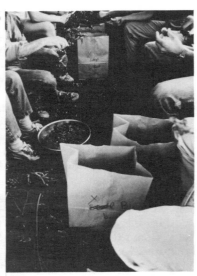

Figure 133. *Left:* For large colas just shear the ends of any leaves that stick out from the cola. *Right:* Large gardens require much labor and organization.

manicure than either fresh or dried marijuana. Much of the manicuring of dried colas can be done easily with your fingers. Just handle the colas gently while manicuring, so that the resin glands aren't knocked from the buds. Before you dry colas, you may prefer to separate the colas from the main stems, and to remove the large fan leaves, which hastens overall drying time.

Manicuring With Electric Shears

Electric shears save considerable time, but you should look into their use only if you're a commercial grower with large quantities of grass to manicure. Electric shears are common grass shears with three top scissor-like blades that slide over three bottom counterparts. Electric shears cut very fast, and the slightest lapse of attention (common among marijuana manicurers) results in a damaged or shredded cola. If you cut off the center blade from both the top and bottom shearing blades, their action is slowed and more easily controlled, although with practice, you can use either two- or three-blade shears.

After you get used to handling shears, you can manicure an intact plant (about half a pound of buds when dried) in about 20 minutes. You need give only a few minutes of touch-up with hand scissors to complete the job. Compare this to the time a careful hand manicure with scissors takes — two to five hours for the same amount. This may sound like a panacea or technological miracle for marijuana growers, but automatic shears present a number of problems.

First, manicurers need a couple of practice plants to get the hang of it. You'll shred some good buds in the learning process.

Second, automatic shears work well only on living or freshly cut plants, because the plants must stand up with turgid, outstretched leaves to facilitate the shearing. This is not a problem indoors, since you can manicure the living plant right in its pot.

Third, most clippers are battery-powered, and in-the-field shearing is limited to the 20-minute charge on portable units and the work must be done in the field. This, of course, is not a problem for indoor gardeners, or you can rewire shears to run on household current if you're handy. Freshly harvested plants do have to be brought quickly to the manicurers for the procedure to work. After only an hour or two wait, cut plants often are too limp to be automatically sheared.

Figure 134. Resin builds up on the fingers when manicuring by hand. Scrape or rub it off for instant hashish.

Fourth, automatic clippers make a lot of noise. Using earplugs or radio headsets might save a manicurist's hearing, but it may make a passer-by or neighbor curious. Remember that the noise is constant, because to use the shears is to use them for mass quantities, which means the shears run continuously.

Drying

Drying Buds and Colas. There are innumerable home-method drying procedures that growers have devised, including using microwave ovens, fruit- and herb-drying boxes, and freeze-drying processes. The best procedure is the simple hang-and-dry procedure at room temperature.

Curing processes are used for preparing tobacco to enhance its bouquet, flavor, and texture. Because curing may degrade the active ingredients of marijuana, it's best left to tobacco farmers. A natural "cure" occurs anytime the marijuana is dried slowly. Some of the chlorophyll disintegrates, and the grass has a milder appearance and taste, since some of the green appearance and taste is lost. To see the effects of curing, fill a jar about half full of leaves. Place the covered jar in sunlight. Every few hours, open the jar to release condensed moisture, and shake the contents. After one or two days, the sun and heat completely degrade the chlorophyll. All that's left is "gold" grass, which is less potent than the original "green" grass. These special curing techniques are best left to other growers who imagine that they're "improving" their grass. Experiment only with leaf or low-grade buds.

Proper drying and drying-time depends on the temperature, humidity, and air circulation. Generally you want warm temperatures: no lower than 60 degrees and no higher than the mid-80's. Humidity should be moderate, but if it's high, **simply raise the temperature into the 70's with space heaters, and use fans and ventilation to keep the air circulating.**

Best drying takes from five to eight days. Dried buds should retain some moisture, and feel supple or pliable, not brittle. A joint should burn evenly and stay lit long enough to be smoked comfortably without needing to be relit. To test for proper dryness, take a bud from the middle of a branch, break it up, and roll a joint for a smoke test. If it burns evenly, it's ready. If not, another day or two of drying is probably all that's needed. Properly dried marijuana retains eight to ten percent water, which is necessary to keep the buds fresh and pliable, and to maintain good taste and fragrance. Dried buds weigh about 14 percent of the weight of fresh buds.

Figure 135. This grower in upstate New York is cutting out rot to save the plants until they reach maturity.

Figure 136. In a damp New England basement, this crop dried perfectly with space heaters and fans to keep the air circulating.

Colas that dry in three days or less are being dried in conditions too hot and dry to produce a smooth smoke. This quick-dried marijuana feels brittle and crumbles when handled. The marijuana is likely to be harsh and gagging to smoke. When drying temperatures are too hot or the humidity is too low, the outside of the buds may be crisp, while the insides remain too moist for even burning. You may be able to correct this condition by sweating (a sweetening or curing process): place the dried colas in a plastic bag for two days to allow the moisture to spread throughout the cola. Open the bag once or twice a day to make sure that no fermentation or mold is developing. Place the colas in a paper bag for a day or two for final drying.

When drying takes longer than eight days, buds may never quite dry sufficiently or evenly. The grass may burn unevenly and constantly need to be relit. Smokers never experience the full potency of their marijuana; some potency is lost, because all the THC doesn't decarboxylate.

Most of the THC in fresh marijuana is in the form of THC-acid (THC-COOH), which is not psychoactive. Drying and burning (heat) transforms (decarboxylates) the acid form of THC to the psychoactive form of THC. This is why all preparations for eating marijuana use heat, such as baking to make marijuana brownies. Burning grass during smoking decarboxylates inactive THC-acid **completely** into the active form of THC, and no special procedure for decarboxylating the marijuana is necessary.

One consequence of smoking joints of freshly dried marijuana is that small, slim joints result in the most efficient use of the THC contained in the grass. Because marijuana often does not burn evenly in an oversized joint, much of the grass and the THC is wasted. Two skinny joints will get you higher than one fat joint with an equivalent amount of marijuana.

In humid areas, such as the Southeast, growers manicure and hang the plants as usual, but sometimes use air conditioners, which extract moisture to cool the air, or they use dehumidifiers to condense the moisture, which dries the grass. Both machines act quickly, and the buds may be dried perfectly in only three days, although the smoke sometimes is harsh. Test your buds twice a day to ensure that they won't be overdried.

Small buds dry quickly as long as they are dried under the same airy conditions described previously. Small buds dry best in a single layer spread on screens or on flats, or placed in a large, closed paper bag to slow the drying process which helps mellow the taste, and improves the burning properties.

Figure 137. Loose buds dry well on flats or on screens.

During wet, rainy weather, colas may reabsorb moisture if they haven't been bagged in moisture-proof containers. Use a fan or mild heat to redry before bagging. **In any high-moisture or humidity situation, colas usually dry well enough if you simply keep the air circulating with fans and raise temperatures into the mild 70's with space heaters.**

Hanging the Colas to Dry

Some growers staple branches for drying to eves or beams in the drying room, but the easiest method is to string strong twine runners between walls or beams, and hang the colas and branches on the runners. Most home gardeners can dry their crop in a closet. Always cut colas or branches so that an overhanging crook of a branch or node is near the end of the piece. This forms a natural hook that makes hanging on twine runners quick and easy. This saves a lot of time by doing away with the need to use wire twists or string to attach the colas to the runners.

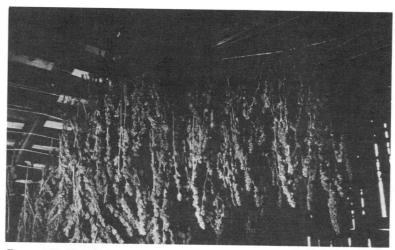

Figure 138. The easiest way to hang the colas is from strong twine runners. These colas dried perfectly in a drafty Pennsylvania barn without the need for space heaters or fans.

Bundle small branches together, and secure and hang them with wire twists or twine. A bundle of small buds cures slightly and dries more slowly because of the containment of moisture within the bundle, and the buds burn better than if they're hung individually. Clothes pins also facilitate the hanging of small branches.

Drying a Sample

To quick-dry a sample, place manicured buds or leaves on a plate sitting on a fluorescent fixture or an HID ballast, or in an oven at 200 degrees. Either way, first break up the buds, or else parts of the bud will turn crisp or burn before other parts are dry enough to smoke. Check the drying often to make sure the grass doesn't burn.

Microwave-drying produces a more even smoke than the oven-drying. Microwave for 30 seconds at medium power. Repeat until dry. Any of these three quick-dry methods are discouraged for anything other than to sample some smoke, but these methods work decently if you need some quick smoke for testing or to supplement a depleted stash. Don't evaluate potency with any of these quick-dry procedures, because they are likely to diminish the actual potency.

Figure 139. *Left:* Make "Thai" sticks from scraggly colas. First, manicure as usual. *Right:* Then strip the grass from the stems.

Figure 140. *Left and Right:* Instead of the unattractive mess on the left, you'll end up with "Thai sticks" like those on the right.

Drying Leaf

To dry leaf, put a six-to-eight-inch layer of leaves in a large paper bag. Once or twice a day, shake and tumble the contents to mix the leaves for an even drying. The average drying time is about three days. Leaves will cure slightly when dried in an enclosed paper bag at room temperature. Leaves quick-dried with heat or a dry atmosphere retain chlorophyll (green color), and they smoke harshly.

Home-Made Thai Sticks

One excellent alternative for growers with large quantities of small buds or scraggly colas is to make Thai sticks. Southeast Asian plants usually don't form tight, distinct colas. This may be one reason why Thai sticks are the popular form in which marijuana is marketed in Southeast Asia.

Thai sticks are quite simple to prepare without any experience. All you need to do is strip the manicured and still wet buds from the stems. Form the wet mass around a slim, reasonably straight, marijuana branch or fireplace matchstick, into a cylinder or Thai Stick shape. Two people working together make processing much easier: one person keeps his or her hands clean of sticky resin for tying; the other handles the marijuana. Use either sewing thread or a hemp fiber stripped from a marijuana stem. Circularly wrap the thread around the mass of buds in loops about half an inch apart. You'll be surprised how well the stickiness of the marijuana keeps the mass stuck together in a cylindrical form around the stem. Dry the sticks by hanging or laying them on flats along with loose buds. Usually it takes two to four days for home-made Thai sticks to dry, and they'll burn beautifully. The procedure actually is very easy to do, and after a few sticks you'll begin to feel like an expert who has made Thai sticks all of his life.

Chapter 25

After the Harvest

Grading

How you grade your harvest depends on what you have grown and your intentions: will you sell your pot; do you get high on leaves or shoots; do you have more than one variety? No matter what you've grown or what your experience is with marijuana, separate and grade your pot very specifically. By separating or grading your harvest, the best grades are not diluted by the weaker parts. Each separation gives you grades of distinctly different strengths, since the strongest compared to the weakest is markedly apparent. By separating varieties, you can experience the different "highs."

Each grower arbitrarily decides on grades, but there is some semblance of continuity in the marijuana market. For instance, sinsemilla buds must be essentially seedless, well-formed buds and colas. Commercial "buds" means matured female flower clusters, whether they're seeded or sinsemilla.

Grades generally break down in the following descending categories: mature sinsemilla buds; seeded buds; bud shake and small buds; shoots and male tops; leaves. Of course the potency of each variety plays a large part in grading. Most experienced smokers can remember a time when they bought beautiful sinsemilla buds that barely gave them a buzz, and yet another time they got wrecked on shoots or leaf. Within these general categories, each variety breaks down into the aforementioned grades.

Table 25.1
Position of Leaf Related to Potency
(THC Content)

Position on Plant	Percentage of THC to Weight of Leaves		
	Plant 1	Plant 2	Plant 3
Top	6.1	6.9	4.8
Middle	3.0	5.5	3.1
Bottom	0.8	4.0	1.5
Ratio (gradient)	8:4:1	1.7:1.4:1	3:2:1

You can see from Table 25.1 that there is a very significant gradient for potency when you compare leaves from the top of the plant to the bottom. Examples #1 and #2 are from the same variety (SP-5). The third sample is another variety (United Nations, UNC-335). Experience shows that example #1 is more typical than examples #2 or #3 are. With a potent variety, the top leaves usually will be six to ten times the potency of the bottom leaves.

For the indoor gardener, shoots make up very little if any of the crop. Shoots usually come from large fields where the growers clip shoots throughout the season. Later in the season, growers also include the flowering tops of male plants. Usually shoots approach, and may actually equal the potency of the female buds. Most often they're disdained by unknowing growers and consumers alike because of their appearance and green/chlorophyll taste. Shoots are becoming more popular and sought after in the marijuana market each summer because the price (about $150 to $250 per pound) just can't be beat considering their substantial potency.

The shoots from high-quality sinsemilla varieties are generally comparable to good-grade Mexican or low-grade (brown) Colombian. Growers need not manicure the shoots; just dry them in a paper bag. With so little labor, its no wonder they are a bargain.

Leaf is the lowest grade of marijuana, and rightfully so. The first lower leaves from a young plant are usually worthless. On the other hand, leaf from the tops of an older, potentially high-grade plant may be quite good for the money. Commercial growers often mix shoots and leaf together, because they can't be bothered with more

Figure 141. Colas from nine different varieties grown in two adjacent gardens. Varietal differences are apparent even though the plants were grown under the same conditions in Oregon.

than the work of caring for their top-grade sinsemilla. Their leaf will be cheap, yet contain some high-grade shoots or immature buds that can be separated by a sharp-eyed dealer.

The buyer's adage of "buyer beware" translates in marijuana buying to "smoke before you buy." Surprisingly, commercial growers often don't know which of their varieties is the most potent before they start to sell their product. Always ask for samples from each variety, and smoke them for evaluation away from the dealer, so that you get a clearer picture of what is the best.

For home-grown gardens, grade your marijuana as follows. First separate the matured sinsemilla buds by variety, and possibly by each plant if you're breeding (you'll want to know if any plant is noticeably more potent than the others). Second will be any seeded buds. Third will be all bud trimmings, immature buds, or shake mixed with any leaf shoots. Last is everything else, which should be mostly leaf. Buds don't have the gradient in potency on each plant shown for leaves in Table 25.1. Buds from the same plant should be near enough in potency to make up one grade. One marijuana myth is that the most potent buds are the topmost or mainstem colas. Actually, any lower, well-developed buds are often slightly more potent. The topmost and largest cola is often leafier than lower buds, and extraneous leaf dilutes potency despite careful manicuring.

Even so, large colas command the highest price in the marijuana market, simply because of appearance and the buyer's belief in the "top potency" myth of top colas.

Storing

The season is over. You've grown your crop, manicured and dried the buds, and now must store your stash, like a squirrel preparing for winter. Put your mind at ease: if you've dried your pot according to the recommendations, all you need to do is to seal and sequester the pot in a cool, dark place, and the stash should stay fresh and potent for several years, if not indefinitely. Both light and air degrade THC to inactive or much-less-active cannabinoids (e.g. CBN). In all of the tables in this chapter, any increase in CBN actually represents a loss in potency. Start with Table 25.2 to see the dramatic loss of THC in stored marijuana that is exposed to light.

Table 25.2
Loss of THC in Marijuana Stored Under Various Conditions

	Storage Conditions					
	41° in Darkness		68° in Darkness		68° in Light	
	THC Present	% of THC Lost	THC Present	% of THC Lost	THC Present	% of THC Lost
Starting	1.37	0	1.37	0	1.37	0
31 Weeks	1.26	8	1.20	12	0.89	35
47 Weeks	1.27	7	1.19	12	0.88	36
73 Weeks	1.21	11	1.10	20	0.68	50
98 Weeks	1.25	9	1.03	25	0.51	63

Table 25.2. *Fairburn*, et al. 1976. *J.* of Pharmaceutical Pharmacology 28 (1).

Many growers store their pot in Zip-lock bags. Seal the bags almost completely, first squeezing the bags to remove most of the excess air. Now draw any remaining air from the bag by sucking the air through a straw or tight, partially closed lips surrounding an opening in the partially sealed top of the bag. When you see the bag reaching a vacuum-like state, quickly seal the bag.

However you seal the bags in preparation for long-term storage, the idea is to remove as much excess air as possible. Some growers use "Seal-a-Meal," which is intended for sealing foods for freezing or other long-term storage. Shrink-wrap processes follow the same principle: remove as much air as possible, then quickly seal the bag in such a way that air doesn't enter the bag. Store the vacuum-sealed pot in a dark, cool, or refrigerated space (freezing is ideal), and don't remove the pot until you need some smoke. Marijuana stored this way maintains its original potency and taste for many years.

Canning jars or any other containers intended for food storage work very well for maintaining original freshness and potency. It is important that, however you seal your marijuana, store it in a light-tight container or place.

Figure 142. A country grower is still smoking from his eight year old stash. He's kept the stash stored in plastic bags, sealed in steel ammunition boxes and buried in the ground.

The worst scenario for degradation of any pot is to break it up, run the grass through a screen, or forcibly compress the pot, and then expose it to light and air. Grass treated these ways loses a good portion of its initial potency within the first year. Table 25.3 shows how breaking up, or compressing the marijuana (breaking the resin glands), causes dramatic losses in stored marijuana.

Table 25.3
Loss of THC Under Various Conditions of Light and Air

Storage Conditions & Preparation of Sample*	THC Present	% of THC Lost	CBN
Freshly prepared	11.6	0	traces
Light and Air			
(1) Loose powder	7.3	37	1.8
(2) Compressed broken mass	5.2	55	2.4
(3) Compressed unbroken lump			
(a) Surface layer	5.2	55	2.3
(b) Next 2-mm layer	10.7	8	1.8
(c) Center	11.4	2	1.6
Darkness and air			
(4) Loose powder	12.0	+3	0.6
(5) Compressed broken mass	10.1	13	1.0
(6) Compressed unbroken lump			
(a) Surface layer	11.1	4	1.9
(b) Next 2-mm layer	10.3	11	1.04
(c) Center	11.0	5	1.47

* All samples stored for one year at 68°F
Fairburn, et al. 1976. J. Pharmaceutical Pharmacology 28 (1).

Never break up the buds, or run buds or leaf through a screen, since this breaks and exposes the THC held in the resin glands to air. Intact buds act as natural storage containers. Properly sealed and protected from light and air, your grass should retain much of its original potency, taste, and fragrance for many years.

Table 25.4
Decomposition of THC in Stored Marijuana

Number of Weeks Elapsed	Percentage of Cannabinoids by Weight in Marijuana [a] Stored at Temperature of									
	0°F		39°F		72°F[b]		97°F		122°F	
	THC	CBN	THC	CBN	THC	CBN	THC	CBN	THC	CBN
Starting	1.3	0.2	1.3	0.2		0.2	1.3	0.2	1.30	0.2
10									0.75	
20									0.20	
30									0.05	
50		1.25			1.21					
60							1.03	0.4	0.04	0.73
70							0.29			0.51
100	1.2	c	1.16	c	1.12	c	0.08	0.67		0.41
% of original THC lost	7.69%		10.76%		13.85%		94.00%		97.00%	

Turner et. al. 1973. J. Pharm. Sci. 62 (10).
a Dried, manicured marijuana stored in amber bottles in darkness.
b This sample received ambient light.
c CBN content increased slightly.

Storing Seeds

Store seeds in any cool, dry, dark place. Your refrigerator or freezer is ideal. Before storing seeds, remove all leaf and extraneous vegetative material. Run seeds through a strainer to remove any vegetation, such as bracts and leaf pieces, or keep them in their intact buds, which act as natural storage containers. Place the intact buds or the cleaned, naked seeds in a clean, dry, airtight, opaque container (e.g., a clean film canister), and store the container in your freezer or refrigerator. Seeds retain their original viability for about two years, and when properly stored, some seeds germinate after more than seven years. Dusting with sulfur and commercial seed dusts for storing grain seeds also helps extend the usable lifetime of stored marijuana seeds. Infection from molds and fungi are the main detriments to long-term viability; anyway you can deter these microbes extends the life of your seeds.

Chapter 26

Some Final Words:
Grow American

Let's face it. Some of the best dope, and by far the best selection grows right here in the U.S.A. More varieties are grown or held as seeds in this country than any other. Traditional pot-growing cultures grow what they have, and they grow the same way their forefathers did. Americans seek and embrace varieties from all over the world. Once we learned that it's better to grow than buy, Americans revolutionized the art and science of growing, and in the process, developed the best marijuana varieties grown anywhere.

The first crop I grew was in 1968, and in that crop a Mexican grew unlike any of its other more conventional brothers and sisters. One plant, named IT, was twice as big as anything else. IT took up a full quarter of the garden, overshadowing and dwarfing its 20 other siblings. IT was IT because IT grew beautiful, large, symmetric female buds in tight rosettes. And beneath each bud hung a cluster of equally impressive large rosettes of male flowers. IT was unlike anything I've seen since.

IT was given the best of care that I could give, but IT was destined to be hung until IT dried. As you've probably guessed, IT was so potent, IT became a new experience. But being a mere novice, I knew nothing of propagating IT.

All of you have the opportunity to find rare and special plants. Learn from my mistake. Propagate any unique plant by breeding or by taking clones. IT is long gone, never to be seen again.

Seeds get around amazingly fast. When growers hear of an especially desirable stock, the seeds soon appear all over the country. In 1978, the United Nations' *Cannabis* seed bank was depleted and in disarray. Let's save and build a stock of prized seeds for future generations. Everyone can contribute. Years from now, your descendants may be indebted to you for the pleasure of smoking and continuing to grow the exotic variety that you developed.

One Last Note

After reading this book, you'll probably realize some information came to me in letters from growers. I value these letters. Personal experiences introduce new ideas and problems I may not have anticipated. Your letters help frame my thinking for future articles and books. I appreciate any feedback, copies of personal or professional plant or marijuana research, and your thoughts or criticisms. Please don't ask me for seeds or marijuana, because I can't and won't respond. Any research material you may wish to send is appreciated and thoroughly examined by me (Mel Frank), and me alone, if addressed to me c/o Red Eye Press, P.O. Box 65751, Los Angeles, California 90065. If you choose to send a return address, I will do my best to keep your name and address strictly confidential and out of reach of anyone else.

Wishing you a fruitful and happy harvest,

Index

358

366

Directory Of Suppliers

The Directory of Suppliers for horticultural equipment has been removed because of Operation Green Merchant. Operation Green merchant was a Drug Enforcement Administration (DEA) effort to curb domestic marijuana growing in 1989. The Operation received scant notice by most media, except for the *New York Times* and *High Times*.

The DEA, in conjunction with local law enforcement agencies, padlocked warehouses, froze bank accounts, searched offices, and confiscated customer lists from companies that advertised legitimate horticultural supplies in *High Times* magazine. Although the actions were arguably unconstitutional, the lack of public outcry and the fear fomented by the Operation discouraged companies from challenging such actions in court. Many companies could not secure adequate legal representation because their assets were frozen, or prospective litigation costs were too high. Some companies dissolved, others now fear any affiliation with marijuana.

Confiscated customer lists subsequently were used to secure search warrants or simply led to unsanctioned visits of customers receiving legitimate horticultural supplies. Other tactics the DEA employed included examining utility company records looking for unusual increases in electrical consumption (to power indoor marijuana gardens), as well as scrutinizing United Parcel Service (UPS) records of horticultural supply companies in the hope of locating growers.

There were 337 Operation Green Merchant cases, ranging from possession of drug paraphernalia to drug possession with intent to distribute. Until February, 1990, most cases had proceeded smoothly with convictions. However, Missouri attorney Dan Dotson filed a motion to suppress prosecution evidence on behalf of his client. He argued that the warrant used to obtain evidence that incriminated his client was illegally obtained, because it was based solely on UPS records of a legal transaction. The essence of this and subsequent successful defense motions is that horticultural supply companies distribute legitimate equipment and advertise in many publications. Simply receiving products advertised in a magazine such as *High Times* is not grounds for issuing a search warrant. Such evidence was ruled inadmissible by the court. This ruling may pave the way for similar successful defenses of victims of Operation Green Merchant.

Commentary on Drug Policy by Mel Frank

September 1990

Last month a California Advisory Commission recommended that California legalize marijuana and marijuana growing for personal use. State Attorney General John Van de Kamp responded by refusing to publish the report, thus hampering access to a state-supported study of public import. However, his action goes far beyond questions of the public's right to information; it speaks to the heart of what is wrong with our drug policy.

The penchant to ignore or dismiss the advice of independent experts is nothing new. This country has suffered more than 50 years of propaganda about drugs and, particularly, about marijuana. Officials continue to deny the facts, including the findings of independent researchers sponsored by the government. Repeated calls for decriminalization and/or findings that marijuana is probably the least harmful drug known to humankind go unheeded. No one has ever died of a marijuana overdose, a claim that can be made for practically no other drug. The most dangerous consequence of smoking marijuana remains that it is illegal.

The Safer Commission, appointed by President Nixon, recommended in 1972 that marijuana be decriminalized. Canada's *Le Dain* Commission made the same recommendation. A decade later, a panel from the National Academy of Sciences also recommended decriminalization. These prestigious bodies concluded that criminalizing marijuana does far more harm than good.

For many years, officials cautioned that there were no long-term health or social studies with large numbers of smokers. This seemingly reasonable position also was not true. There were several valid studies, all officially ignored. The exhaustive British study of hemp smokers in India near the turn of the century, the LaGuardia report in New York between 1938 and 1944, and the 1970s Jamaican report were shunned because they concluded the same thing: no long-term debilitating effects were associated with marijuana use; and, the drug did not cause violent behavior (a central question in the studies).

The headlines of the 1960s and 1970s ominously warned of birth defects, brain damage, and impending long-term medical problems from marijuana use. That was 20 years ago. Where are the malformed, the brain-dead, the dying? Where are the millions of incapacitated or deranged from the flower generation? Our own experience in the United States with 20 million regular smokers and 60 million having used marijuana has yet to justify earlier apprehension.

If the government has not produced conclusive evidence that marijuana is harmful, it is not for lack of trying. Of the more than 7,000 research papers published on marijuana between 1976 and 1986, the majority addressed health questions. When the National Institute of Drug Abuse (NIDA) produced its 1988 report, the body was criticized for not stating that marijuana was addictive or unequivocally harmful. One NIDA official was moved to comment, "Never has so much money been spent trying to find something wrong with a drug and produced so few results." (*Scientific American*, November 1988).

One legitimate concern about smoking marijuana is that the smoke is carcinogenic. All carbon-based smoke is carcinogenic, whether it comes from tobacco, *Cannabis,* or wood fires. But the point is moot because marijuana was synthesized 25 years ago and could be taken in a pill form (generically known as Dronabinol). Marijuana users also do not smoke "a pack a day," and if marijuana were legalized, selective breeding could lead to high potency marijuana varieties with very low tar and resin content. Officials today often lament that marijuana is ten-times as potent as it was in 1970, as if this means marijuana is ten times as harmful. The opposite is true. In 1970, typical Mexican marijuana was about 0.5 to 1.5 percent THC. One would smoke two or three joints, inhale deeply, and hold the smoke in the lungs until nearly turning blue. With marijuana of 10 percent THC, two gentle tokes exhaled almost immediately produced the same result.

Marijuana has the longest legacy of positive usage of any drug or plant known to humankind. It was prescribed to alleviate depression and melancholia, rheumatic pain, lack of appetite, menstrual cramps, and headaches. Before the 20th century, marijuana was routinely prescribed for hundreds of ailments, probably because it made people feel better.

Modern scientists have found marijuana to have therapeutic effects on asthma, epilepsy, spasticity, hypertension, and pain. Still, potential medical applications of marijuana remain thwarted by our drug policy. A 1976 federal directive forbids any independent research or federal health program to investigate marijuana for medical applications. Politically, this might be known as the ostrich axiom: *it is better to bury one's head in the sand than to face a controversial truth.*

Fifty years ago, marijuana was relegated to a Schedule I classification. Schedule I means that a substance is dangerous with no medicinal purposes. And yet during the past 25 years, our government has been growing marijuana at the University of Mississippi at Oxford. Government marijuana has been issued to cancer victims for alleviation of nausea associated with chemotherapy (anti-emetic), and for the relief of pain suffered by glaucoma victims (relieves interocular pressure). While raising and dispensing marijuana for these valid medical purposes, our government has doggedly upheld marijuana's Schedule I.

The idea that marijuana was harmful did not take root until the Prohibitionist era. During the 1920s and 1930s, Hearst newspapers barraged readers with stories of marijuana-crazed Negroes compromising white women. Even Jazz music ("voodoo-satanic") became a target of hate. The stories intensified to include all people of color, and all sorts of violent crime. These headlines and editorials tying violence with marijuana use and race became the basis for testimony leading to the Marijuana Tax Act of 1937 that in effect made *Cannabis* illegal.

Hearings on the Tax Act were confined to committees that spent portions of five days in the House and less than two hours in the Senate. The question before the committees was not whether *Cannabis* should be criminalized, but rather how it would be criminalized. The hearings were dominated by Henry Anslinger who was head of the Federal Bureau of Narcotics (FBN). It was the FBN's contention that marijuana induced users to commit violent, aggressive crimes, and second, to go insane. The FBN gave no studies to support these these claims. Testimony was limited to the reading of sensational headlines and editorials, and three anecdotal cases of violence allegedly connected with marijuana.

The American Medical Association (*Cannabis* extracts were a standard medicant) was not consulted until passage of the 1937 Tax Act was all but ensured. AMA representatives voiced strong objections inasmuch as medicinal marijuana was safely used since colonial times, and since new medical uses were likely to be found.

The National Oil Seed Institute (NOSI) also spoke strongly against the Tax Act. In 1935, 58,000 tons of hemp seed oil were used in the United States to make paints, varnishes, and high quality lubricants. NOSI representatives rightfully argued that the law was too inclusive and would crush the industries based on hemp oil.

Hemp is the strongest and most durable natural fiber and is used to make products ranging from hardy sail and rope to the finest quality cloth and paper. The hemp fiber industry, second only to cotton and decimated by the Civil War, never recovered due to a lack of mechanization. The industry could have been resurrected by the invention of a machine that economically separated fiber from cortex. Unfortunately, such a machine was introduced in 1938, after cultivation of hemp was made illegal. The USSR, France, Italy, Chile, and Japan, among many countries, maintained their hemp industries. The American hemp oil and fiber industries are no more.

In the following ten years, Anslinger continued to testify before congressional committees and through his lecture circuit that marijuana caused uncontrolled violence among users. But in 1948, while congress was obsessed with its anti-communist agenda, Anslinger asserted that marijuana caused users to be peaceful and pacifistic, and that

372

communists could use marijuana to weaken the resolve of America's fighting men. He thus contradicted his argument that led to making marijuana illegal in the first place.

We may snicker at the ridiculous propaganda films such as *Reefer Madness* and *Marijuana--Assassin of Youth,* or the naive, racist headlines of the early Hearst newspapers, but we still pay the price. Much of the population believes such silliness in the absence of documented facts and opposing opinions. Those of us growing up from the 1920s through the 1950s heard nothing else. No wonder many from the elder generations remain confused about drug issues.

(Sample--Warning card to be placed in R. R. Trains, Buses, Street Cars, etc.)

Beware! Young and Old — People in All Walks of Life!

This ▪ may be handed you

by the **friendly stranger.** It contains the Killer Drug "Marihuana"-- a powerful narcotic in which lurks

Murder! Insanity! Death!

WARNING!

Dope peddlers are shrewd! They may put some of this drug in the 🫖 or in the *Cocktail* or in the tobacco cigarette.

WRITE FOR DETAILED INFORMATION, ENCLOSING 12 CENTS IN POSTAGE — MAILING COST

Address: THE INTER-STATE NARCOTIC ASSOCIATION
(Incorporated not for profit)

53 W Jackson Blvd.   **Chicago, Illinois, U. S. A.**

The result is a drug policy that seeks solutions to health and social issues through Big Brother. The Drug Enforcement Agency (DEA) relies on interdiction and quasi-legal measures that the public would not have tolerated twenty years ago. Military personnel are being sent within South and Central America, and to our borders to perform drug duty. The dangerous precedent of using the military in place of the police has expanded this summer to include our country, where troops hunt the countryside for marijuana growers.

In the Fall of 1989, the DEA launched the first phase of Operation Green Merchant (OGM). The objective was to curtail indoor marijuana growing. OGM targeted horticultural companies primarily that advertised in *High Times.* Tactics employed stretched the Constitution to new bounds (see statement on page 368).

The DEA continues to expand the scope of domestic surveillance. Aircraft outfitted with infra-red equipment now probe homes for heat emanating from indoor grow-lights. Helicopters search private property at new low-level altitudes. We have come to the point where people and vehicles that simply look suspicious (drug profiles) can be stopped and searched.

In the name of controlling drugs, our right to privacy has been infringed, search provisions broadened, property confiscated without due process, and through pre-trial seizure and/or freezing of assets, the right to adequate legal defense enjoined. Clearly, fundamental constitutional rights and protections are being eroded.

Current policy presents a bleaker vision for the future. We are moving toward the day when new drugs and their effects will be depicted through computer projections (designer drugs), and any competent chemist could synthesize them. How will the government control the future black market? Secret clearances for chemists and chemistry students? Permits for computers?

We need only heed the lesson of tobacco usage, which is declining not because of government propaganda, but rather because of credible Surgeon Generals' reports. Smoking tobacco has become socially undesirable. We no longer idolize Bogart and Bacall with cigarettes dangling.

If we are ever to curb the destructive use of drugs the government must begin by informing citizens with honest information. Blanket condemnations and hypocritical policies toward selected drugs discredited government warnings during the 1960s. Propaganda in place of education created the climate for dangerous experiments with all drugs and nurtured the rise of today's powerful smugglers and dealers. Attorney General Van de Kamp may think his action correct or politically expedient, but he is merely perpetuating a policy that created our present drug dilemma in the first place.

Organizations Concerned with Sane Drug Policies

The following organizations provide information to the public regarding drug policies, political action activities, health concerns, crime statistics, or questions of law. The addresses are included as a public service, and such inclusion should not be construed as advocacy of marijuana use by any of the organizations. Contact Red Eye Press to include your organization in this listing.

National Organization for Reform of Marijuana Laws (NORML)

NORML
1636 R Street NW, Suite 640
Washington, D.C. 20009

(West Coast)
879 Holloway
West Hollywood, CA 90069

2215-R Market Street, Suite 278
San Francisco, CA 94114

National Council on Crime and Delinquincy (NCCD)

NCCD
S.I. Center at Rutgers
15 Washington St., 4th Floor
Newark, NJ 07102

(West Coast)
685 Market Street, Suite 620
San Francisco, CA 94105

(Midwest)
6409 Odana Road
Madison, WI 53719

Drug Policy Foundation (DPF)
4801 Massachusetts Avenue NW
Suite 400
Washington, D.C. 20016-2087

Legalise Cannabis Campaign
BM Box 2455
London WC1N 3XX England

Coordination Radicale Antiprohibitionniste (CORA)
93, Rue Belliard-R.E.M. 508
1040 Bruxelles (Belgium)

High Times Magazine

High Times (Subscriptions)
P.O. Box 410
Mt. Morris, IL 61054

WAR ON POT?

JUST SAY...
N**O**RML

The National Organization for the Reform Of Marijuana Laws

The government claims you have no right to smoke marijuana. NORML disagrees. The Constitution guarantees rights to the people, not the drug police.

Look at what the war on marijuana is costing us:
- Over 300,000 arrests a year.
- Paramilitary raids and helicopter surveillance.
- Felony arrests for PERSONAL cultivation.
- Billions of dollars in crop losses.
- Loss of privacy and civil liberties.

The marijuana hemp plant has ecological, industrial, medical and recreational value. Hemp is a uniquely productive source of fiber, oil, protein, pulp for paper and methanol fuel. Marijuana also has medical applications as a treatment for nausea, spasticity, glaucoma, epilepsy, and as an analgesic and tranquilizer. Repeated government studies have recommended decriminalization or legalization of marijuana.

LEGALIZE IT - END THE VIOLENCE

For info on marijuana, the law, drug testing and reform contact:
California NORML: 2215-R Market St. #278, San Francisco, CA 94114 - (415) 563-5858
National Office: 1636 R St., NW, Washington, DC 20009 - (202) 483-5500

NEW! from Red Eye HASHISH!

"Everything I know about hashish I learned from Rob Clark."—Mel Frank

378 pages, 192 B&W Photos, Charts, Maps, Drawings, Tables Dramatic Color Section with **70 Color Photos** , Index, Glossary, Bibliography and Appendix. $29.95 + $3 shipping & Handling. Add $3 for RUSH via Priority Mail. See Order Form on this book's last page.

Rob Clarke, author of *Marijuana Botany,,* culminated thirty years of travel and study to illuminate the world of hashish from growing the marijuana plant to collecting its valuable resin, which makes up hashish, a concentrated form of marijuana's active ingredients. High-quality hashish is a rare find these days, primarily due to political upheaval in hashish-making countries such as Lebanon, Afghanistan, and Nepal. If you weren't one of the fortunate few to experience the pleasures of great hashish during the 1960's and early 1970's, you probably don't know how good hashish can be. In the 1970's, sinsemilla revolutionized the marijuana market by replacing low-grade imported marijuana with exceptionally high-grade home-grown sinsemilla. In the next few years, this book will revolutionize the market again when high-quality, home-made hashish appears.

HASHISH! is divided into six Parts:

Part I. traces the **History** of hashish from prehistoric times through 1997.

Part II. describes **Traditional hashish manufacture**, worldwide, past and present.

Part III. covers **Hashish Cultures** in Asia, Africa, Europe, and the Americas.

Part IV. **Hashish Constituents**, explains what hashish is, what is in it, the psychoactive ingredients, non-active ingredients, what makes you high, and different highs. Readers learn how to recognize high-quality hashish, how to determine the presence of adulterants and binders, and how to perform simple, visual tests to determine quality.

Part V. **Consumption of Hashish**, shows the many ways hashish can be consumed. The author explains the psychoactivity of smoking compared to eating, why eating hashish is a different experience than smoking, and why there are different highs. Healthful ways to smoke, and innovative techniques for medical users and recipes also are included.

Part VI. **High-tech Hashish**, illustrates new innovations in hashish-making, improvements that can produce hashish much more potent than ever before. The author concludes with novel ways to make hashish with common kitchenware found in any home. All the hashish-making techniques are **safe, non-chemical, practical**, and **easily performed** with very **simple tools**. Anyone can make extremely high-quality hashish if they know how, and this book explains everything a hashish-maker needs to know.

The NEW Marijuana Grower's Insider's Guide
by Mel Frank, from Red Eye Press

400 pages, 200 photos/charts/drawings/THC graphs, with Index

"The Insider <u>is</u> the definitive guide to growing marijuana."
High Times

...a book that will make a master grower out of everyone who follows it.

The Insider is for anyone who grows, particularly indoors, in greenhouses, or in backyard plots. Frank explains the merits and installation of the best of horticultural lights, as well as light balancers, CO_2 systems, hydroponics, nutrient formulas, and climate controls. Every aspect of growing--from selecting and planting your seeds to drying and storing the harvest--is throughly covered.

With plain text and illustrative photographs and drawings, the author helps you pian your garden--from a basic backyard plot with organic soil, to a high-tech, hydroponic, indoor-grow-room--then guides you to a successful harvest.

Special attention is paid to increasing potency and yields, and harvesting and drying for optimum potency. No other author reveals such insight into the practical aspects of breeding for super-potent varieties, while making the art of breeding and cloning workable for every grower.

Fast Service: Order in--Order out on Same Day!
Or order from your local bookstore by ISBN # 0-929349-00-8.

Send this Red Eye logo (or a copy of it) to get your book autographed by the author.

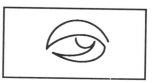

$19.95 plus $3.00 Shipping & Handling (22.95 total). California residents add $1.50 tax per book.

Also available, the Marijuana Grower's Guide Deluxe at $19.95.
Spiral bound edition of Deluxe for $23.95, plus $3.00 S&H.

Make your check or money order payable to:

For Rush Order sent Priority Mail add $2.00

Send to: Red Eye Press
P.O. Box 65751
Los Angeles, CA 90065

deluxe
MARIJUANA
Grower's Guide

by mel frank

MARIJUANA GROWER'S GUIDE DELUXE *NEW* COLOR EDITION

The *Marijuana Grower's Guide Deluxe* has a newly revised color section with 51 new color photos (64 total), informative new captions, and new cover. This classic treatise is known as the "grower's bible" and is revered by growers for being the most comprehensive work ever published on marijuana botany, chemistry and indoor and outdoor cultivation.

"...an extremely clear and interesting essay in practical horticulture, as accessible a study of a single plant at this high level of seriousness as one is likely to find." **NEW YORK TIMES BOOK REVIEW**

"...the writing will help put drug literature on the road to respectability." **LOS ANGELES TIMES**

"...a very wise and masterful book." **WEST COAST REVIEW OF BOOKS**

330 pages, 64 COLOR and 129 B&W photos, drawings, maps, index, bibliography	**376,000** in print **1st** printing new Color edition **33rd** printing all editions	$19.95 0-929349-03-2 Perfect $23.95 0-929349-04-0 Spiral

deluxe   REVISED COLOR EDITION

MARIJUANA
Grower's Guide

by mel frank

RED EYE PRESS 👁
Publishers of Brave New Books™

MARIJUANA GROWER'S INSIDER'S GUIDE

The *Marijuana Grower's Insider's Guide* is the classic guide for indoor, greenhouse and backyard gardeners. Mel Frank simplifies the latest high-tech gardening techniques, while blending home-spun experience for backyard, organic tillers. The clear text and illustrative photographs guide novices to professional results, while botanists learn practical points of horticulture not taught in class. *The Insider* covers everything a novice needs to know and answers questions only experienced professionals would know to ask, in concise, easily understood text.

The Insider's Guide is THE definitive guide to growing." **HIGH TIMES MAGAZINE**

"...all the answers are here in the Marijuana Grower's Insider's Guide." **THE OCCIDENTAL**

330 pages, 200 B&W photos, drawings, graphs, index	**90,000** in print **10th** printing	$19.95 trade paperback 0-929349-00-8 perfect

RED EYE PRESS — *Fast* — Mail Order Books
Order in—Order Out on same day when paid with Money Order or Cashier's Check. Mel Frank will autographs his books (# 1, 2, 3) for FREE. Just ask and write name of person Mel will sign book to.

1. **Marijuana Grower's Insider's Guide   112,000 in print   Our Current Best Seller $19.95**
   by Mel Frank from Red Eye Press. This is the complete guide to indoor, greenhouse, and backyard gardening. Readers tell us that this is the best, most detailed, easy-to-follow growing book. Covers every aspect of growing from planning personal or commercial-size gardens, planting to drying, natural and all electric lights, hydroponics, organics, breeding, clones, treating nutrient deficiencies and insects, maximizing potency. 380 pages, 200 Photos, THC Charts, Drawings, Tables, with Index.   **Consistently praised.**
   "The Insider is THE definitive guide to growing."   **High Times Magazine**

2. **Marijuana Grower's Guide Deluxe Color edition** by Mel Frank   **$19.95**
   Published by Red Eye Press.   **410,000 in print Our all-time Best Seller**
   Botany, Chemistry, History, Indoor and Outdoor Cultivation. This is the classic treatise, known as the Grower's Bible. Updated periodically and new color section inserted in 1997. 330 pages. **60 Color Photos,** 170 B&W Photos, Charts, Drawings, and Maps. Index and bibliography.
   " *... extremely clear and interesting.*"   **New York Times Book Review**
   " *... this is a very wise and learned book.*"   **West Coast Review of Books**

3. **Marijuana Grower's Guide Deluxe Color edition,** with Spiral Binding   **$23.95**
   #2. with wire binding that lays flat for easy reference and years of sturdy use.

4. *HASHISH!* by Rob Clarke, author of Marijuana Botany, from Red Eye Press.   **$29.95**
   "Everything I know about hashish I learned from Rob Clarke." —**Mel Frank**
   This new book became a classic immediately. Unlike any other hashish book, this book tells the whole story. Traces hashish History and describes hashish-using Cultures, Recreational and Medicinal use. Covers how-to of traditional hashish-making. Introduces new, high-tech hashish-making and home-made using kitchenware. Teaches expert evaluation and buying, and healthful ways of smoking and eating, with recipes. Explains potency and what makes you high. All hashish-making shown is by practical, non-chemical, easy-to-perform techniques using simple tools or, none at all. An amazing, beautiful book! 378 pages, **70 Color photos,** 188 B&W Photos, THC graphs, Maps, Drawings, Index, Bibliography. **Highly Recommended.**

5. **Closet Cultivator, revised edition** by Ed Rosenthal, published by Last gasp.   **$16.95**
   An easy-to-handle book on marijuana cultivation. Shows hidden mini-gardens by examples. Describes low-cost, personal gardening under lights. 128 pages, 55 illustrations.

6. **Marijuana Growers Handbook by Ed Rosenthal** from Quick Publishing   **$19.95**
   A handbook for gardening under lights. Details the set-up of high-yield gardens. Includes addendum on photoperiod. 232 pages, 100 photos, drawings, Index.

7. **Indoor Marijuana Horticulture by Jorge Cervantes** published by Interport USA.   **$21.95**
   A user-friendly guide to indoor growing under High-Intensity (HID) lights. Revised and expanded. 288 pages, well illustrated with drawings, photos. Index, Glossary. A popular guide.

8. **Marijuana Botany by Rob Clarke,** published by And/Or Press.   **$21.95**
   Clearly explains marijuana propagation and breeding. Clones, layering, breeding seeds for high potency and yield. Includes growing pointers. Beautifully illustrated with the author's excellent, clear drawings. 220 pages, index, glossary, bibliography. **Recommended!**

9. **Cannabis Alchemy by D. Gold,** published by Ronin Publishing.   **$12.95**
   Extraction and preparation of hashish and hashish oil. The art of making extremely potent *Cannabis* products. Includes isomerization. 110 pages, illustrated, Glossary, Index.

10. **Marijuana Chemistry** $22.95
   by Michael Starks, Ronin Publishing
   Explains marijuana chemistry. Describes extraction, preparation of marijuana
   and hashish; enhancing potency of plant and products.
   200 pages, photos, charts, tables, drawings.

11. **Marijuana Hydroponics** $16.95
   by Daniel Storm, Published by And/Or Books
   A guide to growing without soil from basic systems to computer control.
   Covers nutrient solutions, light, atmosphere, temperature controls.
   117 pages, illustrated, glossary.

12. **Marijuana Question? Ask Ed** $19.95
   by Ed Rosenthal, Quick American Publishing
   A compendium of questions and answers by the infamous answer man for
   High Times. Ed answers hundreds of reader queries on growing, preparing,
   smoking, health, and legal concerns. A wealth of information clearly explained.
   284 pages, 70 photos, index, bibliography.

13. **Marijuana The Law and You: A Guide to Minimizing Legal** $24.95
   Consequences by Rosenthal, Logan and Steinborn, Quick American. In
   this excellent new book, the authors give sound advice and present real-life
   experiences and outcomes from arrests, trials and hearings. Being arrested
   does not mean the end of the world if you are prepared, and this book prepares
   you. Tactics, procedures, and most important, how to avoid arrest. HIGHLY
   RECOMMENDED. The wisest ¢19.95 investment you could make.

14. **CO$_2$, Temperature, & Humidity** $12.95
   by D. Gold and Ed Rosenthal from Quick American Publishing
   A newly revised guide to increasing yields with simple, practical techniques
   for indoor and greenhouse gardens. 80 pages, illustrated.

15. **Psilocybin Magic Mushroom Grower's Guide** $16.95
   by O.T. Oss and O.N. Oeric from Quick American
   Revised and expanded edition of this classic how-to guide to psilocybin
   mushroom home cultivation. 90 pages, illustrated, bibliography and glossary.

16. **The Mushroom Cultivator** $29.95
   by P. Stamets and J.S. Chilton from Agarikon Press
   This is the definitive guide to mushroom cultivation in the home. Covers
   15 species including psilocybin. All you need to know from start to finish.
   412 pages, well illustrated with index, glossary and bibliography.

ORDER FORM—Please indicate books and charges. Return this order form or print clearly the titles, shipping charges, (and tax if California resident) on separate paper and send with payment to Red Eye Press.

1. Marijuana Grower's Insider's Guide $19.95_____
2. Marijuana Grower's Guide Deluxe Color $19.95_____
3. Marijuana Grower's Guide Deluxe Spiral $23.95_____
4. *HASHISH!*   **NEW!** $29.95_____
5. Closet Cultivator $16.95_____
6. Marijuana Grower's Handbook $19.95_____
7. Indoor Marijuana Horticulture $21.95_____
8. Marijuana Botany $21.95_____
9. Cannabis Alchemy $12.95_____
10. Marijuana Chemistry $22.95_____
11. Marijuana Hydroponics $16.95_____
12. Marijuana Questions? Ask Ed $19.95_____
13. Marijuana the Law and You $24.95_____
14. CO_2 Temperature and Humidity $12.95_____
15. Psilocybin Magic Mushroom Grower's Guide $16.95_____
16. The Mushroom Cultivator $29.95_____
17. Psychedelic Encyclopedia (400+pp. **Excellent**) $24.95_____
18. The Emperor Wears No Clothes   (HEMP) $19.95_____
19. Hemp Today   (HEMP) $19.95_____

Regular Shipping and Handling (all USA orders) $ 3.00_____
RUSH via Priority Mail (USA only)   additional $ 3.00_____
Each additional book, all USA orders $ 1.00_____
Only California residents must add 8¼% tax (Total X .0825)_____
Total Enclosed   _____

Send Order and payment to: **Red Eye Press**
P.O. Box 65751
Los Angeles, CA 90065-0751

Foreign Orders: All orders sent outside of the USA are sent Air Mail. No tax. No regular or Priority shipping outside of the USA. Add only these shipping charges to the price of each book.
Canada and Mexico: $6 first book; $2 each additional book.
Europe, South and Central America; $10 first; $6 each additional book.
Australia, Asia, Pacific: $12 first book, $9 each additional book.
All orders must be paid in US$. Bank checks and Money Orders must be international or have US branch imprinted. Postal Money Orders accepted. Send cash (US dollars only) by registered mail to protect yourself from theft or loss.
Please **PRINT** your complete address clearly.
Your name _____
Street and Apt.#_____
City/State/Postal Code/Country_____

1. Orders are private and discreet. We do not sell, share, or buy mailing lists. In the USA, orders are sent in a plain envelope or box with our P.O. Box, not publisher's name, for return address.
2. We will replace, free of charge, any book received damaged. You must return damaged book.
3. No C.O.D. or telephone orders. Mail a check or money order. Registered mail is not necessary for any orders except cash. Your canceled check or money order receipt is proof of purchase.
4. **FASTEST SERVICE** in the USA is by Priority mail paid with a money order, cashier's check, or cash. Customers usually receive such orders within one to three days from the day we receive the order. Personal checks require a two to three week wait to verify clearance.